A THEORY OF
THE CONSUMPTION FUNCTION

NATIONAL BUREAU OF ECONOMIC RESEARCH
NUMBER 63, GENERAL SERIES

A Theory of
the
Consumption Function

MILTON FRIEDMAN
University of Chicago

A STUDY BY THE
NATIONAL BUREAU OF ECONOMIC RESEARCH, NEW YORK

PUBLISHED BY
PRINCETON UNIVERSITY PRESS, PRINCETON
1957

Published 1957 by Princeton University Press
London: Oxford University Press

L.C. CARD 57–5454

Composition by The Universities Press, Belfast
Printed in the United States of America

To Janet and David

Preface

THE theory of the consumption function proposed in this book evolved over a number of years. During most of this period, I was not engaged in empirical work on consumption. Indeed, prior to writing this book, I had done none since 1935–37, when I was connected with the planning of the Study of Consumer Purchases. I nonetheless kept in close touch with empirical research on consumption, thanks to the combined accident of my wife's occasional interest in the field and of our joint friendship with Dorothy Brady. Mrs. Brady's unrivaled knowledge of the empirical evidence from family budget data, penetrating insights into their explanation, and deep understanding of the scientific problems involved in their analysis occasioned a series of conversations on the interpretation of consumption data, in which discussions Margaret Reid subsequently joined. Miss Reid, with characteristic enthusiasm, persistence, and ingenuity proceeded to put to a critical test the hypothesis that had been evolving out of these conversations[1] (see Chapter VII). When it seemed to be passing the test with flying colors, she pressed me to write up the underlying theory so that she could refer to it in a paper presenting her conclusions. This book is the result, and though my hand held the pen, and though I am fully responsible for all its defects, it is in essential respects a joint product of the group, each member of which not only participated in its development but read and criticized the manuscript in its various stages.

The origin of the book may explain some features of it, in particular the extensive reliance on secondary sources for data and the almost complete absence of statistical tests of significance. An hypothesis like the one presented below is typically a by-product of original empirical work; so it is in this case, but the original work was Mrs. Brady's and Miss Reid's, not my own. What systematic empirical work I did came after the development of the hypothesis, not before, and was directed at bringing together as wide a variety of data as I could with which to confront the hypothesis. It is a defect of this confrontation that I make so little use of objective statistical tests of significance. There are several reasons for this defect. First, many of the data do not lend themselves readily to such tests. For example, it would be necessary in some cases to go back to individual

---

[1] The earliest written version of the hypothesis I can find in my files is in a four page typescript dated June 8, 1951.

observations rather than to be content, as I have been, with means of groups. Secondly, sampling fluctuations seem to me a minor source of error, particularly in interpreting family budget data for rather large samples, compared to both biases in the samples and inadequacies for my particular purpose in the definitions used and the kind of information collected. In consequence, I have preferred to place major emphasis on the consistency of results from different studies and to cover lightly a wide range of evidence rather than to examine intensively a few limited studies.

I am indebted to Phillip Cagan for overseeing the computation of the aggregate consumption functions described in section 3b of Chapter V, as well as for much help in deciding what to compute, and to Gary Becker for overseeing some of the computations in Chapter IV, as well as for helpful comments and suggestions on the whole manuscript. Raymond Goldsmith was generous in making available to me much material from his pathbreaking study of savings before it was in print as well as in commenting on an earlier manuscript. James Tobin read an early draft of section 4 of Chapter VI, corrected a number of errors I had made in it, provided some additional computations now contained in that section, and made helpful suggestions on other parts of the manuscript; I appreciate very much both his assistance and the scientific and objective spirit that animated it. James Morgan kindly made available some of the data used in Chapter IV, and contributed some valuable comments on them; Julius Margolis and Lawrence Klein were also helpful in this connection. I am indebted to the Division of Research and Statistics, Board of Governors of the Federal Reserve System, in particular to Homer Jones, Irving Schweiger, and John Frechtling for making available to me data from the Surveys of Consumer Finances and helping me to interpret them. In addition, Frechtling read the entire manuscript and made many helpful criticisms.

A number of other friends have also read one or another version of the manuscript and have been generous with helpful comments. The late Richard Brumberg read an early version of the manuscript in its entirety and made numerous valuable suggestions for its improvement and expansion. Others to whom I am indebted for a similar service are Morris Copeland, Solomon Fabricant, Malcolm Fisher, Irwin Friend, Ruth Mack, Geoffrey Moore, S. J. Prais, George Stigler, and Frederick Waugh.

The reader shares my debt to the editors of the National Bureau of Economic Research and the Princeton University Press for their editorial assistance and to H. Irving Forman for the preparation of the charts.

MILTON FRIEDMAN

February 23, 1956

Contents

xi

List of Tables

List of Figures

A THEORY OF
THE CONSUMPTION FUNCTION

CHAPTER I

Introduction

THE relation between aggregate consumption or aggregate savings and aggregate income, generally termed the consumption function, has occupied a major role in economic thinking ever since Keynes made it a keystone of his theoretical structure in *The General Theory*. Keynes took it for granted that current consumption expenditure is a highly dependable and stable function of current income—that "the amount of aggregate consumption mainly depends on the amount of aggregate income (both measured in terms of wage units)." He termed it a "fundamental psychological rule of any modern community that, when its real income is increased, it will not increase its consumption by an equal *absolute* amount," and stated somewhat less definitely that "as a rule, . . . a greater *proportion* of income . . . (is) saved as real income increases."[1]

Theoretical interest stimulated empirical work. Numerical consumption functions were estimated from two kinds of data: first, time series on consumption, savings, income, prices, and similar variables available mostly for the period after World War I; second, budget data on the consumption, savings, and income of individuals and families available from numerous sample surveys made during the past century and a half.[2] Both sources of data seemed at first to confirm Keynes's hypothesis. Current consumption expenditure was highly correlated with income, the marginal propensity to consume was less than unity, and the marginal propensity was less than the average propensity to consume, so the percentage of income saved increased with income. But then a serious conflict of evidence arose. Estimates of savings in the United States made by Kuznets for the period since 1899 revealed no rise in the percentage

[1] J. M. Keynes, *The General Theory of Employment, Interest and Money* (New York and London: Harcourt, Brace and Co., 1936), pp. 96, 97.
[2] See Faith M. Williams and Carle C. Zimmerman, *Studies of Family Living In the United States and Other Countries* (Department of Agriculture, Miscellaneous Publication 223, 1935); George J. Stigler, "The Early History of Empirical Studies of Consumer Behavior," *The Journal of Political Economy*, LXII (April 1954), pp. 95–113.

of income saved during the past half-century despite a substantial rise in real income. According to his estimates, the percentage of income saved was much the same over the whole of the period. The corresponding ratio of consumption expenditure to income—the constancy of which means that it can be regarded as both the average and the marginal propensity to consume—is decidedly higher than the marginal propensities that had been computed from either time series or budget data.[3] Examination of budget studies for earlier periods strengthens the appearance of conflict. The average propensity to consume is roughly the same for widely separated dates, despite substantial differences in average real income. Yet each set of budget studies separately yields a marginal propensity decidedly lower than the average propensity. Finally, the savings ratio in the period after World War II was sharply lower than the ratio that would have been consistent with findings on the relation between income and savings in the interwar period. This experience dramatically underlined the inadequacy of a consumption function relating consumption or savings solely to current income.

The conflict of evidence stimulated a number of more complex hypotheses. Brady and Friedman suggested that a consumer unit's consumption depends not on its absolute income but on its position in the distribution of income among consumer units in its community. They presented a good deal of evidence, mostly from budget data, in support of this relative income hypothesis.[4] Duesenberry based the same hypothesis on a theoretical structure that emphasizes the desire to emulate one's neighbors and the demonstration by neighbors of the qualities of hitherto unknown or unused consumption goods. In addition, he suggested that the relative income hypothesis could be used to interpret aggregate data by expressing the ratio of consumption to income as a function of the ratio of current income to the highest level previously reached.[5] Duesenberry computed such a regression for the United States for 1929–1941 and obtained reasonably good results. Modigliani independently made essentially the same suggestion for the analysis

[3] For a summary of Kuznets's estimates and an analysis of their implications, see Simon Kuznets, "Proportion of Capital Formation to National Product," *American Economic Review, Papers and Proceedings*, XLII (May 1952), pp. 507–526.

[4] Dorothy S. Brady and Rose D. Friedman, "Savings and the Income Distribution," *Studies in Income and Wealth*, X (New York: National Bureau of Economic Research, 1947), pp. 247–265.

[5] James S. Duesenberry, *Income, Saving, and the Theory of Consumer Behavior* (Cambridge, Mass.: Harvard University Press, 1949). A crucial chapter of Duesenberry's book appeared earlier in *Income, Employment and Public Policy; Essays in Honor of Alvin H. Hansen* (New York: W. W. Norton & Co., 1948), pp. 54–81.

of aggregate data, submitted it to extensive and detailed statistical tests, and concluded that it gave excellent results.[6]

Tobin has recently examined the consistency of the relative income hypothesis and the earlier absolute income hypothesis with a limited body of empirical evidence. Though he finds neither hypothesis entirely satisfactory, he concludes that the weight of evidence favors the absolute income hypothesis, and he tentatively suggests that changes in wealth may explain the rough constancy over time in the fraction of income saved.[7] Tobin's analysis is examined in more detail below (Chapter VI, section 4).

The doubts about the adequacy of the Keynesian consumption function raised by the empirical evidence were reinforced by the theoretical controversy about Keynes's proposition that there is no automatic force in a monetary economy to assure the existence of a full-employment equilibrium position. A number of writers, particularly Haberler and Pigou,[8] demonstrated that this analytical proposition is invalid if consumption expenditure is taken to be a function not only of income but also of wealth or, to put it differently, if the average propensity to consume is taken to depend in a particular way on the ratio of wealth to income. This dependence is required for the so-called "Pigou effect." This suggestion was widely accepted, not only because of its consistency with general economic theory, but also because it seemed to offer a plausible explanation for the high ratio of consumption to income in the immediate postwar period.

One empirical study, by William Hamburger, finds that the ratio of wealth to income is closely correlated with the ratio of consumption to income, as judged by aggregate time series data for the interwar and post-World War II period.[9] Other studies, particularly some by Klein, have used budget data to investigate the role of particular kinds of wealth, especially liquid assets.[10]

---

[6] Franco Modigliani, "Fluctuations in the Saving-Income Ratio: A Problem in Economic Forecasting," *Studies in Income and Wealth*, XI (New York: National Bureau of Economic Research, 1949), pp. 371–441. For further discussion of the relative income hypothesis, see Chap. VI, below.

[7] James Tobin, "Relative Income, Absolute Income, and Savings," in *Money, Trade, and Economic Growth, in honor of John Henry Williams* (New York: Macmillan Co., 1951), pp. 135–156.

[8] Gottfried Haberler, *Prosperity and Depression*, 3rd ed. (Geneva: League of Nations, 1941), pp. 242, 403, 498–502; A. C. Pigou, "The Classical Stationary State," *Economic Journal*, LIII (December 1943), pp. 343–351.

[9] William Hamburger, "Consumption and Wealth," unpublished Ph.D. thesis at the University of Chicago; "The Relation of Consumption to Wealth and the Wage Rate," *Econometrica*, XXIII (January 1955), pp. 1–17.

[10] Lawrence R. Klein, "Estimating Patterns of Savings Behavior from Sample Survey Data," *Econometrica*, XIX, No. 4 (October 1951), pp. 438–454; George Katona,

This brief sketch may convey something of the flavor of the work that has been done in the past few decades on the consumption function. It cannot properly convey the wealth of detailed empirical evidence on consumption behavior that has been added during this period to earlier material, or the extraordinary number and variety of analytical studies that have been made of this evidence.

This monograph presents yet another hypothesis to explain the observed relation between consumption expenditure and income. The justification for doing so is that the new hypothesis seems potentially more fruitful and is in some measure more general than either the relative income hypothesis or the wealth-income hypothesis taken by itself. It incorporates fully the wealth-income effect and explains why the relative income hypothesis should be valid under special conditions. The hypothesis follows directly from the currently accepted pure theory of consumer behavior, seems consistent with existing empirical evidence, and has observable implications capable of being contradicted by additional evidence. Its essential idea is to combine the relation between consumption, wealth, and income suggested by purely theoretical considerations with a way of interpreting observed income data that I developed earlier for what at first glance seems a completely different purpose, namely the analysis of changes in relative income status.[11] This way of interpreting income data can be extended to consumption data, and in the process, the problem of changes in relative income status can be linked intimately with the problem of the determinants of consumption expenditure. The hypothesis thus enables much of the wide range of statistical evidence accumulated about the distribution of income to be brought to bear directly on the interpretation of consumption behavior.[12]

Lawrence R. Klein, John B. Lansing, and James N. Morgan, "Statistical Estimation of Economic Relations from Survey Data," *Contributions of Survey Methods to Economics* (New York: Columbia University Press, 1954), pp. 189–240.

[11] Milton Friedman and Simon Kuznets, *Income from Independent Professional Practice* (New York: National Bureau of Economic Research, 1945), Chap. V.

[12] After completing an earlier draft of this monograph, I saw two recent papers by Franco Modigliani and Richard Brumberg on the consumption function that embody a very similar approach, but that develop its implications in a rather different direction. The similarity of approach reflects, I believe, the influence of a common intellectual environment. See Modigliani and Brumberg, "Utility Analysis and the Consumption Function: An Interpretation of Cross-Section Data," *Post-Keynesian Economics*, ed. by Kenneth K. Kurihara (New Brunswick: Rutgers University Press, 1954), pp. 383–436. Also, "Utility Analysis and Aggregate Consumption Functions: An Attempt at Integration," (to appear in a Supplement to *Econometrica*).

CHAPTER II

The Implications of the Pure Theory of Consumer Behavior

THE relation between the theoretical constructs used in consumption research and the observable magnitudes regarded as approximating them has, I believe, received inadequate attention. It therefore seems desirable to start by setting forth in considerable detail the implications of the pure theory of consumer behavior, even though this involves repetition of some familiar material.

1. *Complete Certainty*

Let us consider first the behavior of a consumer unit under conditions of complete certainty. It knows for certain, we suppose, that it will receive a definite sum in each of a definite number of time periods; it knows the prices that will prevail for consumer goods in each period and the rate of interest at which it can borrow or lend. Under these conditions there are only two motives for spending on consumption less or more than it receives in any time period. The first is to "straighten out" the stream of expenditures— by appropriate timing of borrowing and lending, the unit can keep its expenditures relatively stable even though its receipts vary widely from time period to time period. The second is to earn interest on loans, if the interest rate is positive, or to receive payment for borrowing, if the interest rate is negative. How it will behave under the influence of these motives depends, of course, on its tastes—the relative utility it attaches to consumption at different points of time.[1]

To facilitate graphic presentation, consider the special case of two discrete time periods, say years 1 and 2.[2] The relevant features of a consumer unit's tastes at a point in time, say year 1, can then

---

[1] See Irving Fisher, *The Rate of Interest* (New York: Macmillan, 1907), esp. Chap. VI, pp. 87–116; *The Theory of Interest* (New York: Macmillan, 1930), esp. Chaps. X and XI.
[2] The analysis of this special case is essentially identical with that given by Fisher, *The Rate of Interest*, pp. 387–392, and by Kenneth E. Boulding, *Economic Analysis*, Rev. ed. (New York: Harper, 1948), pp. 734–741.

7

be summarized by a two-dimensional system of indifference curves, as in Figure 1. c_1, measured along the vertical axis, is the money value at year 1 prices of services consumed in year 1; c_2, measured along the horizontal axis, is the money value at year 2 prices of services consumed in year 2. A point on the diagram thus represents a particular combination of consumption in the two years. Underlying each such point is already a prior maximization process: the expenditures represented by the corresponding c_1 and c_2 are supposed optimally distributed among the various consumption services for the given prices. As always, a single indifference curve

FIGURE I

Hypothetical Indifference Curves and Budget Lines of a Consumer Unit
for Consumption in Two Time Units

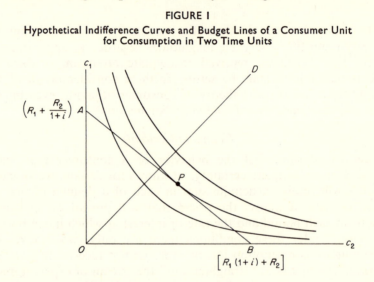

is the locus of combinations of c_1 and c_2 among which the consumer unit is indifferent—as it views the situation in year 1. The slope of the indifference curve at any point gives the rate at which it is willing to substitute consumption in year 2 for consumption in year 1. For the usual reasons, the indifference curves can be taken to be negatively sloped and convex to the origin.

Let R_1 and R_2 be the consumer unit's expected receipts in year 1 and 2 respectively, and i the interest rate. The maximum amount the unit can spend in year 1 if it spends nothing in year 2 is $R_1 + [R_2/(1 + i)]$, that is, its receipts in year 1 plus the maximum loan it can repay with its receipts in year 2. The maximum amount it can spend in year 2 if it spends nothing in year 1 is $R_1(1 + i) + R_2$ or its receipts in year 1 plus the interest it would earn if it loaned out the whole of its year 1 receipts, plus its receipts in year 2. A straight line between these two points (AB in Figure 1) then defines the combinations of consumption in the two years that are open to the consumer unit; it can attain any point in the triangle OAB. If we suppose that the two years stand for the whole future for which plans are being made, there is nothing that the unit can gain by not spending all it receives, so that the combination chosen will be on the budget line AB. The optimum combination is, of course, the point at which the budget line is tangent to an indifference curve, point P in Figure 1.

We have introduced three variables to describe the consumer unit's opportunities: R_1, R_2, and i. However, it is clear from the diagram that consumption in year 1 depends in any meaningful way not on three variables but only on two: the slope of the budget line and its position. Changes in R_1 or R_2 affect consumption in year 1 only through their effect on what we may term the consumer unit's wealth in year 1, or

$$(2.1) \qquad\qquad W_1 = R_1 + \frac{R_2}{1 + i}.$$

Changes in R_1 and R_2 that do not affect its wealth do not affect its consumption. To put it differently, it appears at first that we need to know three things to determine c_1, namely, R_1, R_2, and i; in fact, we need to know only two, namely, a particular combination of R_1, R_2, and i; and i itself. There are different combinations of R_1, R_2, and i that we could use; that is, different ways of collapsing the three original variables into two. One way, already suggested, is to take W_1 and i as the two variables[3] and to write the consumption function as

$$(2.2) \qquad\qquad c_1 = f(W_1, i).$$

This elementary formulation already sheds considerable light on the usual view about the consumption function. What we have been calling receipts in year 1 (R_1) or some slight modification thereof,

---

[3] This is equivalent to the usual way of writing the demand curve for a particular good as a function of its price, for given money income and other prices. Changes in wealth shift the budget line parallel to itself, and the resulting points of tangency trace out the effect of changes in wealth on consumption. Changes in the interest rate pivot the budget line about the point A, and the resulting points of tangency trace out the effect of changes in the interest rate for a given wealth. This procedure has the disadvantage of the usual demand curve procedure that it does not separate substitution effects fully from the effect of a general increase or decrease in available opportunities—income effects in the usual demand analysis. An alternative that would be comparable to the real income demand curve I have discussed elsewhere is to define the wealth variable so that a change in the interest rate pivots the budget line about the initial point of equilibrium P. Since our interest here is primarily in the relation of c to W, rather than to i, these issues are neglected in the text. See "The Marshallian Demand Curve," *Journal of Political Economy*, LVII (December 1949), pp. 463–495, reprinted in my *Essays in Positive Economics* (Chicago: University of Chicago Press, 1953), pp. 47–99.

is usually, and particularly in statistical budget studies, called "income" and taken as the variable on which consumption depends. Now in our simple case it is clear that consumption in year 1 does not depend directly on R_1 at all; a change in R_1 affects consumption only through its effect on W_1 and, if accompanied by an appropriate opposite change in R_2, may not affect consumption at all. This is clearly eminently sensible: if a consumer unit knows that its receipts in any one year are unusually high and if it expects lower receipts subsequently, it will surely tend to adjust its consumption to its "normal" receipts rather than to its current receipts. On the other hand, if savings are defined as the difference between current receipts and current consumption, they do depend on current receipts, for, from (2.2), savings are then given by

$$(2.3) \qquad s_1 = R_1 - c_1 = R_1 - f(W_1, i).$$

Equation (2.3) is the formal rationalization for the frequently expressed view that savings are a "residual."

The designation of current receipts as "income" in statistical studies is an expedient enforced by limitations of data. On a theoretical level, income is generally defined as the amount a consumer unit could consume (or believes that it could) while maintaining its wealth intact.[4] On our analysis, consumption is a function of income so defined. In the simple example considered here, W_1 is the consumer unit's wealth in year 1 and iW_1, its income in this sense for year 1. If receipts in year 1 exceed iW_1, the difference must be set aside as a "depreciation allowance" to be added to receipts in year 2 in order that wealth in year 2 be the same as in year 1. If receipts in year 1 fall short of iW_1, the difference is the amount that the unit can borrow to spend in addition to its receipts without reducing wealth in year 2 below its level in year 1.[5]

---

[4] The well-known problems raised by this definition are not relevant to the analysis that follows. For a discussion of some of them see J. R. Hicks, *Value and Capital* (Oxford, 1939), pp. 171–188.

[5] The use of discrete points of time raises difficulties of timing that disappear if the receipts are considered as continuous. Perhaps the simplest way to show the arithmetic involved in the discrete case is to suppose that R_1 and R_2 are received at the beginning of the respective time periods and that the expenditures are made at the end of the time periods. Then R_1 will have grown to $R_1(1 + i)$ by the end of the first period. The depreciation allowance is $R_1(1 + i) - iW_1$, or

$$R_1(1 + i) - i\left(R_1 + \frac{R_2}{1 + i} \right) = R_1 - \frac{iR_2}{1 + i}.$$

Total wealth at the beginning of the second period is this sum plus receipts at the beginning of the second period, or R_2, which gives

$$W_2 = R_1 - \frac{iR_2}{1 + i} + R_2 = R_1 + \frac{R_2}{1 + i} = W_1.$$

A similar problem arises about the meaning of "consumption." We have been using the term consumption to designate the value of the *services* that is it *planned* to consume during the period in question, which, under conditions of certainty, would also equal the value of the services actually consumed. The term is generally used in statistical studies to designate actual expenditures on goods and services. It therefore differs from the value of services it is planned to consume on two counts: first, because of additions to or subtractions from the stock of consumer goods, second, because of divergencies between plans and their realization.

Let us use the terms "permanent income" and "permanent consumption" to refer to the concepts relevant to the theoretical analysis, so as to avoid confusion with the frequent usage of income as synonymous with current receipts and consumption as synonymous with current expenditures, and let us designate them by y_p and c_p respectively, with an additional numerical subscript to denote the year in question.[6] We can write the consumption function as

$$(2.4) \qquad c_{p1} = f\left(\frac{y_{p1}}{i}, i\right) = g(y_{p1}, i) = g(iW_1, i),$$

since $y_{p1} = iW_1$.

This approach seems somewhat forced for the present simple case of a horizon of only two years. Initial wealth is then spent on consumption during the two years, rather than being maintained. It makes much more sense if (2.4) is regarded as a generalization from this special case to a longer horizon.[7]

The only empirical restrictions that have been imposed on the indifference curves up to this point are that they be negatively sloped (to be consistent with the observed absence of a tendency for individuals to give their wealth away indiscriminately) and convex to the origin (to be consistent with the observed absence of a tendency for individuals to spend their entire wealth on

[6] The adjective "planned" would perhaps be more appropriate in the present context than "permanent." The reason for using the latter will appear in Chap. III below.

[7] The transformation used to convert (2.2) into (2.4) raises difficulties for $i = 0$. If there is a finite perpetual income stream, the value of wealth is then infinite for the consumer unit, and it can satisfy its desires for current consumption without limit—it is in the economic *nirvana* where the economic problem disappears. If the income stream is limited in duration, the value of wealth is finite. A finite level of consumption can then be maintained only for a finite period and the implicit generalization of (2.2) to a (2.4) regarded as referring to a perpetual stationary state, in which it is possible to assign stationary flows without specifying their duration, is impossible. These are the usual difficulties that arise in connection with a zero interest rate supposed applicable to *all* sources of services. They may not arise if the interest rate is zero only for some sources of services, for example, only for nonhuman sources of services.

11

consumption in a single time period). These restrictions on the indifference curves impose only rather mild restrictions on the shape of a consumption function described by (2.2) or (2.4). To get a more specific hypothesis about the shape of the consumption function we shall have to go farther.

Suppose money prices are the same in the two years so that a point on the 45 degree line OD in Figure 1 represents equal opportunities in the two years. Suppose also that the unit is regarded as the same in the two years (thus abstracting from "aging" and similar phenomena). It then seems reasonable to suppose that if, in year 1, the consumer unit correctly assesses the relative value of consumption in the two years, the indifference curves will be symmetrical around OD so that c_1 and c_2 could be interchanged without altering the curves—alternatively, this can be taken as the definition of the absence of "time preference proper."[8]

This type of symmetry implies that all indifference curves have a common slope of -1 where they intersect OD—that is, that the consumer unit is willing to substitute one dollar of consumption this year for one dollar of consumption next year when both dollars will buy the same things and when it is consuming the same real amount in the two years, and that this is true regardless of the level of consumption. The convexity of the indifference curves then implies that when the unit is consuming more in year 1 than in year 2, it is willing to give up more than one dollar of consumption in year 1 for a dollar of consumption in year 2; when it is consuming less in year 1 than in year 2, it requires more than a dollar of additional consumption in year 2 to compensate it for giving up one dollar in year 1. It follows that if $R_1 = R_2$ so that the initial position is on the 45 degree line, the consumer unit consumes more than its receipts in year 1 if the interest rate is negative; exactly its receipts, if the interest rate is zero; and less than its receipts, if the interest rate is positive, as it is for the hypothetical budget line AB in Figure 1.

For a zero interest rate, the conditions so far imposed make consumption the same fraction of wealth ($1/2$ in our special case) at all levels of wealth. It seems reasonable to generalize this relation to other interest rates; that is, to suppose that, just as the indifference curves all have a common slope where they intersect the 45 degree line through the origin, so also they have a common slope where

---

[8] It should be noted that our special assumptions eliminate some of the usual reasons assigned for time preference, in particular, the possibility that the consumer unit will not live to engage in consumption in subsequent years, or that equally satisfactory consumer goods will not for one reason or another be available then as now.

12

they intersect any other straight line through the origin—mathematically, to suppose that the utility function is not only symmetrical but also homogeneous in c_1 and c_2. For our special case, this means that the rate at which the individual is willing to substitute consumption in year 2 for consumption in year 1 depends only on the ratio of consumption in the two years, not on the absolute level of consumption. Doubling, let us say, the level of consumption in year 1 may diminish in some sense the urgency of additional consumption in year 1 relative to consumption in year 2, which, by itself, would tend to lower the additional year 2 consumption required to compensate the consumer unit for giving up one dollar of year 1 consumption; however, if the level of consumption in year 2 is simultaneously doubled, this would have the opposite effect, diminishing the urgency of additional consumption in year 2 relative to consumption in year 1, and so, by itself, tending to raise the amount of year 2 consumption required to compensate the consumer unit for giving up one dollar of year 1 consumption. These two effects need not exactly offset one another; but there seems no a priori reason why the first should systematically or generally tend to exceed the second or conversely; the things being compared are of the same stuff, differing only in dating; it is hard to see any reason why this difference in dating should have an asymmetrical effect.[9] There seems nothing unreasonable, therefore, in supposing the two effects exactly to offset one another, and this is surely the simplest hypothesis. We shall, therefore, tentatively accept it, subject as always, of course, to the possibility that empirical evidence will be discovered that turns out to be inconsistent with it and that will therefore require complicating the hypothesis.

[9] This simple argument is the basic reason for questioning the initially plausible conjecture that the ratio of consumption to income decreases with income, if income is appropriately defined as a flow that can be permanently maintained. To put it differently, the ratio of consumption to permanent income is dimensionally free from any absolute units, even if the numerator and denominator are regarded as physical quantities of goods, rather than as value sums, for the physical units in numerator and denominator are the same. One would expect this ratio to depend on dimensionally similar variables or at least on variables that are free of the physical units common to numerator and denominator (like the rate of interest, the reciprocal of which has the dimension of time units). Why should it depend in any obvious way on such a dimensionally different variable as the absolute level of income? Note that this argument does not justify the conclusion that the ratio of one kind of consumption to another can be expected also to be independent of the absolute level of income. Regarded in terms of physical quantities, such a ratio has, for example, the dimensions, pounds of sowbelly per pound of steak, and might readily depend on such dimensionally comparable variables as the ratio of absolute prices of steak to sowbelly (also having the dimensions, pounds of sowbelly per pound of steak) or absolute income (capable of being regarded as the total number of pounds of sowbelly or of steak that could be consumed and so having the dimensions of pounds of sowbelly or pounds of steak).

For indifference curves satisfying these assumptions, the consumption function defined by (2.4) assumes a particularly simple form, namely,

$$(2.5) \qquad c_{p1} = k(i, u) \cdot y_{p1} = k(i, u) \cdot i W_1 ,$$

where the function has been written so that it can be regarded as applying to an indefinitely long horizon, and not merely to two years. While k does not depend on the level of wealth or permanent income, it obviously does depend on the interest rate. It also depends on any factors that determine the shape of the indifference curves, symbolized in (2.5) by the variable u (for utility factors).[10]

If u is regarded as including such factors as age, family composition, and the like, we can drop the earlier assumption that the consumer unit is the same in the two (or more) years considered, and along with it the special assumption that if $i = 0$, $c_1 = c_2$ in the two year case. That is, the preceding analysis can be interpreted as referring to consumer units of a given kind in a particular year.

The simple function (2.5), though derived from such elementary and abstract considerations, is a cornerstone of the theory of the consumption function presented in this monograph. We shall see that the introduction of uncertainty gives no reason to alter it fundamentally, and that it is not inconsistent with existing empirical evidence on consumption behavior, provided that its variables are appropriately identified with observable magnitudes.

2. *The Effect of Uncertainty*

Uncertainty about the future has effects of two kinds on the preceding analysis: first, it complicates the interpretation of the indifference curve diagram; second, it introduces an additional reason for saving that requires distinguishing among different kinds of wealth.

a. THE INDIFFERENCE CURVE DIAGRAM

Under conditions of certainty, the alternatives open to the consumer unit in year 2 for each level of consumption in year 1 can be described completely by a single number, namely, the maximum level of real consumption attainable in year 2, or the abscissa of the budget line AB in Figure 1. Under conditions of uncertainty, such a simple description is impossible; it must be replaced by a probability distribution of possible maximum levels of real

---

[10] Duesenberry reaches the same conclusion, that consumption is proportionate to income in long-run comparative statics, on the basis of a somewhat different line of reasoning. *Income, Saving, and the Theory of Consumer Behavior* (Cambridge, Mass.: Harvard University Press, 1949), pp. 32–37.

14

consumption in year 2, the dispersion among the possible levels reflecting both the direct effect of uncertainty about future receipts and future prices and the indirect effect of this uncertainty on the possibility of lending or borrowing.

Suppose that there is no uncertainty about future tastes (as viewed from the present), and that the c_2 axis continues to be interpreted as showing actual consumption. The indifference curves are then unaffected by the introduction of uncertainty. However, the budget line is significantly altered in meaning. The probability distribution of possible future consumption associated with each level of consumption in year 1 has some utility to the consumer unit, and there is in general some single value of consumption that has the same utility. The locus of such "certainty equivalents" traces out a curve comparable to the budget line in the sense that its point of tangency with an indifference curve is the optimum position. But there is no reason for this curve to be a straight line, and it cannot be computed solely from knowledge of the opportunities open to the unit; it depends also on its tastes. The sharp dichotomy between tastes and opportunities that is the central attraction of the indifference analysis under certainty is shattered.

An alternative is to interpret the c_2 axis of Figure 1 as referring to expected consumption in year 2, where "expected" is used in the sense of "mean value" rather than of "anticipated." If there were no disagreement about probability distributions, so that expected receipts could be borrowed or loaned at a fixed rate of interest, the budget line would be unaffected and would remain a straight line. The indifference curves would now, however, be significantly altered in meaning. The utility attached to a given expected value depends on the probability distribution yielding that expected value. The indifference curves can therefore be drawn only if the probability distribution yielding each expected value is specified; once again, any sharp separation between opportunities and tastes is destroyed.

The introduction of uncertainty thus blurs the sharp lines of the above analysis, and suggests additional factors that may produce departures from the shape of the consumption function specified in (2.5). However, on the present level of analysis, there seems no way to judge whether these factors would tend to make consumption a larger or a smaller fraction of wealth the higher the absolute level of wealth. Accordingly, this effect of uncertainty establishes no presumption against the shape assigned to the consumption function, and thus casts no shadow on the "simplicity" that recommends it.

b. MOTIVES FOR HOLDING WEALTH

The introduction of uncertainty adds a new reason for holding wealth to the two motives present under certainty—straightening out the consumption stream and earning interest. This new motive is the availability of a reserve for emergencies—for unexpectedly low receipts, on the one hand, or unexpectedly high levels of consumption on the other. If all forms of wealth were equally satisfactory as a reserve for emergencies, this motive could be regarded as producing simply an alteration in the shape of the indifference curves of Figure 1 and otherwise completely covered by that figure. Any part of wealth not used for current consumption would be available as a reserve for emergencies. Provision for future consumption would therefore be valued not only for its own sake but also because it provided such a reserve. The result would be that the indifference curves would be steeper at each point than otherwise; that is, the consumer unit would be willing to give up a larger amount of current consumption than otherwise to add a dollar to future consumption.

All forms of wealth are not, however, equally satisfactory as a reserve for emergencies. The major general distinction is between human and nonhuman wealth. In a nonslave society, there is no market in human beings comparable to the market for nonhuman capital. It is in general far easier to borrow on the basis of a tangible physical asset, or a claim to one, than on the basis of future earning power. Accordingly, current consumption may be expected to depend not only on total permanent income and the interest rate, but also on the fraction of permanent income derived from nonhuman wealth, or—what is equivalent for a given interest rate—on the ratio of nonhuman wealth to permanent income. The higher this ratio, the less need there is for an additional reserve, and the higher current consumption may be expected to be.[11] The crucial variable is the ratio of nonhuman wealth to permanent income, not the absolute amount of nonhuman wealth. A reserve is needed for protection against unexpected occurrences threatening the realization of a planned level of consumption, or making it urgent to consume at a higher level than that initially planned. A common proportional increase in nonhuman wealth and in permanent income increases both the reserve available and the level of consumption to be protected; it is like a change in scale. In consequence, there seems no a priori reason why such a common proportional increase

---

[11] To incorporate this effect formally into Figure 1 would require the addition of another axis showing the amount of nonhuman wealth.

16

in nonhuman wealth and in permanent income should systematically or generally raise the importance attached to increasing the size of the reserve, or conversely.[12] This effect of uncertainty therefore, like the other, establishes no presumption against the form assigned to the consumption function in (2.5). It requires only that the ratio of nonhuman wealth to income be included as a variable determining k, the ratio of consumption to permanent income. This converts (2.5) into

$$(2.6) \qquad c_p = k(i, w, u,)y_p = k(i, w, u)iW \,,$$

where w stands for the ratio of nonhuman wealth to permanent income and, for simplicity, the subscript 1 has been dropped from c, y, w, and W, with the understanding that all variables refer to the same point in time.

The importance attached to a reserve for emergencies depends, of course, on the degree of uncertainty that the consumer unit foresees. The variable u may be taken to include any objective factors that affect its anticipations. For example, the degree of inequality of wealth or income in the community may very well be related to the anticipated degree of uncertainty about receipts and so be a relevant variable.

All forms of nonhuman wealth are not equally satisfactory as a reserve for emergencies; this is the reason why certain kinds of nonhuman wealth, such as so-called "liquid assets," have been singled out for special attention in some empirical studies. But none of the other distinctions among forms of wealth seems as pervasive and fundamental as the distinction between human and nonhuman wealth, or even sufficiently fundamental to justify including it in the consumption function at the present stage.

The distinction among different kinds of wealth implies a corresponding distinction among different rates of interest. The rate of interest at which an individual can borrow on the basis of his future earnings may be different from the rate at which he can borrow on the basis of nonhuman capital; and the rate at which he can borrow may differ from the rate at which he can lend. We shall, however, neglect these complications, letting i stand for the whole complex of rates of interest.

---

[12] The dimensional argument of footnote 9 applies here.

It is at first glance tempting to suppose that the "law of averages" makes the same ratio of nonhuman wealth to permanent income more adequate, the higher the absolute level of both. This does not, however, follow if the increase in both takes the form of a common proportional increase in each possible future receipt, with the probabilities unchanged. In this case, the standard deviation is increased in the same ratio as the mean.

3. *The Relation between the Individual and the Aggregate Consumption Function*

The preceding theoretical analysis has been for an individual consumer unit. Equation (2.6) to which it leads ostensibly describes the behavior of such a unit for different values of its variables. In order to use this equation in interpreting group behavior, we must take the additional step of regarding the same equation as applicable to all members of the group—not merely the same form of equation, but the same functional relation. This is, however, a less drastic step than it may at first appear. The variables in equation (2.6), particularly w and u, are designed precisely to allow for differences among consumer units. If i, w, and some particular specification of u are the same for a number of consumer units and yet the ratio of consumption to permanent income differs among the consumer units by enough to be regarded as significant for the purpose at hand, than either the equation itself must be regarded as deficient, or the particular specification of u as inadequate. The acceptance of (2.6) and a particular specification of u for an individual consumer unit is thus equivalent to its acceptance for all members of a group.

Given that (2.6) applies to every consumer unit in a group, the ratio k of consumption to permanent income will nonetheless vary from consumer unit to consumer unit because of differences among them in the values of i, w, and u; and the absolute amount of consumption will vary because of differences in y_p as well. Aggregate consumption depends therefore not only on the precise form of equation (2.6) but also on the distribution of consumer units by these variables. Let

$$(2.7) \qquad f(i, w, u, y_p)\,di\,dw\,du\,dy_p$$

be the number of consumer units for whom the interest rate is between i and $i + di$, the ratio of nonhuman wealth to permanent income is between w and $w + dw$, the taste determining factors are between u and $u + du$, and permanent income is between y_p and $y_p + dy_p$. Then aggregate consumption is

$$(2.8) \qquad c_p^* = \int\!\!\int\!\!\int\!\!\int_{i,w,u,y_p} f(i, w, u, y_p)k(i, w, u)y_p\,di\,dw\,du\,dy_p .$$

Suppose that the distribution of consumer units by income is independent of their distribution by i, w, and u, so that

$$(2.9) \qquad f(i, w, u, y_p) = g(i, w, u)\cdot h(y_p) .$$

18

Equation (2.8) then reduces to

$$(2.10) \qquad\qquad c_p^* = k^*(\qquad\quad)\cdot y_p^* ,$$

where c_p^* is aggregate permanent consumption; y_p^*, aggregate permanent income; and

$$(2.11) \qquad k^*(\qquad\quad) = \iiint_{i,w,u} g(i, w, u)k(i, w, u)didwdu .$$

k^* depends on the function k, and also on the function g which describes the distribution of individuals by i, w, u. As an approximation, k^* could be expressed as a function of the mean values of i, w, and u, their variances, and the co-variances among them, or other similar parameters describing the distribution. The coefficients of these variables would be determined by the parameters of k. The parenthesis containing the variables has been left blank in (2.10) and (2.11) because there is no way of specifying on the present level of generality a limited number of variables to stand for the functions k and g.

Equation (2.10) is obviously unchanged if both sides are divided by the same number, such as total population or a price index, so in using (2.10), c_p^* and y_p^* can be taken to refer equally to money aggregates, real aggregates, money per capita figures, or real per capita figures.

The assumption used in passing from (2.8) to (2.10), namely, that the distribution of consumer units by income is independent of their distribution by i, w, and u, is obviously false in a descriptive sense. The variable u, for example, covers such factors as age, size of family, perhaps education, and these are all known to be connected systematically with the distribution of income; indeed, we shall have occasion at a later point to use some of these connections to explain certain observed features of consumption behavior. At the same time, although the interdependence between these variables and the distribution of income may be important for some problems, it may not be for this aggregation. The interdependence enters in a rather complex way and equation (2.10) remains an approximation even when interdependence exists. If, as we shall see to be the case, equation (2.10) is a good approximation of the relation among observed magnitudes, this must be interpreted to mean that the interdependence is of only secondary importance.

CHAPTER III

The Permanent Income Hypothesis

THE magnitudes termed "permanent income" and "permanent consumption" that play such a critical role in the theoretical analysis cannot be observed directly for any individual consumer unit. The most that can be observed are actual receipts and expenditures during some finite period, supplemented, perhaps, by some verbal statements about expectations for the future. The theoretical constructs are *ex ante* magnitudes; the empirical data are *ex post*. Yet in order to use the theoretical analysis to interpret empirical data, a correspondence must be established between the theoretical constructs and the observed magnitudes.

The most direct way to do so, and the one that has generally been followed in similar contexts, is to construct estimates of permanent income and permanent consumption for each consumer unit separately by adjusting the cruder receipts and expenditure data for some of their more obvious defects, and then to treat the adjusted *ex post* magnitudes as if they were also the desired *ex ante* magnitudes. Cash expenditures during a particular time period that are regarded as expenses of earning income can be deducted from cash receipts during the corresponding time period; accrual methods of accounting can be substituted for cash accounting for some or all income items; expenditures on durable consumer goods can be regarded as capital expenditures and only the imputed value of services rendered included as consumption; and so on. These adjustments clearly reduce the difference between the statistical estimates and the theoretical constructs and are therefore highly desirable. But even when they are carried as far as is at all feasible, the resulting magnitudes, interpreted as estimates of permanent income and permanent consumption, are not consistent with equation (2.6): measured consumption turns out to be a smaller fraction of measured income for high than for low measured incomes even for groups of consumer units for whom it does not seem reasonable to attribute this result to differences in the values of i, w, or u.

We are thus driven either to reject equation (2.6), which is what earlier workers have done, or to resort to more indirect means of establishing a correspondence between the theoretical constructs and the observed magnitudes, which is what I propose to do. One indirect means is to use evidence for other time periods and other consumer units to interpret data for one consumer unit for one period. For example, if Mr. A's measured income fluctuates widely from year to year while Mr. B's is highly stable, it seems reasonable that Mr. A's measured income is a poorer index of his permanent income than Mr. B's is of his. Again, suppose Mr. A's measured income in any period is decidedly lower than the average measured income of a group of individuals who are similar to him in characteristics that we have reason to believe affect potential earnings significantly—for example, age, occupation, race, and location. It then seems reasonable to suppose that Mr. A's measured income understates his permanent income.

The following formalization of the relation between the theoretical constructs and observed magnitudes is designed to facilitate the use of such evidence. Its central idea is to interpret empirical data as observable manifestations of theoretical constructs that are themselves regarded as not directly observable.

1. *The Interpretation of Data on the Income and Consumption of Consumer Units*

Let y represent a consumer unit's measured income for some time period, say a year. I propose to treat this income as the sum of two components: a permanent component (y_p), corresponding to the permanent income of the theoretical analysis, and a transitory component (y_t),[1] or

$$(3.1) \qquad\qquad y = y_p + y_t.$$

The permanent component is to be interpreted as reflecting the effect of those factors that the unit regards as determining its capital value or wealth: the nonhuman wealth it owns; the personal attributes of the earners in the unit, such as their training, ability, personality; the attributes of the economic activity of the earners, such as the occupation followed, the location of the economic activity, and so on. It is analogous to the "expected" value of a probability distribution. The transitory component is to be interpreted as reflecting all "other" factors, factors that are likely to be treated by the unit affected as

---

[1] The terminology, and much of the subsequent analysis, is taken from Friedman and Kuznets, *Income from Independent Professional Practice*, pp. 325–38, 352–364.

"accidental" or "chance" occurrences, though they may, from another point of view, be the predictable effect of specifiable forces, for example, cyclical fluctuations in economic activity.[2] In statistical data, the transitory component includes also chance errors of measurement; unfortunately, there is in general no way to separate these from the transitory component as viewed by the consumer unit.

Some of the factors that give rise to transitory components of income are specific to particular consumer units, for example, illness, a bad guess about when to buy or sell, and the like; and, similarly, chance errors of measurement. For any considerable group of consumer units, the resulting transitory components tend to average out, so that if they alone accounted for the discrepancies between permanent and measured income, the mean measured income of the group would equal the mean permanent component, and the mean transitory component would be zero. But not all factors giving rise to transitory components need be of this kind. Some may be largely common to the members of the group, for example, unusually good or bad weather, if the group consists of farmers in the same locality; or a sudden shift in the demand for some product, if the group consists of consumer units whose earners are employed in producing this product. If such factors are favorable for any period, the mean transitory component is positive; if they are unfavorable, it is negative.[3] Similarly, a systematic bias in measurement may produce a nonzero mean transitory component in recorded data even though the transitory factors affecting consumer units have a zero effect on the average.

Similarly, let c represent a consumer unit's expenditures for some time period, and let it be regarded as the sum of a permanent component (c_p) and a transitory component (c_t), so that

$$(3.2) \qquad c = c_p + c_t.$$

Again, some of the factors producing transitory components of consumption are specific to particular consumer units, such as unusual sickness, a specially favorable opportunity to purchase, and the like; others affect groups of consumer units in the same way, such as an

---

[2] This division is, of course, in part arbitrary, and just where to draw the line may well depend on the particular application. Similarly, the dichotomy between permanent and transitory components is a highly special case. See *ibid.*, pp. 352–364, for a generalization to a larger number of components.

[3] Note the difference from *ibid.*, p. 326, where the mean transitory component can be taken to be zero without loss of generality. The difference reflects a narrower definition of transitory component in *ibid.* plus the use of the concept to compare the same group in two years.

unusually cold spell, a bountiful harvest, and the like. The effects of the former tend to average out; the effects of the latter produce positive or negative mean transitory components for groups of consumer units; the same is true with chance and systematic errors of measurement.

It is tempting to interpret the permanent components as corresponding to average lifetime values and the transitory components as the difference between such lifetime averages and the measured values in a specific time period. It would, however, be a serious mistake to accept such an interpretation, for two reasons. In the first place, the experience of one unit is itself but a small sample from a more extensive hypothetical universe, so there is no reason to suppose that transitory components average out to zero over the unit's lifetime. In the second place, and more important, it seems neither necessary nor desirable to decide in advance the precise meaning to be attached to "permanent." The distinction between permanent and transitory is intended to interpret actual behavior. We are going to treat consumer units *as if* they regarded their income and their consumption as the sum of two such components, and *as if* the relation between the permanent components is the one suggested by our theoretical analysis. The precise line to be drawn between permanent and transitory components is best left to be determined by the data themselves, to be whatever seems to correspond to consumer behavior.

Figure 2 is designed to bring out more explicitly the wide range of possible interpretations of permanent income. This figure refers to a single consumer unit, the head of which is assumed to be 30 years of age on the date in 1956 for which the figure is drawn. We may suppose the unit to have been formed when the head was aged 20. Measured income experience from 20 to 30, as recorded in the solid jagged line, is a datum; so also, of course, are other items not recorded in the figure, such as the amount of nonhuman wealth possessed, the occupation of the head and of other members of the unit, location, and so on. Future measured income experience is uncertain. The scatter of dots for later ages is intended to represent the possibilities as *viewed* by the unit; for each future date, there is some anticipated probability distribution of measured income. Because of the limitations of a two-dimensional figure, this scatter diagram seriously misrepresents the situation in one important respect. It suggests that the probability distributions at different ages are independent, whereas in general they might be expected to be interdependent. The distribution anticipated for age 40, for example, if a high measured income is realized at age 31 would presumably be different from

23

the distribution expected if a low measured income is realized.[4] But this defect of the figure is not serious for our present limited purpose.

The scatter in the figure should not be confused conceptually with the corresponding scatter that would be generated by plotting the contemporaneous incomes of a large number of units with heads of different age. The scatter in the figure is the anticipated experience of one unit, not the realized experience of many. In forming its

FIGURE 2

Illustration of Alternative Interpretations of Permanent Income

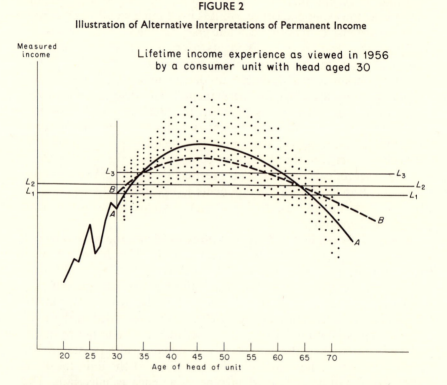

anticipations, the one unit may well take into account the contemporaneous experience of units which are of different age but alike in respect of other factors such as occupation, nonhuman wealth, etc.; and it may for some purposes usefully be regarded as doing so by simply accepting the contemporaneous differences as describing its own future possibilities. On the conceptual level, however, there is no

[4] The most general description would be in terms of a probability distribution of alternative age-measured-income functions. It should be noted that the generalized analytical formulation in *ibid.*, pp. 352–364, allows fully for interdependence.

need to foreclose the possibility that the unit will take other information into account as well.[5]

The solid curve AA in Figure 2 is the mean of the probability distributions anticipated for future years. It is one possible interpretation of the permanent income to which consumption is adapted. The horizontal line L_1L_1 is the mean lifetime income as anticipated at age 20; L_2L_2, as anticipated at age 30, taking into account realized experience from age 20 to age 30; L_3L_3, mean income anticipated at age 30 for the remaining lifetime of the unit. Each of these is another possible interpretation of permanent income, and almost at the opposite extreme of the spectrum from AA. No one of these has very great intuitive appeal as *the* permanent income to which consumption is adapted; AA, because it implies an exceedingly short time horizon; L_1L_1, L_2L_2, and L_3L_3, not only because they imply an extremely long time horizon, but also because they imply that units can borrow on the basis of anticipated receipts from both human and nonhuman wealth at the same interest rate at which they can lend accumulated nonhuman wealth. L_3L_3 has the further objection that it supposes no carry-over into the present of past adaptations. The dashed curve BB is an intermediate interpretation, intended to be something of an average of AA and L_1L_1 or L_2L_2. Something like this seems intuitively the most plausible interpretation, but intuitive plausibility gives little guidance to the exact kind of average, or length of horizon. For this, we must rely on the empirical evidence. (See Chapter VII, where a tentative estimate is made on the basis of existing evidence.)

Figure 2 is drawn for a particular date. There is nothing about the concept of permanent income that requires the relevant parts of the figure to remain the same for any later date. Aside from the point already made, that in advance the probability distribution for any future date depends on the measured income actually experienced, the whole joint probability distribution may be shifted by occurrences that were entirely unanticipated at the date in question. In our empirical work, we shall sometimes find it desirable to suppose that permanent income, or the age pattern of permanent income, remains unchanged over a period of years, but it should be clear that this is an empirical specialization of a more general concept.

2. *A Formal Statement of the Permanent Income Hypothesis*

In its most general form our hypothesis about the consumption function, which we shall hereafter refer to as the permanent income

---

[5] For example, in sec. 3 of Chap. IV below, the unit is interpreted as modifying contemporaneous experience by information on the secular trend of income.

hypothesis, is given by the three equations (2.6), (3.1), and (3.2):

(2.6) $$c_p = k(i, w, u)y_p,$$

(3.1) $$y = y_p + y_t,$$

(3.2) $$c = c_p + c_t.$$

Equation (2.6) defines a relation between permanent income and permanent consumption. It specifies that the ratio between them is independent of the size of permanent income but does depend on other variables, in particular: (1) the rate of interest (i) or sets of rates of interest at which the consumer unit can borrow or lend; (2) the relative importance of property and nonproperty income, symbolized by the ratio of nonhuman wealth to income (w); and (3) the factors symbolized by the portmanteau variable u determining the consumer unit's tastes and preferences for consumption versus additions to wealth. The most significant of the latter factors probably are (a) the number of members of the consumer unit and their characteristics, particularly their ages, and (b) the importance of transitory factors affecting income and consumption, measured, for example, by the "spread" or standard deviation of the probability distributions of the transitory components relative to the size of the corresponding permanent components. Equations (3.1) and (3.2) define the connection between the permanent components and the measured magnitudes.

In this most general form the hypothesis is empty, in the sense that no empirical data could contradict it. Equations (3.1) and (3.2) are purely definitional; they add two equations but also two additional unknowns, the transitory components. There are a variety of ways to specialize the hypothesis so that it is capable of being contradicted by observed data. The one I shall use is to specify some of the characteristics of the probability distributions of the transitory components. A particularly simple specification, yet one that seems adequate to explain existing evidence, is to suppose that the transitory components of income and consumption are uncorrelated with one another and with the corresponding permanent components, or

(3.3) $$\rho_{y_t y_p} = \rho_{c_t c_p} = \rho_{y_t c_t} = 0,$$

where ρ stands for the correlation coefficient between the variables designated by the subscripts.

The assumptions that the first two correlations in (3.3)—between the permanent and transitory components of income and of consumption—are zero seem very mild and highly plausible. Indeed, by themselves, they have little substantive content and can almost be regarded as simply completing or translating the definitions of transitory and permanent components; the qualitative notion that the transitory component is intended to embody is of an accidental and transient addition to or subtraction from income, which is almost equivalent to saying an addition or subtraction that is not correlated with the rest of income. The merging of errors of measurement with transitory components contributes further to the plausibility that these correlations are zero.

For a group of individuals, it is plausible to suppose that the absolute size of the transitory component varies with the size of the permanent component: that a given random event produces the same percentage rather than the same absolute increase or decrease in the incomes of units with different permanent components. This may make more convenient an alternative definition of transitory component that is suggested below; it is not, however, inconsistent with zero correlation. Zero correlation implies only that the *average* transitory component—the algebraic average in which positive and negative components offset one another—is the same for all values of the permanent component. For example, suppose that the transitory component is equally likely to be plus or minus 10 per cent of the permanent component. The average transitory component is then zero for all values of the permanent component, although the average absolute value, which disregards the sign of the components, is directly proportional to the permanent component.

The plausibility of taking our definition of transitory components to imply a zero correlation for a group of consumer units depends somewhat on the criteria determining membership in the group. The clearest example is a classification of units by the size of their measured income. For each such group, the correlation between permanent and transitory components is necessarily negative, since with a common measured income the permanent component can be relatively high only if the transitory component is relatively low, and conversely.[6]

The assumption that the third correlation in (3.3)—between the transitory components of income and consumption—is zero is a much stronger assumption. It is primarily this assumption that introduces important substantive content into the hypothesis and makes it susceptible of contradiction by a wide range of phenomena capable of being observed. The ultimate test of its acceptability is of course whether such phenomena are in fact observed, and most of what follows is devoted to this question. It is hardly worth proceeding to such more refined tests, however, unless the assumption can pass— or at least not fail miserably—the much cruder test of consistency

[6] See *ibid.*, pp. 326 and 327.

with casual observation of one's self and one's neighbors, so some comments on the intuitive plausibility of the assumption are not out of order.

The common notion that savings, or at least certain components of savings, are a "residual" speaks strongly for the plausibility of the assumption. For this notion implies that consumption is determined by rather long-term considerations, so that any transitory changes in income lead primarily to additions to assets or to the use of previously accumulated balances rather than to corresponding changes in consumption.

Yet from another point of view, the assumption seems highly implausible. Will not a man who receives an unexpected windfall use at least some part of it in "riotous living," i.e. in consumption expenditures? Would he be likely to add the whole of it to his wealth? The answer to these questions depends greatly on how "consumption" is defined. The offhand affirmative answer reflects in large measure, I believe, an implicit definition of consumption in terms of purchases, including durable goods, rather than in terms of the value of services. If the latter definition is adopted, as seems highly desirable in applying the hypothesis to empirical data—though unfortunately I have been able to do so to only a limited extent—much that one classifies offhand as consumption is reclassified as savings. Is not the windfall likely to be used for the purchase of durable goods? Or, to put it differently, is not the timing of the replacement of durable goods and of additions to the stock of such goods likely to some extent to be adjusted so as to coincide with windfalls?

Two other considerations argue for the plausibility of the assumption that transitory components of income and consumption are uncorrelated. First, the above identification of a windfall with transitory income is not precise. Suppose, for example, inheritances are included in a particular concept of measured income. Consider a consumer unit whose receipts remain unchanged over a succession of time periods except that it receives an inheritance in the final period. If the inheritance was expected to occur some time or other, it will already have been allowed for in permanent income; the transitory component of income is only the excess of the inheritance over this element of permanent income. There seems no reason why the receipt of the inheritance should make consumption in the final period different from that of preceding periods, except through inability to borrow in advance on the strength of the inheritance. But this implies that the receipt of the inheritance changes w (the ratio of wealth to income) in (2.6); it is therefore already taken into account in the hypothesis. There is no essential difference if the inheritance is unexpected. The effect of the inheritance is then to increase the permanent income of the unit, and this will justify a higher consumption in the final period; again the transitory component is only the excess of the windfall over this element of permanent income, and it is no longer intuitively obvious that it should lead to an increase in current consumption.[7] The second consideration is that just as there are instances in which one would expect a transitory increase in income to produce a transitory increase in consumption, so also there are instances in which one would expect the reverse. The simplest example is when a transitory increase in income reduces opportunities for consumption as when it is obtained by working longer hours or going to a backward country. Such negative and positive correlations will tend to offset one another.

The preceding remarks abstract from errors of measurement. Yet, as noted, in any statistical analysis errors of measurement will in general be indissolubly merged with the correctly measured transitory components. The effect on the correlation between statistically recorded transitory components of income and consumption depends critically on how the statistical data are obtained. If income and consumption are measured independently, the errors of estimate might be expected to be independent as well and therefore to contribute toward a small or zero observed correlation between transitory components of income and consumption. On the other hand, if consumption is estimated, as it frequently is, by measuring independently savings and income and subtracting the former from the latter, then measured consumption and measured income have common errors of measurement. This tends toward a positive observed correlation between transitory components of income and consumption.

The purpose of these remarks is not to demonstrate that a zero correlation is the *only* plausible assumption—neither evidence like that alluded to nor any other can justify such a conclusion. Its purpose is rather to show that common observation does not render it absurd to suppose that a hypothesis embodying a zero correlation can yield a fairly close approximation to observed consumer behavior. The assumption that the correlation between transitory components of income and consumption is zero could, of course, be replaced by the less restrictive assumption that it is a positive number between zero and unity, but this would greatly weaken the hypothesis and reduce its potential usefulness for predicting behavior. It seems highly undesirable to do so until and unless a significant contradiction

[7] I owe this point to Modigliani and Brumberg, "Utility Analysis and the Consumption Function," pp. 405–406.

arises between the stronger hypothesis and empirical evidence on consumer behavior.

A particularly simple special case of the hypothesis arises if, in addition to (3.3), it is assumed that the mean transitory components of consumption and income are zero, or

$$(3.4) \qquad\qquad \mu_{y_t} = \mu_{c_t} = 0 ,$$

where μ stands for the mean of the variable designated by its subscript. This assumption is eminently reasonable if the probability distribution in question is sufficiently comprehensive. In general, however, we shall want to use conditional probability distributions, for example, the distribution of transitory components in a particular year, or for members of a particular group. In such cases, it will generally be undesirable to assume that (3.4) holds, just as for the single consumer unit viewed *ex post* it is undesirable to assume that the transitory components themselves are necessarily zero.

It may be desirable or necessary to impose additional conditions on the probability distributions to facilitate the estimation of the parameters of the system from observed data. I shall, however, largely neglect the problem of statistical estimation, and so we need not go into such conditions.

A more important qualification is that, for simplicity of exposition, equations (3.1) and (3.2) express the relation between observed income and its permanent and transitory components as additive. The form of the relation is important because it may affect the empirical validity of such specifications of the characteristics of the probability distributions as (3.3) and (3.4), as well as the validity of using specifications of other characteristics of the distribution that are convenient statistically. From this point of view, I conjecture that a multiplicative specification is preferable for income and consumption data. If we let capital letters stand for the logarithms of the variables designated by the corresponding lower case letters, the equations defining the hypothesis then take the following alternative form:

$$(2.6') \qquad\qquad C_p = K(i, w, u) + Y_p,$$

$$(3.1') \qquad\qquad Y = Y_p + Y_t,$$

$$(3.2') \qquad\qquad C = C_p + C_t,$$

$$(3.3') \qquad\qquad \rho_{Y_t Y_p} = \rho_{C_t C_p} = \rho_{Y_t C_t} = 0.$$

Many of the results that follow apply equally to both forms of the hypothesis, requiring only that the same symbol be interpreted in one case as an absolute value, in the other, as a logarithm. For any significant results for which this is not true, the logarithmic expressions are given in footnotes.

3. *The Relation between Measured Consumption and Measured Income*

Suppose we have observations on consumption and income for a number of consumer units, for all of whom the k of equation (2.6) can be taken to be numerically the same. Let us proceed, as is usually done in family budget studies, to estimate from these data a relation between consumption and income. For simplicity, let the relation to be estimated be linear, say:

$$(3.5) \qquad c = \alpha + \beta y,$$

where c is to be interpreted as the mean consumption for a given value of y, it being understood that the consumption of individual units deviates from this value by chance.[8] The least squares estimates of α and β (call these a and b), computed from the regression of c on y, are

$$(3.6) \qquad b = \frac{\Sigma(c - \bar{c})(y - \bar{y})}{\Sigma(y - \bar{y})^2},$$

$$(3.7) \qquad a = \bar{c} - b\bar{y},$$

where $\bar{c}$ and $\bar{y}$ stand for the mean consumption and income respectively of the group of consumer units, and the summation is over the group. In the numerator of the expression for b, replace y and c by the right hand sides of (3.1) and (3.2), and $\bar{y}$ and $\bar{c}$ by the corresponding sums of means. This gives

$$
\begin{aligned}
(3.8) \quad \Sigma(c - \bar{c})(y - \bar{y}) &= \Sigma(c_p + c_t - \bar{c}_p - \bar{c}_t)(y_p + y_t - \bar{y}_p - \bar{y}_t) \\
&= \Sigma(c_p - \bar{c}_p)(y_p - \bar{y}_p) + \Sigma(c_p - \bar{c}_p)(y_t - \bar{y}_t) \\
&\quad + \Sigma(c_t - \bar{c}_t)(y_p - \bar{y}_p) + \Sigma(c_t - \bar{c}_t)(y_t - \bar{y}_t).
\end{aligned}
$$

From (2.6),

$$(2.6) \qquad c_p = ky_p.$$

Inserting (2.6) in (3.8) yields

$$
\begin{aligned}
(3.9) \quad \Sigma(c - \bar{c})(y - \bar{y}) &= k\Sigma(y_p - \bar{y}_p)^2 + k\Sigma(y_p - \bar{y}_p)(y_t - \bar{y}_t) \\
&\quad + \frac{1}{k}\Sigma(c_t - \bar{c}_t)(c_p - \bar{c}_p) + \Sigma(c_t - \bar{c}_t)(y_t - \bar{y}_t).
\end{aligned}
$$

[8] On our hypothesis, the relation between the mean value of c and y will be linear only under special conditions. For example, it will be if y_p, y_t, and c_t are distributed according to a trivariate normal distribution. See D. V. Lindley, "Regression Lines and the Linear Functional Relationship," *Journal of the Royal Statistical Society, Supplement,* IX (1947), pp. 218–244.

Given the zero correlations specified in (3.3), the final three terms will differ from zero only because of sampling fluctuations: they will approach zero as the sample size is increased, or average zero over many similar samples. Since our present concern is not with the problem of statistical estimation but with the interpretation of the results, let us suppose the sample to be sufficiently large so that sampling error can be neglected. In that case

$$(3.10) \qquad b = k \frac{\Sigma(y_p - \bar{y}_p)^2}{\Sigma(y - \bar{y})^2} = k \cdot P_y \, ,$$

where P_y is the fraction of the total variance of income in the group contributed by the permanent component of income. More generally, of course, b can be regarded as an estimate of the righthand side of (3.10).[9]

The algebraic relation in (3.10) lends itself directly to meaningful interpretation in terms of the permanent income hypothesis. The regression coefficient b measures the difference in consumption associated, on the average, with a one dollar difference between consumer units in measured income. On our hypothesis, the size of this difference in consumption depends on two things; first, how much of the difference in measured income is also a difference in permanent income, since only differences in permanent income are regarded as affecting consumption systematically; second, how much of permanent income is devoted to consumption. P_y measures the first; k, the second; so their product equals b. If P_y is unity, transient factors are either entirely absent or affect the incomes of all members of the group by the same amount; a one dollar difference in measured income means a one dollar difference in permanent income and so produces a difference of k in consumption; b is therefore equal to k. If P_y is zero, there are no differences in permanent income; a one dollar difference in measured income means a one dollar difference in the transitory component of income, which is taken to be uncorrelated with consumption; in consequence, this difference in measured income is associated with no systematic difference in consumption; b is therefore zero. As this explanation suggests, P_y, though *defined* by the ratio of the variance of the permanent component of income to the variance of total income, can be *interpreted* as the fraction of any difference in measured income that on the average is contributed by a difference in the permanent component. This point is developed more fully below.

Substitute (3.10) in (3.7), replace $\bar{c}$ by $\bar{c}_p + \bar{c}_t$, $\bar{y}$ by $\bar{y}_p + \bar{y}_t$, and

---

[9] In the special case of the preceding footnote, $\beta = kP_y$.

$\bar{c}_p$ by $k\bar{y}_p$. The resulting expression can then be written:

$$(3.11) \qquad a = \bar{c}_t - kP_y\bar{y}_t + k(1 - P_y)\bar{y}_p .$$

The elasticity of consumption with respect to income at the point (c, y) is

$$(3.12) \qquad \eta_{cy} = \frac{dc}{dy} \cdot \frac{y}{c} = b \cdot \frac{y}{c} = kP_y \cdot \frac{y}{c} .$$

Suppose that the mean transitory components of both income and consumption are equal to zero, so that $\bar{y} = \bar{y}_p$, $\bar{c} = \bar{c}_p$. In this special case

$$(3.13) \qquad \frac{\bar{y}}{\bar{c}} = \frac{1}{k} .$$

It follows that if the elasticity is computed at the point corresponding to the sample mean:

$$(3.14) \qquad \eta_{cy} = P_y .$$

Consider, now, the regression of y on c, say

$$(3.15) \qquad y = a' + b'c .$$

By the same reasoning it can be shown that, sampling errors aside,

$$(3.16) \qquad b' = \frac{1}{k} P_c ,$$

where P_c is the fraction of the variance of consumption contributed by the permanent component, and

$$(3.17) \qquad a' = \bar{y}_t - \frac{1}{k} P_c \bar{c}_t + \frac{1}{k}(1 - P_c)\bar{c}_p .$$

The elasticity of consumption with respect to income computed from this regression is

$$(3.18) \qquad \eta'_{cy} = \frac{dc}{dy} \cdot \frac{y}{c} = \frac{1}{b'} \cdot \frac{y}{c} = \frac{k}{P_c} \cdot \frac{y}{c} .$$

Again, if $\bar{y}_t = \bar{c}_t = 0$,

$$(3.19) \qquad \eta'_{cy} = \frac{1}{P_c} ,$$

if evaluated at the point corresponding to the sample mean.[10]

[10] For the logarithmic alternative described by (2.6'), (3.1'), (3.2'), and (3.3') the analogues to the results given in the text are

$$(3.10') \qquad B = P_Y,$$

$$(3.11') \qquad A = K + \bar{C}_t - \bar{Y}_t P_Y + \bar{Y}_P(1 - P_Y),$$

Some of these results are presented in graphic form in Figure 3 for the special case in which the mean transitory components of income and consumption are zero.

Consider the consumer units with a particular measured income, say y_0, which is above the mean measured income for the group as a whole. Given zero correlation between the permanent and transitory components of income, the average permanent income of these units

FIGURE 3

Hypothetical Relation between Measured Consumption and Measured Income
(mean transitory components equal zero)

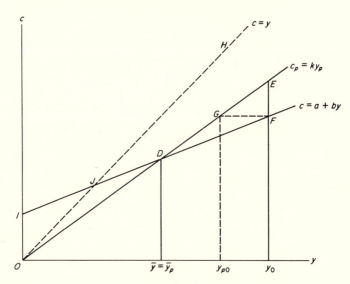

is less than y_0; that is, the average transitory component is positive. These units have been classified together precisely because their measured income is a certain amount *above* the average income of the group; such a relatively high measured income could have been

$$(3.12') \qquad \eta_{cy} = \frac{dC}{dY} = B = P_Y,$$

$$(3.16') \qquad B' = P_C,$$

$$(3.17') \qquad A' = -K + \bar{Y}_t - \bar{C}_t P_C + \bar{C}_v(1 - P_C),$$

$$(3.19') \qquad \eta'_{cy} = \frac{1}{P_C}.$$

These results are in some ways simpler and more appealing than those in the text, since the elasticity of consumption with respect to income is the same everywhere and hence equal to P_Y or $1/P_C$ without the necessity of assuming the mean transitory components to be zero.

34

received despite unfavorable transitory effects; clearly, it is more likely to have been received because of favorable transitory effects; the winners in any particular set of races may well be better on the average than the losers but they are also likely to have had more than their share of good luck. Put more rigorously, the transitory component of income is positively correlated with the sum of itself and a variable (the permanent component) with which it is itself uncorrelated.[11] What about the average transitory component of consumption for these units? The corresponding component of their income is positive because the transitory component of income helped to determine which units had a measured income of y_0 and so were classified together; given, however, that the transitory components of income and consumption are uncorrelated, a classification by income is random with respect to transitory components of consumption; in consequence, the latter tend to average out to the average for the group as a whole, which is assumed to be zero. The average consumption of units with a measured income y_0 is therefore equal to their average permanent consumption. On our hypothesis, this is k times their average permanent income. If y_0 were not only the measured income of these units but also their permanent income, their mean consumption would be ky_0 or y_0E. Since their mean permanent income is less than their measured income, their average consumption, y_0F, is less than y_0E.

By the same reasoning, for consumer units with an income equal to the mean of the group as a whole, or $\bar{y}$, the average transitory component of income as well as of consumption is zero, so the ordinate of the regression line is equal to the ordinate of the line OE which gives the relation between permanent consumption and permanent income. For units with an income below the mean, the average transitory component of income is negative, so average measured consumption is greater than the ordinate of OE. The regression line therefore intersects OE at D, is above it to the left of D, and below it to the right of D.

Let us return to the income class y_0. Draw a horizontal line through F. The abscissa of the point G, where this line intersects OE, is the permanent income associated with a permanent consumption y_0F. This income, labelled y_{p0} on the figure, is therefore the average permanent component of the income of the members of the income class y_0, and $(y_0 - y_{p0})/(y_0 - \bar{y})$ is the fraction of the deviation of their average income from the average for the group attributable to the transitory component. If this fraction is the same for all income classes, IF is a straight line, and the common value of the fraction is

[11] See Friedman and Kuznets, *op. cit.*, pp. 327–332, esp. footnotes 10 and 13.

$1 - P_y$.[12] The higher this fraction, the flatter *IF* and conversely. At one extreme, if P_y is zero, that is, if all members of the group have the same permanent component, average consumption is the same for all income classes and *IF* is horizontal. At the other extreme, if $P_y = 1$, so transitory components are all zero, *IF* coincides with *OE*.

If k is less than unity, permanent consumption is always less than permanent income. As is clear from the figure, however, it does not follow that measured consumption is necessarily less than measured income. The line *OH* on the figure is a 45 degree line along which $c = y$. The vertical distance between this line and *IF* is average measured savings. Point *J* is the "break even" point at which average measured savings are zero. To the left of *J*, average measured savings are negative, to the right, positive; as measured income increases, so does the ratio of average measured savings to measured income. Our hypothesis thus yields a relation between measured consumption and measured income that reproduces the broadest features of the corresponding regressions that have been computed from observed data.

For the special case for which Figure 3 is drawn, k could be readily computed from observed data on the measured consumption and measured income of a group of consumer units, since average measured consumption and average measured income then equal the corresponding average permanent components. The line *OE* in the figure therefore goes through the point describing the mean income and consumption of the group, so $k = \bar{c}/\bar{y}$. P_y could then be computed from the relation between the regression of c on y (the line *IF*) and the line *OE*, and P_c from the corresponding relation between the regression of y on c and the line *OE*.[13]

If the mean transitory component of consumption is not zero, the curve *IF* is shifted vertically by a corresponding amount—upwards, if the mean transitory component is positive, downwards, if it is negative. Clearly, there is no way of distinguishing such a shift from a change in k. Similarly, a positive mean transitory component of income shifts *IF* to the right, a negative mean, to the left. For a straight line, there is no way of distinguishing such horizontal shifts from vertical shifts produced by a mean transitory component of

[12] See *ibid*. pp. 332–336, 358. Figure 3 is essentially the same as Chart 28 on p. 333.

[13] The estimation problem is the classical one of "mutual regression" or regression when "both variables are subject to error." See D. V. Lindley, *op. cit.*, for an excellent analysis of the problem and survey of the literature. Many of our equations duplicate equations in his paper. As Lindley points out, there are no efficient statistics for estimating all the parameters in the model from sample data. The method described in the text is therefore not statistically efficient. The usual solution is to assume the ratio of the variance of y_t to the variance of c known, in which case efficient statistical procedures do exist.

consumption. It follows that, if the mean transitory components cannot be set equal to zero, data for one group for one time period are inadequate to estimate all the parameters. Some other source of information is required as well.

Our hypothesis gives a major role to certain features of the income distribution generally neglected in consumption studies. It asserts that some of the most strikingly uniform characteristics of computed regressions between consumption and income are simply a reflection of the inadequacy of measured income as an indicator of long-run income status. In consequence, differences among various groups of consumer units in observed marginal propensities to consume may not reflect differences in underlying preferences for consumption and wealth at all; they may reflect primarily the different strength of random forces, including errors of measurement, in determining measured income. Fortunately, considerable evidence is available on the importance of transitory components of income from studies of changes over time in the relative income status of individuals or consumer units. One of the attractive features of our hypothesis is that it enables us to bring this independent body of evidence to bear on the interpretation of consumption behavior; such evidence can provide some of the additional information required when transitory components of income and consumption cannot be supposed to be zero.

Before examining these data, however, we shall first examine the consistency of the hypothesis with some of the major general findings of empirical studies of consumption behavior and its relation to the relative income hypothesis suggested by Brady and Friedman, Duesenberry, and Modigliani. This will serve the double purpose of bringing out more fully the implications of the hypothesis and of suggesting the evidence that recommends its acceptance as a provisional working hypothesis.

CHAPTER IV

Consistency of the Permanent Income Hypothesis with Existing Evidence on the Relation between Consumption and Income: Budget Studies

ONE of the aims of this and the next chapter is to document the consistency of our hypothesis with a number of broad empirical findings that strikingly contradict the impression that consumption is a stable function of absolute real income and that this function can be identified with the regression of consumption on income computed from either budget studies or time series. These findings, cited at the outset, are: (a) the rough constancy of the average propensity to consume in the United States over the past half-century, as measured by time series data, despite a substantial rise in real income; (b) the rough similarity of the average propensity to consume in budget studies for widely separated dates, despite substantial differences in average real income; (c) the sharply lower savings ratio in the United States in the period after World War II than would have been consistent with the relation between income and savings computed from data for the interwar period. Another finding of the same kind is (d) the apparent decline over time in the inequality of income despite the possibility of interpreting the consumption-income relation from time series or budget data as showing that the rich are getting richer and the poor, poorer.

But consistency with such broad findings would by itself not be much of a recommendation. Accordingly, these chapters examine the consistency of the permanent income hypothesis also with more detailed evidence on consumption behavior. This chapter compares it with evidence from budget studies; the next, with evidence from time series. Although the empirical evidence examined is by no means exhaustive, it covers a fairly wide span of time and a fairly broad range of phenomena. Its chief defect is that so much of the evidence is for the United States. This is partly because more empirical work has been done for the United States, particularly in recent years; partly because my knowledge of the work that has been done in other countries is more limited, and I have relied mainly on material that was fairly readily available.

As noted in the preceding chapter, the permanent income hypothesis accounts for the broader features common to observed regressions of measured consumption expenditures on measured income computed from budget data: the tendency for expenditures to exceed income at low incomes, and to fall short of income above some point; the uniform tendency for the ratio of consumption to income to be lower, the higher the income. We turn now to consider the consistency of the hypothesis with (1) temporal changes in the inequality of income; (2) differences among regressions for (a) widely spaced dates, (b) different countries, (c) farm and nonfarm families, (d) different occupational groups and (e) Negro and white families; (3) the relation between savings and age; and (4) the effect of changes in income on the relation of measured consumption to measured income.

1. *Temporal Changes in Inequality of Income*

A tendency for the inequality of income to increase over time has frequently been inferred from the regressions of consumption on income computed from budget data. These regressions show savings to be negative at low measured income levels, and to be a successively larger fraction of income, the higher the measured income. If low measured income is identified with "poor" and high measured income with "rich," it follows that the "poor" are getting poorer and the "rich" are getting richer.

The identification of low measured income with "poor" and high measured income with "rich" is justified only if measured income can be regarded as an estimate of expected income over a lifetime or a large fraction thereof. One step in this direction is taken when the computed regressions are regarded as estimates of a stable function relating consumption to income, since, in our terminology, this is equivalent to regarding them as estimates of the relation between the permanent components of consumption and income. It requires only the additional step of giving "permanent" the special meaning of expected income over a large fraction of a lifetime to make increasing inequality of income a valid inference from the observed regressions.

On the permanent income hypothesis, the observed regressions give no evidence on the secular behavior of the inequality of income. Negative savings at low measured incomes reflect precisely the fact that measured income is not a valid index of wealth; that many people have low incomes in any one year because of transitory factors and can be expected to have higher incomes in other years. Their negative savings are financed by large positive savings in

39

years when their incomes are abnormally large, and it is these that produce the high ratios of savings to measured income at the upper end of the measured income scale. The existence of large negative savings is a symptom that the observed inequality of measured income overstates substantially the inequality of permanent income. It is not a harbinger of a widening gap between rich and poor.

Empirical data show no tendency for inequality of income to increase. If anything, inequality seems to have been decreasing in recent decades.[1] This fact has been widely recognized, and so has the possibility of reconciling it with the observed regressions of consumption on income by considerations very similar to those embodied in our hypothesis. But this has not prevented these regressions from being treated as describing a relation between permanent components in other contexts where the contradiction with available evidence is less obvious.

2. Consumption-Income Regressions for Different Dates and Groups

Table 1 summarizes some of the salient findings of budget studies for a wide range of dates and groups of consumer units. The studies summarized in this table are a major source of the evidence examined in this section.

For the United States, the average propensity to consume is remarkably similar for different studies covering either nonfarm groups alone or all consumers (Table 1). Eight of nine values are between .89 and .92, and these are for years as much as six decades apart; the one deviant is for 1944, and reflects the extraordinarily high level of savings during World War II. Time series data show both the same similarity of the average propensity for different periods of time and an average propensity very nearly the same in magnitude (see Table 12 in the next chapter). On a definition of consumption like that used in these budget studies—one which treats as consumption, expenditures on consumer durable goods other than housing—the average propensity for the period 1897 through 1949 computed from estimates by Raymond Goldsmith is .892. It would be preferable for our purposes to use a definition of consumption that included only the use value of durable goods as consumption and treated increases in the stocks of consumer durable goods as increases in wealth. According to Goldsmith's

[1] See Simon Kuznets (assisted by Elizabeth Jenks), *Shares of Upper Income Groups in Income and Savings*, (New York: National Bureau of Economic Research, 1953); Selma Goldsmith, George Jaszi, Hyman Kaitz, and Maurice Liebenberg, "Size Distribution of Income since the Mid-Thirties," *The Review of Economics and Statistics*, XXXVI, No. 1 (February 1954), pp. 1–32.

TABLE 1

Relation between Consumption and Income Based on Budget Data,
for Different Countries, Dates, and Groups
of Consumer Units

	Date	Consumer Units	Average Income	Average Propensity to Consume	Marginal Propensity to Consume	Income Elasticity of Consumption
		United States *(income given in dollars)*				
1.	1888–90	Selected wage-earner families	682	.90	.67	.74
2.	1901	Selected wage-earner normal families	651	.92	.68	.75
3.	1917–19	Selected wage-earner families	1,513	.91	.78	.86
4.	1935–36	Nonrelief nonfarm families	1,952	.89	.73	.82
5.	1941	Urban families	2,865	.92	.79	.87
6.	1944	Urban families	3,411[a]	.82	.57	.70
7.	1947	Urban families	3,323[a]	.92	.78	.85
8.	1950	Nonfarm families	4,084[a, b]	.91	.73	.80
9.	1950	Spending units of one or more persons, urban plus rural	3,220[a, b]	.92	.75	.82
10.	1935–36	Nonrelief farm families	1,259	.87	.57	.65
11.	1941	Farm families	1,680	.83	.57	.69
		Great Britain *(income given in pounds sterling)*				
12.	1938–39	Middle-class families with one earner				.89
13.	1951–52	Income units of one or more persons, urban plus rural	369	.99	.86	.87
		Sweden *(income given in Swedish kronor)*				
14.	1913	Industrial workers and low-grade employees	744	.99	.90	.91
15.	1923	Industrial workers and low-grade employees	1,232	1.00	.96	.96
16.	1923	Middle-class families	2,692	1.00	.92	.92
17.	1933	Industrial workers and low-grade employees	1,236	.98	.94	.95
18.	1933	Middle-class families	2,341	.96	.88	.91
19.	1933	Small farmers	577	.95		
20.	1933	Farm and forestry workers	504	.99		

(cont. on next page)

TABLE 1 (cont.)

ᵃ After personal taxes.

ᵇ Difference reflects not only inclusion or exclusion of farm families and of single individuals but also difference in definition of consumer unit. Line 8 is for families defined by relationship, line 9, by pooling of income. The latter, "spending units" in the terminology of the Survey of Consumer Finances, are more numerous than the former.

General Notes: 1. Concepts of consumption and income vary among studies. Consumption uniformly includes expenditure on durable consumer goods other than owned homes. For United States data, consumption includes gifts, contributions, and personal taxes except where noted; it excludes life insurance premiums, which are treated as savings. Income is personal income before personal taxes, except where otherwise noted.

2. Average propensity to consume is ratio of average consumption of group to average income.

3. Income elasticity of consumption is slope of straight line regression of logarithm of consumption on logarithm of income. For most studies, regression was estimated graphically.

4. Marginal propensity to consume is product of average propensity and income elasticity. It is therefore marginal propensity at point corresponding approximately to mean income of group.

5. Definition of family varies among studies. Uniformly refers to group of two or more persons sharing same dwelling unit; beyond this, some studies use criterion of relationship, others, of pooling of income.

Source:

United States: Lines 1, 2, 3, 6, 7

Income and consumption by income classes used in computing elasticity, from Dorothy S. Brady, "Family Saving 1888–1950," Part II of Raymond W. Goldsmith, Dorothy S. Brady, and Horst Mendershausen, *A Study of Saving in the United States, III*, (Princeton University Press, 1956), pp. 182–183; average income and average expenditure for all income classes furnished by Brady, based on same data.

Lines 4, 5, 10, 11

See notes to Table 3 below. Income and consumption include nonmoney items, except that elasticities for lines 4 and 5 were computed from data by income classes excluding nonmoney items.

Line 8

Data provided by Division of Research, Board of Governors of the Federal Reserve System, based on the 1951 Survey of Consumer Finances. "Family" is defined by relationship, in contrast to line 9, where unit is "spending unit," as defined in Survey of Consumer Finances.

Line 9

H. F. Lydall, "National Survey of Personal Incomes and Savings: Part IV," *Bulletin of the Oxford University Institute of Statistics*, XV (October and November, 1953), p. 388, gives basic data by income classes, derived from Supplementary Table 8, "1952 Survey of Consumer Finances, Part III," *Federal Reserve Bulletin*, September 1952; Table 1, "1951 Survey of Consumer Finances, Part III," *ibid.*, August 1951; and Appendix Table 1, "1951 Survey of Consumer Finances, Part IV," *ibid.*, September 1951. Unit is "spending unit." Classification of units is by income before taxes; elasticity is computed from relation between consumption and income after taxes for such gross income classes; comparison of this result for corresponding British figures with result obtained from relation between consumption and income for net income classes indicates that use of gross income classes yields same result as use of net, presumably because of extremely high correlation between tax (as computed by surveys) and gross income.

Great Britain: Line 12

H. S. Houthakker, "The Econometrics of Family Budgets," *Journal of the Royal Statistical Society*, Series A (General) CXV, Part I, 1952, p. 20.

(cont. on next page)

TABLE 1 (cont.)

Line 13

Lydall gives mean income and expenditure, and mean income and savings for net income classes. The elasticity cited is computed from slope of graphically fitted log-log straight line.

Sweden:

Average income and average propensity for all studies, Herman Wold in association with Lars Jureen, *Demand Analysis* (Almquist and Wiksell; Stockholm, 1952), p. 20; elasticities, *ibid.*, p. 226. The elasticities cited are those obtained by "direct pooling."

figures, the average propensity computed on this definition is only moderately lower than those so far cited; for 1897 through 1949 it is .877 rather than .892.[2]

The average propensities are much higher for the British and Swedish studies than for the American studies, and very much the same for those two countries; for Sweden, the average propensities are much the same for different dates for comparable groups. Since these studies cover only personal consumption and savings, this difference between the United States and the other countries—even if statistically reliable—does not necessarily mean a corresponding difference in the fraction of aggregate income devoted to savings or capital formation. In all countries, capital formation is financed not only by personal savings but also by business and governmental saving, and the importance of the different sources of savings doubtless varies from country to country.

The marginal propensities vary somewhat more widely than the average propensities and so do the income elasticities of consumption, which are the ratios of the marginal propensities to the average propensities. The major differences are, however, between the farm and the other regressions and between countries, rather than among dates. For the United States, if we exclude the two farm regressions, eight of nine marginal propensities are between .67 and .79, eight of nine elasticities, between .74 and .87. The deviant is again 1944, for which both the marginal propensity and elasticity are decidedly lower than for the other studies. These differences are by no means negligible and we shall examine below (in section a) why they should have occurred. But they are small enough to justify regarding a marginal propensity of about .75 and an income elasticity of about .83 as reasonably typical values for broad groups of nonfarm families in the United States. For both Britain and Sweden, the corresponding values are systematically higher (section b). For farm families in the United States, the corresponding values are systematically lower (section c);

[2] See Table 12 below for sources of time series estimates.

unfortunately, no farm-nonfarm comparisons are available for the other countries.

a. TEMPORAL DIFFERENCES

For every regression in Table 1, the marginal propensity is less than the average propensity so that the elasticity of consumption with respect to measured income is uniformly less than unity. It is this feature, of course, that makes it impossible to regard these regressions as estimates of a stable relation between consumption and income. An income elasticity of less than unity implies that a rise in income produces a decline in the ratio of consumption to income; yet the average propensities are the same over the six decades spanned by the table despite a sextupling of average income. This stability in average propensities is therefore inconsistent with stability in the relations themselves.

For a more detailed examination of these temporal differences, let us restrict our attention to the first eight lines of Table 1—for the United States and for wage-earner or nonfarm or urban families. For these regressions, the marginal propensities and elasticities are quite similar, except for 1944, so the differences among them that produce the common average propensity is primarily in their height. The variation in height is shown by column (4) of Table 2, which gives consumption at a common dollar income of $2,000 as estimated from the regressions for the different studies. Computed consumption is lower for the 1901 study than for the 1888-90 study, along with average income, but then rises steadily—except for 1944—from $1,360 in 1901 to $2,160 in 1950 or from 68 per cent of income to 108 per cent.[3]

Much of this difference in heights of the regressions is accounted for by differences in the price level in the various years and thus reflects simply a difference in the unit of measure. The values of average income shown in Table 1 and repeated in column (2) of Table 2 are in current prices: prices of the date when the study was made. Expressing them in constant prices reduces drastically the differences among them—from a range of 6 to 1 to a range only a little more than 2 to 1 [column (3) of Table 2]. Similarly, expressing the regressions in a common unit—a dollar of 1935-39 purchasing power—reduces drastically the differences in their heights. Computed consumption at an income of $2,000 varies from $1,565 for

[3] No special importance is to be attached to the figure $2,000. It was chosen rather arbitrarily as a convenient figure somewhat in the middle of the span of observed income. Comparison at some such figure is better than comparison of the constant terms in the logarithmic regressions (i.e. logarithm of consumption at an income of $1), because the latter is subject to much greater sampling error.

TABLE 2

Comparison of Heights of Regressions in Current and Constant Prices,
Eight Studies from 1888–90 to 1950

Date	Average Income		Estimated Consumption at Income of $2,000[a]		Ratio of Consumption to Income at Average Income in 1935–39 Prices Computed from Regression for		Income Elasticity of Consumption
	Current Prices	1935–39 Prices	Current Prices	1935–39 Prices	1888–90	1950	
(1)	(2)	(3)	(4)	(5)	(6)	(7)	(8)
1. 1888–90	$682	$1,236	$1,385	$1,610	.91	1.07	.74
2. 1901	651	1,135	1,360	1,565	.94	1.09	.75
3. 1917–19	1,513	1,402	1,755	1,735	.89	1.04	.86
4. 1935–36[b]	1,952	1,980	1,875	1,880	.82	.98	.82
5. 1941[b]	2,865	2,723	1,945	1,930	.76	.93	.87
6. 1944	3,411	2,714	1,625	1,915	.75	.92	.70
7. 1947	3,323	2,082	2,055	1,920	.80	.97	.85
8. 1950	4,084	2,376	2,160	1,945	.77	.94	.80

[a] Computed from regressions of logarithm of consumption on logarithm of income.
[b] The entries in columns (2) and (3) are for money plus nonmoney income. The remaining entries are based on regressions and averages for money income and consumption only. The effect of excluding nonmoney income is minor.

1901 to $1,945 for 1950, or from 78 per cent of income to 97 per cent.

Though price changes account for the greater part of the differences in the heights of the regressions, sizable differences remain even after the regressions are expressed in the same units, as is shown by the steady rise from 1901 to 1941 in the entries in column (5). It is shown, also, in columns (6) and (7) in a slightly different way, a way that is more closely connected with the observed stability in the average propensity to consume. If the 1888–90 regression had been valid throughout the period and for the different groups, consumption at the arithmetic mean income would have fallen from 94 per cent of income in 1901 to 77 per cent in 1950; if the 1950 regression had been valid, consumption would have fallen from 109 per cent of income in 1901 to 94 per cent in 1950; in fact, of course, the shift in the regressions was enough to keep consumption roughly the same percentage of the mean income.[4]

On our hypothesis, it is no accident that the computed regressions

[4] It will be noted that the ratio of consumption to income at the arithmetic mean income is not equal to the average propensity, which we have defined as the ratio of the arithmetic mean consumption to the arithmetic mean income. The reason is that we are using logarithmic regressions. Arithmetic regressions necessarily pass through the point

shifted by just these amounts; the shifts do not indicate any change in tastes or in the underlying factors affecting consumption; they are a direct result of the change in average real income. The interpretation of the results by our hypothesis is suggested by Figure 4. Unlike the earlier figures, the scales in this one are logarithmic, since the logarithmic variant of our hypothesis conforms better to observed data. The heavy line is an assumed relation between permanent components:

$$\text{Permanent consumption} = .9 \text{ (permanent income)}$$

or

$$\log c_p = \log .9 + \log y_p.$$

If mean transitory components of income and consumption were zero for each study separately, and if the value of k stayed the same over time, because changes in the determinants of k had been either negligible or offsetting (see section 2d below and section 1b of Chapter V for further comments on this point), the points defined by mean income and mean consumption would, on our hypothesis, fall on a line such as this. The crosses and solid symbols, which plot these mean points, clearly huddle very closely around the line. The one point that is decidedly off the line is for 1944, a year for which the mean transitory component of income was almost certainly positive and of consumption, negative; and this point is off the line in the direction that would be produced by mean transitory components with these signs.[5]

Consider now average consumption for different measured income classes in a single year, such as the points plotted in Figure 4 for 1888–90 and 1950. These cannot be expected to huddle around the heavy line since mean incomes for such classes are not mean permanent incomes; for the low measured income classes, mean measured income is less than mean permanent income but mean

---

defined by mean consumption and mean income so that the ratio of consumption computed from the regression at the mean income to mean income necessarily equals the average propensity. The logarithmic regression passes through the point defined by the geometric means but not in general through that defined by the arithmetic means, so the equality no longer holds.

[5] One feature of the figure and this interpretation should be noted. The means plotted are arithmetic means, whereas consistency with logarithmic plotting might seem to require geometric means. This is not, however, so; the question is solely what is to be meant by the "averaging out" of transitory components. Suppose the relation $c_p = k y_p$ holds for every consumer unit; then it holds *both* for the arithmetic mean of the *permanent* component and the geometric mean of the *permanent* component. The question then becomes how to estimate the one or the other of these means from data on *measured* income and consumption; and this depends on whether the arithmetic mean of the transitory components themselves or of the logarithmic transitory components can more appropriately be regarded as zero. In the present case, there is little choice; the data are not in a form in which geometric means can be readily computed with any accuracy.

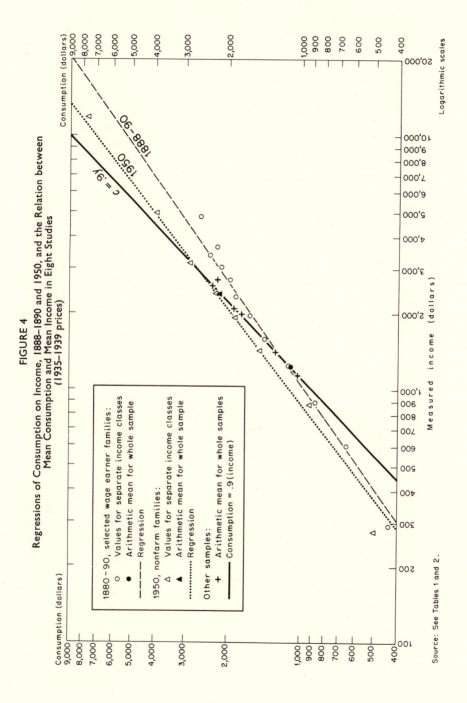

FIGURE 4

Regressions of Consumption on Income, 1888–1890 and 1950, and the Relation between
Mean Consumption and Mean Income in Eight Studies
(1935–1939 prices)

Source: See Tables 1 and 2.

47

consumption is equal to mean permanent consumption, so the observed points will be above the heavy line, and conversely for the high measured income classes. The regression of consumption on measured income is flatter than the heavy line and cuts it in the neighborhood of mean measured income.[6] On our hypothesis the slope of these regressions tells us something about the importance of random factors in the distribution of income but nothing about consumption behavior. As mean measured income and consumption rise along the heavy line, they carry this regression along with them.

Points for individual measured income classes are plotted on Figure 4 only for the earliest and latest study in order to keep the figure readable. If the points for the other studies were plotted, they would for the most part fall within the area bounded by the two regressions, though some of course would be outside. The general picture would be the same but blurred by much random variation. For each study the set of points starts for low incomes above the heavy line and ends below it for high incomes, crossing in the neighborhood of the mean measured income; the later the time period, in general, the higher the set of points.

One detailed feature of the 1888–90 and 1950 points that is rather characteristic of these and similar regression data is the deviation of the points for the lowest and highest measured income classes from the pattern of the remaining points: for the lowest income class, consumption is abnormally high, for the highest, abnormally low. This pattern holds for six of the eight regressions covered by Table 2 and Figure 4, for one of the two points in one of the remaining regressions and for neither point in only one.

On our hypothesis, points like those plotted for 1888–90 and 1950 will fall on a straight line if random factors affect all income classes alike in the sense that the fraction of the deviation of the measured income of an income class from the mean measured income of the group as a whole accounted for by the deviation of the transitory component from its mean is the same for all income classes.[7] It should be recalled that a common effect in this sense

[6] Again, attention should be called to the difference between arithmetic and geometric means. The regressions are something of a mixture: the mean expenditures and incomes plotted for the separate income classes are arithmetic means; the regression is fitted to their logarithms and so passes through a point corresponding to the geometric mean of the class means rather than through the plotted arithmetic means. Again it might be—though it is not entirely certain that it would be—preferable to use logarithms and geometric means throughout; however, this is impossible without going back to the original data. The differences are not, however, large, as can be seen from the closeness of the arithmetic mean points to the fitted regressions.

[7] With logarithmic lines, all quantities should be expressed in logarithms.

implies that measured income itself (as contrasted with the deviation of measured income from the mean) understates permanent income by successively larger percentage margins the farther measured income is below the mean, and overstates permanent income by successively larger percentage margins the farther measured income is above the mean. The abnormally high consumption in the lowest income class means that permanent income for this class is even higher than the level consistent with a common effect of random factors. The abnormally low consumption in the highest income class means that permanent income is even lower than the level consistent with a common effect. Thus both deviations from the pattern reflect a disproportionate importance of transitory components of income at the extremes of the permanent income scale.

Two alternative explanations of this phenomenon suggest themselves: first, that it mirrors an important and basic feature of the income structure of the population; second, that it reflects the nonrepresentativeness of the samples or errors in recorded responses rather than a characteristic of the population.[8] While the first explanation can by no means be ruled out, I do not believe that the budget studies themselves can be regarded as providing much evidence for or against it, because the second explanation is so clearly important for such studies that the only question is whether it tells the whole story.[9]

Consider, first, the lowest income class. One source of bias is

[8] For the upper point, some part may also be played by a purely technical explanation which arises from the mixture of arithmetic and geometric operations in the figure and regression. Suppose that all income classes are affected alike by transitory factors when all quantities are expressed in logarithms. The log-log regression will then be a straight line throughout. Now compute the arithmetic mean income and consumption of the units with measured incomes above some value. The point defined by the logarithms of these two quantities will be below, on, or above the log-log straight line according as its slope is less than, equal to, or greater than unity. For the regressions in question, the slope is uniformly less than unity, so that if the relation between the logarithms were strictly linear, a point computed like our final points would fall below the line. This same bias affects all our points, but it is much smaller for the intermediate points than for the end point which is generally for an open-end class covering a rather wide range of incomes.

[9] There is some independent evidence on the first explanation. See in particular, Friedman and Kuznets, *Income from Independent Professional Practice*, pp. 309–319, 325–352; Horst Mendershausen, *Changes in Income Distribution during the Great Depression*, Studies in Income and Wealth, VII (New York: National Bureau of Economic Research, 1946), pp. 101–113; Frank A. Hanna, "The Accounting Period and the Distribution of Income" in Frank A. Hanna, Joseph A. Pechman, Sidney M. Lerner, *Analysis of Wisconsin Income*, Studies in Income and Wealth, IX (New York: National Bureau of Economic Research, 1948), pp. 241–250.

This evidence is mixed: that in the first reference cited is contradictory to the explanation; that in the second reference supports it rather strongly; and that in the third, supports it slightly. A thorough analysis of the scattered evidence now available on this question is much to be desired.

the so-called "eligibility requirements" used in deciding which consumer units to include in the sample. The 1935–36 study is the clearest example. The main body of expenditure data from this study is for families not on relief; relief families were excluded to eliminate the "abnormal" cases left in the wake of the Great Depression. Even with a representative sample, the lowest measured income classes are unduly populated with units that do not "belong" there permanently; this effect is already allowed for in the linear regression. With a sample restricted to nonrelief families, the lowest measured income classes must be almost exclusively populated with units that "belong" higher up the permanent income scale, and it is not surprising that their mean consumption is decidedly higher than the level computed from a regression fitted to the intermediate income classes. The three earlier wage-earner studies— for 1888–90, 1901, and 1917–19—all had eligibility requirements that had similar objectives though they were different in detail, and less clear in effect. It seems very likely that their effect would be much the same, though for the 1917–19 study, consumption for the lowest income class is not out of line with the pattern for the rest of the classes. Perhaps the reason is that the eligibility requirements for this study were more restrictive than for any of the others, going so far as to exclude families with large transitory incomes, so that the bias in this direction offset the bias in the direction of excluding families with unusually low permanent incomes.[10] The later studies—for 1941, 1944, 1947, and 1950—were directed more explicitly at getting a representative sample and hence deliberately avoided imposing eligibility requirements of the kinds used in the earlier studies. Yet even without explicit requirements, much the same result is likely to flow from the problems of field sampling and interviewing. The consumer unit with temporarily low income is more likely to be a temporally stable unit, to be included in the directory used for sampling, and so on, therefore more likely to be included in the sample than the unit with permanently low income. It may also be more willing and able to respond; the units that are abnormal by virtue of very low permanent incomes are likely to be abnormal in other respects.

In the highest income classes, a rather different problem arises. This is the problem of "refusals," "not at homes," and so on; and here my interpretation of the source of bias in the final sample is perhaps more conjectural. For family surveys of the kind under

[10] See *Cost of Living in the United States*, Bureau of Labor Statistics Bulletin 357, (Washington, 1924), or the summary in H. Gregg Lewis and Paul H. Douglas, *Studies in Consumer Expenditures*, (Chicago: University of Chicago Press, 1947), p. 7.

discussion, it is fairly well established that the refusal rate rises with measured income and is particularly high in the high income groups. The crucial question for our purpose is whether the key variable is measured income itself or permanent income so that the refusal rate rises with measured income only because permanent income rises with measured income. The latter is highly plausible, implying, as it does, that a person who this year has a high measured income thanks to good fortune, so that his measured income is substantially higher than his customary income, is more likely to respond than a person who has the same measured income but whose measured income this year is about equal to his customary income. The former tends to live in a different neighborhood, move in a different social circle, and in general to have the habits of his cultural and geographical neighbors rather than of his accidental measured income neighbors. If this interpretation of the differential refusal rate is correct, it means that those units with high measured income who reply have been even more favorably affected by transitory factors than the whole population of that measured income class. In consequence, their consumption tends to be lower than that of the whole class, which would explain why the observed point for the top income class tends to be below the regression fitted to the intermediate points.[11]

The final feature of these data that requires interpretation is the elasticity of consumption with respect to income—the slope of the regression of the logarithm of consumption on the logarithm of income. On our hypothesis, this elasticity measures the fraction

---

[11] These doubts about the significance of the initial and terminal points partly explain why graphic methods were used so extensively in determining the elasticities presented in the tables. I experimented with fitting least-squares regressions to all the points and to all but the first and last points. In general, my graphic fits seemed to me to be better and to come closer to giving the end points some weight without allowing them to distort the regression. The following comparison for three of the studies indicates the quantitative magnitude of the problem.

	Income Elasticity of Consumption from:		
	Computed Regression		
Study	Using All Points	Excluding First and Last Points	Graphically Fitted Regression
1935–36	.767	.840	.825
1941	.851	.892	.868
1944	.630	.698	.701

My trials and tribulations with these data are an excellent illustration of the dictum attributed to Frederick Macaulay: the best method of curve-fitting is the freehand graphical method; the only difficulty is that it takes too much time.

of the variance of measured income attributable to variation in the permanent component: the higher the elasticity, the smaller the importance of transitory factors relative to permanent factors in producing income differences in the group considered, and conversely. Except for 1944, the earliest study has the lowest elasticity, and the next earliest, the next to the lowest. One interpretation is that this reflects a secular decline in the importance of chance or transitory factors in our economy, and one that proceeded with special rapidity from 1888 to the first World War—a result that is most plausible in view of the changes in the character of the private economy in the period before World War I and in the governmental arrangements for providing security to individuals in the later period. We cannot, however, be sure that the difference between the imputed elasticities may not be more simply explainable by differences in the kinds of groups covered and in the way the data were collected. In both the first two studies, the eligibility requirements almost certainly operated to narrow the range of variation in permanent components of income more than in transitory components. For example, restriction of the samples to wage-earners, to certain industries, and to families of specified demographic characteristics would all have this effect. Some indication of the possible quantitative importance of this factor is available for 1901 from separate tabulations by income classes for "all" families and "normal" families; the latter including families which had "(1) a husband at work; (2) a wife; (3) not more than five children and none over fourteen years of age; (4) no dependent, boarder, lodger, or servant; and (5) expenditures reported for rent, fuel, lighting, food, clothing, and sundries."[12] (1), (2), (3), and (4) might all be expected to reduce the variation in permanent components; only (1), to reduce the variation in transitory components. As our hypothesis would lead us to expect, the elasticity for "normal" families is lower than for "all families": .75 as compared with .81.[13] Unfortunately, however, this difference cannot be regarded as the effect solely of the factors listed; the elementary observations for "all families" are averages for small groups of families, rather than data for individual families; and this, too, would tend to make the elasticity for all families higher than for "normal"

---

[12] Quoted from Lewis and Douglas, *op. cit.*, p. 6.

[13] The value for normal families (.75) is taken from Table 1. The value for all families (.81) is the slope of a straight line regression of the logarithm of consumption on the logarithm of income estimated graphically from data given by Dorothy S. Brady, in "Family Saving, 1888–1950," Part II of Raymond W. Goldsmith, Dorothy S. Brady, and Horst Mendershausen, *A Study of Saving in the United States*, III (Princeton University Press, 1956), p. 182.

families. The difference between the elasticities for "all" and for "normal" families is almost the same as the difference between the elasticities in Table 1 for the 1888–90 and the 1935–36 studies, and of the same order of magnitude as most of the other differences between elasticities. On the basis of this evidence, therefore, there is little firm basis for supposing any underlying secular change, though what evidence there is argues for a diminution in the relative importance of transitory variation in income.

The extremely low elasticity for 1944 is readily explained on our hypothesis. This was a wartime period involving unprecedented geographical, industrial, and occupational mobility of income recipients. It seems eminently reasonable that transitory components should account for some 30 per cent of the variation in income under such circumstances rather than for the approximately 15 per cent they account for in the preceding and succeeding peacetime years.

This interpretation of the 1944 elasticity makes the 1917–19 elasticity seem decidedly out of line. This, too, was a war period; yet the elasticity is higher than for the other wage-earner studies. It seems likely that the explanation is to be found in the eligibility requirements which were particularly stringent for this study and some of which operated especially to rule out large transitory components; for example, the requirement that the family have kept house in the locality for the entire year covered. The high elasticity for this study may well be simply a resultant of rules that retained a much larger fraction of the variation in the permanent than in the transitory component. One piece of evidence in favor of this explanation is a study not included in Table 1, a study of the money disbursements of wage earners and clerical workers for a year within the period 1934–36 but which varied in exact dating for different groups. This study is very comparable to the 1917–19 study, and used highly similar and equally restrictive eligibility requirements. The elasticity derived from this study is .89,[14] which is decidedly higher than the value of .82 for nonrelief, nonfarm families derived from the contemporaneous 1935–36 study and recorded in Table 1. The 1935–36 study was much broader in scope than the wage-earner study and had less restrictive eligibility

[14] Based on data from Faith M. Williams and Alice C. Hanson, *Money Disbursements of Wage Earners and Clerical Workers, 1934–36, Summary Volume,* Bureau of Labor Statistics Bulletin No. 638 (Washington, 1941), pp. 12 and 22.

This report also contains a special tabulation for a subsample selected so as to match, so far as possible, the 1917–19 sample in cities covered and type of family included (pp. 345–346). This subsample yields the same value of the elasticity (.89) as the entire sample.

requirements. Further, the elasticity for the 1934–36 wage earner study is moderately higher than the elasticity of .86 recorded in Table 1 for the 1917–19 study, so consistent with a reduced elasticity during a wartime period.

The lower elasticity for the 1935–36 study than for the 1941 and 1947 studies, which also cover all occupational groups, is readily explained by the exclusion of relief families and the consequent reduction in the variation attributable to permanent components of income.

This final point may well be gilding the lily. 1888–90 and 1944 aside, the outstanding fact about the remaining elasticities is that they are so similar. Though I have not tried to make a formal test of the proposition, I strongly suspect that the differences are within the range of sampling variation. One must, therefore, beware of trying to explain too much.

It should perhaps be explicitly noted that the constancy of the average propensity to consume over the period, while consistent with our hypothesis, is not required by it. On our hypothesis, this average—for groups and dates for which transitory effects can be regarded as averaging out to zero—is determined by such variables as the rate of interest, the ratio of wealth to income, the degree of uncertainty contemplated, etc., and there is no reason why these need either stay the same or change in such a way as to offset one another. This point is considered in more detail in section 2b below and in section 1b of Chapter V.

b. DIFFERENCES AMONG COUNTRIES

Both the elasticity of consumption with respect to income and the average propensity to consume are higher for the British and Swedish studies in Table 1 than for the United States studies. In addition, the recorded income elasticities are higher for Sweden than for Britain. The evidence on the average propensities is too meager to justify any conclusion about the direction of the difference between Sweden and Great Britain.

On our hypothesis, the differences in income elasticity reflect differences in the relative importance of transitory factors in producing differences in measured income. Taken at their face value, therefore, the elasticities in Table 1 suggest that transitory factors are more important in the United States than in the United Kingdom and more important in the United Kingdom than in Sweden— results that seem not inconsistent with casual observation.

However, the results for Sweden recorded in Table 1 cannot be regarded as strictly comparable with those for the United States and Great Britain, for two reasons: (1) the groups covered are more narrowly defined, covering consumer units in a particular socio-economic class; (2) the regressions were computed from data adjusted for differences in family size by being converted into consumption and income per equivalent unit, rather than per consumer unit. Point (1) might be expected to make the elasticities less than for broader groups, since restriction to a homogeneous socio-economic class presumably reduces the variance attributable to permanent components without affecting systematically the variance attributable to transitory components. Point (2) might work in either direction, depending on the precise characteristics of the scale chosen. Judging from similar data for the United States, I conjecture that the most likely result is that the number of equivalent units assigned to consumer units of different size varies much more widely than their average incomes. If this is so, conversion to a per equivalent basis would widen the differences among the average incomes of families of different size. Since such differences are to be regarded as differences in permanent components, the final effect would be to increase the variance of permanent components relative to that of transitory components and so to make the elasticities higher than they would otherwise be.[15] If this conjecture is correct, points (1) and (2) affect the recorded elasticities in opposite directions, and there is no way of knowing whether their combined effect is to make the recorded elasticities higher or lower than elasticities directly comparable with the British and United States elasticities.

The comparison between Britain and the United States is free from these difficulties. Indeed, the two studies summarized in lines 9 and 13 are about as nearly comparable as could be. The United States study was conducted by the Michigan Survey Research Center under the auspices of the Board of Governors of the Federal Reserve System, the United Kingdom study, by the Oxford Institute of Statistics; the latter explicitly patterned its study on the Federal Reserve study and adopted very nearly the same definitions, sampling methods, schedules, and so on. The one difference that is worth recording is in the definition of the consumer unit: the United Kingdom definition places less emphasis on the "pooling" of income and so would in some cases yield two or more consumer units where the United States definition would yield but one (see section 3 below for a fuller discussion of this difference). It is not at all

---

[15] Unfortunately, Wold does not present the basic data that could provide a check of this conjecture.

clear in what direction this would affect the elasticities, and it seems unlikely that the quantitative effect could be large.

Some of the data from these two studies are plotted in Figure 5. The scales on the figure have been chosen so as to make the arithmetic mean incomes coincide: the mean income in the United States

FIGURE 5

Regressions of Consumption on Income for the United States and the United Kingdom, Spending or Income Units of One or More Persons, Urban plus Rural, United States, 1950, United Kingdom, 1951–1952

(consumption and income in dollars for the U.S., in pounds sterling for the U.K.)

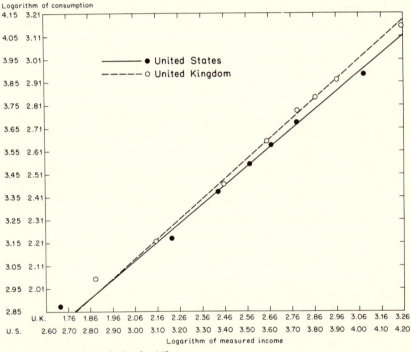

Source: See Table 1, sources for lines 9 and 13.

study in dollars is 8.73 times the mean income in the United Kingdom study in pounds; accordingly, dollar and pound values have been plotted as if the rate of exchange between them were $8.73 to the £. It is interesting that for both sets of data, the initial point is above and the final point below the regression suggested by the intermediate points—a characteristic of such data discussed in the preceding section.

The elasticities of .82 for the United States data and of .87 for the United Kingdom data imply that some 18 per cent of the variance of measured income in the United States but only 13 per cent in the United Kingdom can be regarded as attributable to transitory factors. Since the total variance in measured income relative to the mean is not very different in the two countries or, if anything, somewhat less in the United Kingdom,[16] transitory variation in income must be less important in the United Kingdom not only as a percentage of total variation in income but also as a percentage of mean income itself. On the basis of our theoretical analysis in Chapter II, this would mean that the need for a reserve for emergencies would be less in the United Kingdom than in the United States, and hence might be expected to mean a higher value of k—or a higher average propensity to consume—in the United Kingdom than in the United States.[17] The observed value is decidedly higher, and the greater temporal stability of relative income position in the United Kingdom than in the United States revealed by the income elasticities may well be one important reason why it is.

Two other reasons for the higher average propensity in the United Kingdom come immediately to mind: (1) the more extensive provision of security through governmental channels in the United Kingdom; (2) the absence of a capital gains tax and the associated stimulus to investment by corporations. Both work against personal saving, which is the only kind covered in the studies summarized in Table 1.

One reason for the greater relative importance of transitory factors in the United States may be the higher frequency of farm units, who number some 10 per cent of the United States sample

---

[16] Compare the distributions of gross and net income for the two countries in H. F. Lydall, "National Survey of Personal Incomes and Savings," *Bulletin of the Oxford University Institute of Statistics*, XV, Numbers 2 and 3, (February and March, 1953), pp. 35–84, esp. Table 10, and in "1952 Survey of Consumer Finances, Part III. Income, Selected Investments and Short-Term Debt of Consumers," *Federal Reserve Bulletin*, (September 1952), esp. Table 8.

[17] There is a slip between the lower need for a reserve and the higher value of k that should be noted. Strictly speaking, the smaller magnitude of transitory factors implies, other things the same, a lower equilibrium level of nonhuman wealth relative to total wealth or to income. Given full stationary equilibrium, k would be unity whatever the magnitude of transitory factors, because full adjustment would have been made to it. The value of k depends on the difference between the equilibrium level of nonhuman wealth and the achieved level—or the significance attached to the difference. The assertion that k is higher the smaller the magnitude of transitory variation in income implicitly assumes (1) that we are speaking of a nonequilibrium position, (2) that the discrepancy between the existing position and the full equilibrium position is larger the higher the equilibrium level of nonhuman wealth, so that the higher the latter, the greater the pressure to devote current resources to increasing the level of nonhuman wealth.

and only 1 per cent of the British.[18] However, this can hardly account for much of the difference. The elasticity for United States nonfarm families alone is .80 (line 8, Table 1), compared to .82 for all United States units and .87 for all British units.

c. CONSUMPTION OF FARM AND NONFARM FAMILIES

Figure 6 presents some comparative data for farm and nonfarm families from two studies for the United States—one for 1935–36, the other for 1941. These studies are comparable in coverage, method of collection of data, and concepts used. The only significant differences between the data from them plotted in Figure 6 are that (1) the 1935–36 data are for nonrelief families only, the 1941 data, for all families; (2) the nonfarm figures for 1935–36 are for all nonfarm families whereas those for 1941 are for urban families alone and exclude rural nonfarm families. Table 3 summarizes some numerical data for these two studies and adds some additional data for 1948–50. The 1948–50 figures are derived from the Federal Reserve Board Survey of Consumer Finances conducted by the Michigan Survey Research Center, and differ from the other figures in several important respects: (1) The data were collected differently. In the other studies, data were collected on consumption, savings, and income independently, in this study, only on savings and income. (2) The data are for spending units rather than for families. A spending unit consists of all related persons living in a single household who pool their income for "major" expenses, and it is on the average smaller than a family defined by relationship alone. According to Survey figures, there were about 15 per cent more spending units than families in 1950.[19] The use of the spending unit rather than the family has no effect on the average propensity to consume but does alter the level of mean income and consumption and can affect the regression of consumption on income. (3) The data are for spending units of all sizes combined, including one-person spending units, whereas the other data in Table 3, except for the 1941 farm figures, exclude single individuals. Both the use of the spending unit instead of the family and the inclusion of single individuals make decidedly more difference for nonfarm than for farm units,[20] which explains why only the average propensity to consume is recorded for nonfarm families.

[18] "1951 Survey of Consumer Finances, Part III," *Federal Reserve Bulletin* (August 1950), Table 7; Lydall, *op. cit.*, p. 61.

[19] "1955 Survey of Consumer Finances," *Federal Reserve Bulletin*, (May 1955), p. 472.

[20] Tables 7 and 8 of "1951 Survey of Consumer Finances, Part III," *Federal Reserve Bulletin* (August 1951) report that units headed by a farm operator accounted for 9 per cent of all spending units but 10 per cent of all family units. Unfortunately, these percentages are rounded to too few significant figures to permit a satisfactory estimate

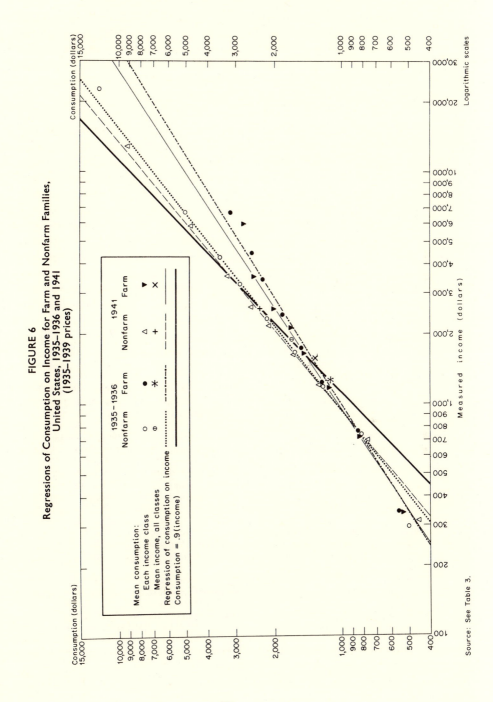

FIGURE 6

Regressions of Consumption on Income for Farm and Nonfarm Families,
United States, 1935–1936 and 1941
(1935–1939 prices)

Source: See Table 3.

59

(4) The data are for money items of income only. (5) Last but by no means least, the data available in published form are much less fully and less conveniently presented than for either of the other studies.[21] Despite these differences, the 1948–50 figures are included to provide some evidence for the period after World War II when the situation was decidedly different than in 1935–36 or 1941, particularly with respect to the income position of farmers.

The figures plotted on the chart are for money income and money consumption expenditures for nonfarm families, but include both money and nonmoney items for farm families. For nonfarm families, the only important source of nonmoney income and consumption is the imputed income from owned homes (the excess of rental value over current housing expenses and depreciation). In consequence, the difference between the money magnitudes and a broader concept of income and consumption that includes nonmoney items as well is not large enough to affect appreciably the kind of results we have been considering. As Table 3 shows, nonmoney items account for only about 5 per cent of total income; accordingly, we have not heretofore found it necessary to distinguish between

---

of the excess of spending units over family units for farmers: taking the reported percentages to be precisely 9 and 10 would imply an excess of spending units of two per cent; allowing for errors of rounding, the excess could be anything at all under the 15 per cent for the country as a whole in 1951 implied by the estimates cited in the preceding footnote.

Footnote f of our Table 3 gives some figures on the relative importance of single individuals among farm consumer units. I have been able to infer no comparable data from the published data on the Survey of Consumer Finances.

[21] Indeed, there is no other American survey I have had occasion to use for which the published material on income and saving is so unsatisfactory for research purposes. The annual publications on the Survey of Consumer Finances in the Federal Reserve Bulletin give primarily frequency distributions, and even these are mostly only one-way distributions and the entries are given to too few significant figures to enable them to be used rather than simply repeated (a striking example is contained in the preceding footnote). Few averages or aggregates are published. Those that are published are mostly for the country as a whole. Even where averages are presented for subgroups, as for different occupational groups, the weights required to combine them into any other grouping cannot be inferred from the reported "number of cases," owing to the sampling methods used, but must be taken from a frequency distribution in which they are given to too few significant figures to be useful. No averages are given for income classes.

As a result of these deficiencies in the published data, I have had to rely almost entirely on data made available to me on special request or on data published in secondary sources in connection with special analyses of the Survey, mostly by members of the Michigan Survey Research Center. The research staff of the Board of Governors of the Federal Reserve System has been extremely cooperative and helpful in meeting such requests, and I am much indebted to them. At the same time, this arrangement is at best a poor substitute for having the basic data available in a form in which one can work with them himself. This is a major reason why these potentially valuable data have been far less useful in this study than they might have been, and why they are referred to so seldom.

the two concepts. For farm families, imputed income from housing is relatively more important than for nonfarmers; in addition, value of food grown for own use, which is of minor importance for nonfarm families, is even larger. The result is that nonmoney items—all of which count as both income and consumption—account for something like a third of total measured income including such items.[22] The broader concept seems more nearly comparable for the two groups of families, so is used in the chart. Table 3 contains data for both: money income and consumption alone, and total income and consumption including both money and nonmoney items.

The differences between the 1935–36 and 1941 studies themselves are primarily of the kind that, as suggested in section a above, would follow, on our hypothesis, from the higher average income in 1941 than in 1935–36: the 1941 regression of consumption on income is a trifle higher in every case than the comparable 1935–36 regression. The 1941 elasticity of consumption with respect to income (the slope of the regressions in the graph) is also a trifle higher in each case; these differences are minor and may well be a result simply of sampling fluctuations, though the consistency of the difference argues against this interpretation. Insofar as they are more than a reflection of sampling fluctuations, they imply that transitory factors were relatively more important in the 1935–36 data than in the 1941 data, a result that, as noted above, might be expected from the restriction of the 1935–36 data to nonrelief families.[23] The 1948–50 figures yield a higher average propensity to consume for both nonfarm and farm units than the earlier figures; it is not clear whether this is a result of differences in methods and definitions or is a significant difference between the two periods (see the additional comments on this point in the next section). The same question arises about the higher elasticity and marginal propensity for farm units in 1948–50, since the use of spending units instead of families would tend to produce higher values for these parameters. The differences among the several studies are, however, minor compared to the remarkably consistent story they tell about the differences between farm and nonfarm families:

[22] In addition to imputed income from housing and the value of food grown for own use, nonmoney income for farmers includes some minor items, such as fuel and ice, and gifts or pay in kind.

[23] This factor may also help to explain why the elasticities differ more for nonfarm than for farm families: about 17 per cent of all nonfarm families but only about 9 per cent of all farm families are estimated to have received relief during 1935–56. See U.S. National Resources Committee, *Consumer Incomes in the United States* (Washington, 1938), pp. 74–75.

TABLE 3

Relation between Consumption and Income for Farm and Nonfarm
Consumer Units, 1935–1936, 1941, and 1948–1950

(*dollar figures in 1935–39 prices*[a])

	Arithmetic Mean		Estimated Consumption at Income of $1,500	Average Propensity to Consume[b]	Income Elasticity of Consumption[c]	Marginal Propensity to Consume[d]
Group and Year	*Income*	*Consumption*				
Money Income and Consumption						
Nonfarm or urban:[e]						
1. Families, 1935–36	$1,896	$1,676	$1,479	.88	.82	.73
2. Families, 1941	2,554	2,325	1,503	.91	.87	.79
3. Spending units, 1948–50				.94		
Farm:						
4. Families, 1935–36	816	657	1,035	.80	.63	.50
5. Families, 1941[f]	1,103	828	1,110	.75	.64	.48
6. Spending units, 1948–50				.88	.69	.61
Money plus Nonmoney Income and Consumption						
Nonfarm or urban families:[e]						
7. 1935–36	1,980	1,760		.89		
8. 1941	2,723	2,494		.92		
Farm families:						
9. 1935–36	1,278	1,118	1,309	.87	.65	.57
10. 1941[f]	1,597	1,322	1,374	.83	.69	.57

[a] Figures in original sources all converted to 1935–39 prices by Bureau of Labor Statistics index of consumer prices.

[b] Ratio of arithmetic mean consumption to arithmetic mean income. For 1948–50, mean income is disposable income after personal taxes.

[c] Slope of graphically fitted straight line regression of logarithm of consumption on logarithm of income.

[d] Average propensity times elasticity.

[e] Nonfarm in 1935–36 and 1948–50, urban in 1941.

[f] Families plus single individuals. However, of the 762 farm consumer units in the sample, only 29 are single individuals, so the results for families alone would differ very little.

Source:

Lines 1, 4, 7, 9

Average income and consumption computed from National Resources Planning Board, *Family Expenditures in the United States* (Washington, 1941), pp. 119, 123, 124, 125, 127, 128, 130, and 131. Data for regression of consumption on income from *ibid.*, p. 51, for line 9; from Dorothy Brady in *A Study of Saving*, Vol. III, p. 182, for lines 1 and 4. Consumption throughout includes gifts and personal taxes.

Lines 2, 5, 8, 10

Average income and consumption from U.S. Bureau of Labor Statistics, *Bulletin No. 822, Family Spending and Saving in Wartime* (Washington, 1945), pp. 71 and 73; income figure used is item recorded in these tables as income plus inheritances and other money receipts; consumption includes gifts and personal taxes. Data for regression of consumption on income from Dorothy Brady in *A Study of Saving*, Vol. III, p. 182, for lines 2 and 5; from Department of Agriculture, Miscellaneous Publication No. 520, *Rural Family Spending and Saving in Wartime* (Washington, 1934), p. 161, for line 10.

Line 3

Based on weighted averages of average income and consumption figures in Table 5 for "independent business" and "others," with a weight of .07 for "independent business" and of .93 for "others." These

(cont. on next page)

TABLE 3 (cont.)

weights were roughly estimated from the averages for each of the three groups in Table 5 separately and all groups combined, plus the percentage of spending units reported as headed by "farm operator" in "1951 Survey of Consumer Finances, Part III," *Federal Reserve Bulletin*, August 1951, Table 7, and "1950 Survey of Consumer Finances, Part III," *ibid.*, August 1950, Table 15.

Line 6
See notes to Table 5.

consumption expenditures of farm families (1) are lower at any absolute income level except, perhaps, at the lowest levels of income observed in the farm samples; (2) increase less rapidly with measured income —both the marginal propensity to consume and the income elasticity of expenditures are decidedly lower; (3) are on the average a smaller fraction of average income—in our terminology, k is lower; this difference is much smaller for the comparison in terms of money plus nonmoney items than for the comparison in terms of money items alone; in all cases, however, it is in the same direction.[24]

Let us consider each of these in turn. On our hypothesis, point (1) follows from the lower average measured income of farm than of nonfarm families in the several studies. To bring this effect alone out in sharp relief, let us depart from the actual data in Figure 6 and instead consider the hypothetical Figure 7, in which differences

[24] For additional discussions of these data see Margaret G. Reid, "Effect of Income Concept upon Expenditure Curves of Farm Families," in Conference on Research in Income and Wealth, *Studies in Income and Wealth*, XV (New York: National Bureau of Economic Research, 1952), pp. 133–174; Brady and Friedman, "Savings and the Income Distribution," pp. 252–253; James N. Morgan, "The Structure of Aggregate Personal Saving," *Journal of Political Economy*, LIX (December 1951), pp. 528–534 especially p. 531.

In his time series savings study, which provides much of the evidence analyzed in the following chapter, Goldsmith estimates savings and the ratio of savings to income separately for nonagricultural and agricultural households. At first glance, his figures suggest that the relatively high savings of farmers shown by the budget studies are a special feature of the period after the mid-1930's and do not apply before then. His estimates give savings-income ratios for periods prior to 1934 that are decidedly lower for farm than for nonfarm families and for some periods even negative [see R. W. Goldsmith, *A Study of Saving in the United States*, Vol. I (Princeton University Press, 1955), pp. 76 and 102]. However, this contradiction is only superficial. It reflects primarily Goldsmith's exclusion of capital gains and losses from income and savings, which affects agriculture particularly strongly because of the large rise in land values during the early decades of the century. Whatever the validity of this treatment for the national aggregate, it is misleading in comparing the saving propensities of different groups. Goldsmith recognizes the difficulty and points out that the situation is rendered even worse by the inclusion, as a negative item of savings, of debt accumulated to purchase land that has risen in value. As some indication of the effect of his treatment, Goldsmith presents estimates of changes in net worth for separate saver groups for selected periods. It is clear from the relation of these to his savings estimates that use of change in net worth— and this seems closer than Goldsmith's concept of savings to the concept relevant in comparing different groups and implicit in budget studies—would yield higher savings-income ratios for agricultural than nonagricultural households for the whole of his period except possibly 1923–33. *Ibid.*, pp. 136–137.

(2) and (3) are supposed not to hold and which, for simplicity of exposition, is in arithmetic rather than logarithmic terms. Let $c_p = ky_p$ be the relation between permanent components, provisionally supposed to hold for both farm and nonfarm groups. Assume that transitory components of both income and consumption average out to zero for the group of farm families and also for the group of nonfarm families. Mean expenditures and mean income for the two groups would then fall on the line $c = ky$, say at P_1 for nonfarm families and at P_2 for farm families. As we saw in

FIGURE 7

Hypothetical Regressions of Consumption on Income
for Farm and Nonfarm Families
(k and P_y assumed same)

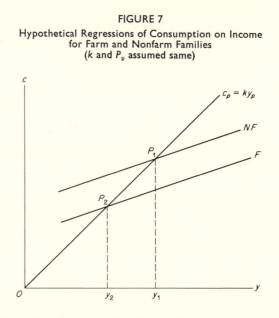

Chapter III, section 3 above, the observed regression of consumption on income tends to be flatter than $c = ky$ and to cut it at the group mean producing two regressions like those labelled *NF* (nonfarm) and *F* (farm) in Figure 7.

The explanation for this difference in observed results is therefore the same as for the differences between regressions for widely spaced points in time (see section a above). The interpretation is, however, somewhat easier to put explicitly in this case. Consider an income equal to y_1, the mean observed income of nonfarm families. Of the nonfarm families at this income, some "belong" there, in the sense that this is their permanent component, some are there because of favorable factors that have made their incomes abnormally high, some, because of unfavorable factors that have made their incomes abnormally low. Because y_1 is the mean income of all nonfarm families, the latter two groups may be expected to be about equally numerous and to offset one another, so that on the average, y_1 correctly describes the permanent income of the class. Their consumption is, therefore, adjusted to this income, at least on the average. Consider now the farm families with an income of y_1. They fall into the same three groups—those who "belong" there, those who are there by good fortune, and those who are there despite bad fortune. But y_1 is an unusually high income for farm families, well above the average for all farm families. Those who are in this income class because of good fortune are therefore likely to be more numerous than those who are in it despite bad fortune. The average permanent income of the class is therefore less than y_1; their consumption is adjusted on the average to this permanent status; it is, therefore, less than the average consumption of the nonfarm families with an income of y_1. Similarly, consider an income equal to y_2, the mean observed income of farm families. This is, on the average, the "permanent" or "normal" income of the farm families classified at this measured income, so on the average their consumption is k times this income. But it is an abnormally low income for nonfarm families, so the average permanent income of nonfarm families classified at this measured income is higher than y_2, and their average consumption is higher than k times this income.

The lower marginal propensity to consume for farm families recorded in point (2) is, on our hypothesis, to be interpreted as a resultant of two more basic factors: the lower income elasticity of consumption and the lower average propensity to consume recorded in point (3). For our hypothesis tells us that the income elasticity is equal to P_y, the fraction of the total variance of income contributed by the variance of the permanent component;[25] and that the marginal propensity is equal to kP_y.[26] In discussing this point, therefore, we shall consider the lower income elasticity as its independent contribution. This lower income elasticity is, of course, reflected in Figure 6 in the steeper slope of the regressions for nonfarm than for farm families. When extended toward lower incomes, the regressions cross, a fact which explains the occasional finding of higher consumption expenditures for farm than for nonfarm families at low observed incomes.

On our hypothesis, the income elasticity itself is a resultant of

[25] If the regression is linear in arithmetic units, this is the elasticity at the mean income, when transitory components average out to zero.
[26] If the regression is linear in logarithmic units, this is the marginal propensity at the mean income when the transitory components average out to zero.

two more basic magnitudes: (a) the differences among families in measured income produced by factors regarded as transitory or temporary; (b) the differences in measured income produced by factors regarded as permanent. It seems plausible that (a) should on the average be larger for farm than for nonfarm families, perhaps not in dollar terms given the lower average income of farm families but certainly as a percentage of income. Variations in weather and the like affect farm income much more than nonfarm income; and farm income has a large entrepreneurial element whereas most nonfarm income is from such relatively stable sources as wages and salaries. The relative size of (b) is less clear: the greater heterogeneity of the nonfarm group tends toward wider differences in permanent components for them; the entrepreneurial character of farm income may well work in the opposite direction. The lower income elasticity for farm families tells us, or reflects the fact that, (a) is larger relative to (b) for farm than for nonfarm families, which is consistent with these speculations though not required by them. But, by itself, it does not tell us anything about each magnitude separately.

We can get estimates of each magnitude separately by combining the estimated income elasticities with the observed variation among families in measured income. Table 4 summarizes the results. Column (2) repeats the income elasticities from Table 3. These are here treated as measuring the fraction of the variance of measured income attributable to the variance of the permanent component. Column (3) is the standard deviation of the logarithms of measured income. Because computed from the logarithms, it is a measure of relative dispersion. It can be regarded as an estimate of the coefficient of variation of the original observations, or the ratio of the standard deviation to the mean.[27] The advantage of a measure of this sort is that it allows for differences in the unit of measure or in average income, and we have already taken account of such

---

[27] The standard deviation of the logarithms is a direct estimate of the coefficient of variation of the original observations provided that natural logarithms (logarithms to the base e) are used. If common logarithms (to the base 10) are used, the standard deviation of the logarithms must be multiplied by $\log_e 10$ to convert it into an estimate of the coefficient of variation.

If the observations are supposed to be distributed according to a logarithmic normal distribution, the maximum likelihood estimate of the coefficient of variation is $(e^{s^2} - 1)^{\frac{1}{2}}$, where s^2 is the variance of the natural logarithms of the observations. It will be seen that this is approximately equal to s for small values of s. I have not used the more precise estimate of the coefficient of variation simply because there is no special reason to prefer the estimated coefficient of variation of the original observations to the standard deviation of the logarithms as a measure of relative dispersion. It is convenient in exposition that the two can be regarded as estimates of one another.

TABLE 4

Dispersion of Measured Income, and its Permanent and
Transitory Components Relative to Mean Measured Income
for Farm and Nonfarm Families, 1935–1936, 1941

Group, Year, Income Concept (1)	Fraction of Variance of Measured Income Attributed to Permanent Component[a] (2)	Relative Dispersion of:		
		Measured Income[b] (3)	Permanent Component[c] (4)	Transitory Component[d] (5)
Nonfarm or urban families:				
1935–36	.82	.78	.70	.33
1941	.87	.82	.76	.29
Farm families:				
Money income:				
1935–36	.63			
1941	.64	1.04	.83	.62
Money plus nonmoney income:				
1935–36	.65	.70	.57	.41
1941	.69	.85	.70	.48

[a] Elasticity of consumption with respect to income from Table 3.

[b] Standard deviation of natural logarithms of measured income. This is an approximate estimate of the coefficient of variation (standard deviation divided by arithmetic mean income) of measured income itself.

[c] Square root of product of elasticity in column (2) and variance of logarithms of measured income [square of column (3)]. Result is an approximate estimate of coefficient of variation of permanent component in absolute units, on assumption that mean transitory income is zero.

[d] Square root of product of unity minus elasticity in column (2) and variance of logarithms of measured income. Result is an approximate estimate of ratio of standard deviation of transitory component to mean measured income.

Source of distributions of measured income: 1935–36, National Resources Planning Board, *Family Expenditures in the United States* (Washington, 1941), p. 120. 1941, urban, U.S. Bureau of Labor Statistics, Bulletin No. 822, p. 68; farm, U.S. Department of Agriculture, Miscellaneous Publication No. 520, pp. 26, 27, and 161. In lieu of detailed information, rather arbitrary approximations were used to distribute negative incomes and incomes in the top open-end class. Logarithmic variances cannot, of course, be computed when there are negative incomes. This difficulty was evaded by combining negative incomes with incomes under $500 and treating the corresponding families as if all had the average income of the group.

differences in our discussion of point (1). The square of the number in column (3) is the variance of logarithms of income, and the product of this and the fraction in column (2) is the estimated variance of the permanent components alone; its square root is the number entered in column (4). Similarly, the product of the variance of logarithms of income and the complement of the fraction in column (2) is the estimated variance of the transitory component and its square root is the number entered in column (5). Our procedure forces equality between the square of column (3) and the sum of the squares of columns (4) and (5). This is, of course, a consequence of the assumption in our hypothesis that permanent and transitory components of income are uncorrelated. In interpreting these figures, it should be noted that the dispersion of permanent and transitory components is measured relative to total income. This seems the appropriate base. No significance can be attached, for example, to the dispersion of transitory components relative to their own mean, which might well be zero or negative.

There is considerable agreement between the studies for 1935–36 and 1941. The differences are in the direction to be expected from the more stringent eligibility requirements for the 1935–36 figures, especially their restriction to nonrelief families. In addition, the 1935–36 figures include nonfarm rural families plus urban families, whereas the 1941 figures include only urban families. Both factors would tend to produce wider variation in the 1941 data than in the 1935–36 data, and this is what Table 4 shows.

The more meaningful comparison between farm and other families is for money plus nonmoney income—only one set of figures is given for nonfarm families because the results are not appreciably different for the two concepts. This comparison shows the expected difference between the two groups in the dispersion of the transitory component: the standard deviation of the transitory component is about 30 per cent of mean income for nonfarm or urban families, and between 40 and 50 per cent for farm families. The difference is in the other direction for the permanent component: the standard deviation of the permanent component is at least 70 per cent of mean income for nonfarm or urban families; at most, 70 per cent for farm families. This means that the lower income elasticity of farm families is produced by both a larger variance of transitory components and a lower variance of permanent components—though the figures for money income show how the same result can occur despite a larger variance of permanent components.

For farm families, money income alone is relatively more dispersed than money plus nonmoney income. This is to be expected. Nonmoney income from housing and from food grown for own use can hardly be expected to vary anything like so much among families as money income.

The greater importance of transitory variation in income for farm than for nonfarm families may also help explain point (3), the lower ratio of average consumption to average income for farm families. The reason is the same as that suggested above for the higher average propensity of British than of United States families: a larger variance in the transitory components of income means that farmers have a greater need for a reserve against emergencies than nonfarmers and so might be expected to have a lower k. Another factor that has often been cited, and that may well play a role, is the possibility that the farmer can earn a higher average rate of interest by direct investment in his own enterprise than nonfarmers can by indirect investment through financial intermediaries. However, it is my impression that savings as a fraction of income have been found to be higher for farmers than for nonfarmers even during periods when farming was a declining industry relative to other industries. If this is so, it suggests that the lower P_y is an independent and quantitatively significant factor producing a relatively high savings ratio.

d. OCCUPATIONAL CHARACTERISTICS OF FAMILIES

Two characteristics of farm families are the keystone of the preceding analysis of their consumption behavior: their decidedly lower average income, at least for the years studied, which accounts for generally lower consumption at given measured incomes; and the entrepreneurial source of their income, which helps to account for both the lower income elasticity of consumption and the lower average propensity to consume by making transitory components a relatively important source of income variation. Owners of nonfarm unincorporated businesses differ from farmers in respect of the first characteristic—their average income is higher than the average income of all families;[28] they are alike in respect of the second. Accordingly, if our hypothesis is valid, we should find that the average propensity to consume is lower for them than for nonentrepreneurial families and that our measures imply higher relative dispersion of transitory components—in this section we examine whether this is so. Negro families as a group are like farmers with respect to the first characteristic—they tend to have a decidedly lower average income than their white neighbors; but they differ with respect to the second. Accordingly, we should find that observed consumption is lower at given measured incomes for them than for white families; but there is no reason, on the basis of the characteristics cited, why the observed elasticities or

[28] See Table 5 below; *Consumer Incomes in the United States*, p. 26;1 "952 Survey of Consumer Finances, Part III. Income, Selected Investments, and Short-Term Debt of Consumers," *Federal Reserve Bulletin* (September 1952), Table 2.

average propensities should differ—in the next section we examine whether this is so.

Figure 8 and Table 5 summarize some evidence on the consumption-income relations for independent business spending units and other

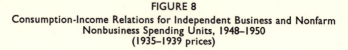

FIGURE 8

Consumption-Income Relations for Independent Business and Nonfarm
Nonbusiness Spending Units, 1948–1950
(1935–1939 prices)

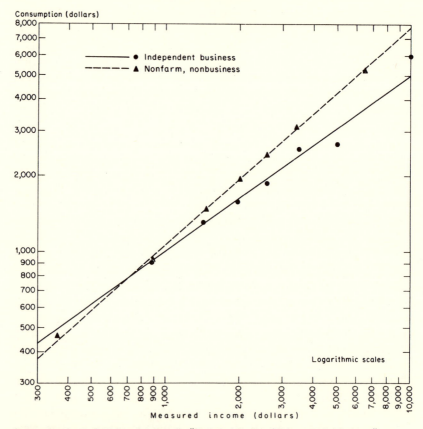

Source: Based on L. R. Klein and J. Margolis, "Statistical Studies of Unincorporated Business,"
Review of Economics and Statistics, February 1954, Table 13, p. 41.

spending units. These data are from the nationwide Surveys of Consumer Finances covering 1948, 1949, and 1950 income. For comparability with earlier figures, the income and expenditure data in Figure 8 have been deflated to 1935–39 prices. The two regressions in the figure are very much like those for farm and nonfarm families in Figure 6: the business regression is flatter,

TABLE 5

Relation between Consumption and Income for Independent Business,
Farm, and Other Spending Units, 1948–1950

Occupational Group	Average Disposable Income		Average Propensity to Consume	Income Elasticity of Consumption
	Current Prices	1935–39 Prices		
Independent business	$4,789	$2,795	.77	.70
Farmers	2,404	1,403	.88	.69
Others	3,038	1,773	.95	.86

Note: Figures are for money consumption and money disposable income.

Source:

Average disposable income and average propensity to consume: Based on data made available by the Board of Governors of the Federal Reserve System. These data gave average saving and average total income for each occupational group in each year but average disposable income only for 1948 and 1950. I estimated average disposable income in 1949 from the other figures plus average total income and disposable income in separate income classes. The average propensity entered is the ratio of average consumption for the three years to average disposable income for the three years, these averages in turn being simple averages of the corresponding figures for the individual years.

Elasticity of consumption for independent business and others: Slope of straight line regression of logarithm of consumption on logarithm of disposable income fitted graphically to data plotted in Figure 8. *Elasticity of consumption for farmers:* Slope of graphically fitted straight line regression of logarithm of consumption on logarithm of disposable income based on data for 1948, 1949, and 1950 made available by the Board of Governors of the Federal Reserve System. These data were for total income rather than disposable income classes and for each year separately.

starts above the other regression, then meets it and falls below it by increasing amounts. As Table 5 shows, the elasticity for independent business spending units is .70, decidedly lower than the elasticity of .86 for nonfarm, nonentrepreneurial spending units in Table 5, but a trifle higher than the values ranging from .63 to .69 recorded in Table 3 for farm families or spending units.

The similar elasticities for farm units and for independent business spending units is interesting; it is not, however, required by our hypothesis. We should expect both farm and independent business units to display a wider relative dispersion of transitory components of income than other units. The value of the elasticity also depends, however, on the size of the relative dispersion of permanent components. It is plausible that permanent components differ more widely for independent businessmen than for farmers. The independent businessmen pursue a wider diversity of activities than the farmers and differ more widely in such attendant circumstances as the amount of capital invested in the business. For similar reasons, it is plausible that permanent components differ more widely for business spending units than for nonbusiness, nonfarm spending units. The crucial question for elasticities, however, is whether differences in the dispersion of permanent components are greater or less than the corresponding differences in the dispersion of transitory components, and about this there is not much a priori basis for formulating any precise expectations. What the elasticities tell us is that if the dispersion of permanent components for business units exceeds that for farm units, the dispersion of transitory components does so by a smaller percentage; whereas, if the dispersion of permanent components for business units exceeds that for nonfarm, nonbusiness units, the dispersion of transitory components does so by an even larger percentage. Unfortunately, there are no reasonably comparable estimates of total dispersion of measured income that could be combined with the elasticities to get estimates of the dispersion of each component separately, as we were able to do in Table 4.[29]

The decidedly lower average propensity recorded in Table 5 for business units (.77) than for nonfarm nonbusiness units (.95)

[29] Klein and Margolis consider explicitly what is in essence the explanation given here for the difference between business and other spending units in the elasticity of the consumption-income relations and in the preceding section for farmers and nonfarmers. They reject this explanation, writing, "Possible explanations for these findings (a lower marginal propensity to consume for farmers than nonfarmers) are differences in the rural way of life, high motivation to invest savings in productive farm assets, or participation by farmers in relatively large income increases just preceding the survey interviews. The last mentioned point would help to explain the differences if savings were positively correlated with income change. To some extent this is true, but the contribution of *large* income *increases* to lower savings rates has been found and can be established on plausible reasoning. Farmers, being entrepreneurs, are said to have more variable income than nonentrepreneurial groups; consequently, income change may be a more strategic variable for the former.

"Similar considerations carry over to our study of unincorporated businessmen. They too show a lower average propensity to consume and a lower marginal propensity than nonfarm, nonbusiness spending units" (p. 41). Later, they write, "The data in Tables 7 and 8, together with the fact that the marginal effect of income change on savings has doubtful size or sign, do not lead us to explain the observed discrepancies by differences in the variability of income for the two groups" (p. 42). Tables 7 and 8 of the Klein-Margolis paper give the distributions of past income change and of a number of other items for independent business and all spending units.

The evidence Klein and Margolis cite does not seem to justify their conclusion. We shall see later, in section 4, that data on the relation of income change to the consumption-income regression, including data from the studies Klein and Margolis use, are directly consistent with our hypothesis; it is hard to see why Klein and Margolis regard them as indirectly inconsistent with it. L. R. Klein and J. Margolis, "Statistical Studies of Unincorporated Business," *Review of Economics and Statistics*, XXXVII (February 1954), pp. 33–46.

conforms with expectations.[30] The propensity for farmers is much more difficult to interpret. It is closer to the propensity for "others" than for business units. Moreover, it is based on money items only. Inclusion of nonmoney items, which would render it more nearly comparable with the other propensities, would probably yield a still higher figure. If the ratio of nonmoney items to money items were the same in 1948–50 as in the 1935–36 and 1941 studies summarized in Table 3, and if, as in those studies, all nonmoney items consisted of consumption in kind, a propensity of .88 for money items would imply a propensity of .92 for money plus non-money items. It is likely that nonmoney items were less important in 1948–50 than in the earlier studies. In addition, the 1948–50 studies excluded some nonmoney saving items.[31] On both grounds, the required upward adjustment is smaller than that indicated. To add to the problem of interpretation, the 1948–50 propensity for farmers, whether or not adjusted for nonmoney items, diverges much more from the propensities computed from the earlier studies than the propensity for nonfarm units (see Table 3). These earlier studies yield propensities of .75 and .80 for money items, of .83 and .87 for nonmoney items. Does the divergence reflect a temporal change? Or does it reflect the sizable differences in the methods, techniques, and definitions of the several studies? I see no way to decide. Whichever interpretation is accepted, the studies agree in setting the average propensity lower for farmers than for nonfarm, nonbusiness units—though this difference is rather small for the 1948–50 data—and higher for farmers than for independent business units—though this difference is non-existent if the money figures for the earlier studies are regarded as comparable to the figures in Table 5.

The only other extensive body of data classified by occupations that I know about is the 1935–36 data from the Study of Consumer Purchases, used as the source of the various data for 1935–36 cited earlier in this chapter. Some evidence from this source is summarized in Table 6. These data have some advantages over those from the Survey of Consumer Finances: data on consumption expenditures were collected directly, whereas in the Survey of

[30] Goldsmith gives estimates of the saving-income ratio of unincorporated business (*op. cit.*, I, p. 169) which are lower than his estimates for nonfarm households. However, these data do not contradict our findings for two reasons: (1) the exclusion of capital gains discussed above in footnote 24; (2) his estimates are for the businesses, not the owners thereof, and in consequence he does not include savings by the owners in forms other than investment in their business.

[31] In particular, changes in farm inventories, which were positive over the period 1948–50. See "1949 Survey of Consumer Finances, Part VIII," *Federal Reserve Bulletin* (January 1950), footnote 7; *National Income, 1954 edition* (Washington, 1954), p. 167.

TABLE 6

Income Elasticity of Consumption, and Relative Dispersion of Measured Income
and its Components by Occupational Groups, Native White Nonrelief
Complete Families in Three Cities, 1935–1936

				Relative Dispersion[a] of:								
	Income Elasticity of Consumption			Measured Income			Permanent Component			Transitory Component		
Occupational Group	N.Y.C.	Col., Ohio	Atl., Ga.	N.Y.C.	Col., Ohio	Atl., Ga.	N.Y.C.	Col., Ohio	Atl., Ga.	N.Y.C.	Col., Ohio	Atl., Ga.
Wage earner	.94	.78	.83	.54	.54	.61	.52	.47	.56	.14	.25	.26
Clerical	.81	.83	.86	.51	.52	.56	.46	.47	.52	.22	.21	.21
Salaried business	.88	.78	.88	.72	.56	.57	.68	.50	.53	.25	.26	.20
Salaried professional	.87	.76	.78	.66	.54	.50	.61	.47	.44	.23	.26	.23
Independent business	.90	} .73	.82	.85	} .87	.90	.80	} .75	.82	.26	} .45	.38
Independent professional	.84			.92			.85			.37		
All families	.89	.81	.84	.77	.68	.70	.73	.61	.65	.26	.30	.28

[a] For meaning and computation of measures of relative dispersion see notes b, c, and d to Table 4.
Source:
Income elasticity of consumption: Slope of graphically fitted straight line regression of logarithm of consumption on logarithm of income. Basic data from Department of Labor, Bulletin No. 648, *Family Expenditures in Selected Cities, 1935–36, Volume VIII, Changes in Assets and Liabilities* (Washington, 1941), Table 2.
Relative dispersion of measured income: Standard deviation of natural logarithms of income computed from frequency distributions in Department of Labor, Bulletin No. 643, *Family Income and Expenditure in New York City, 1935–36, Volume I, Family Income* (Washington, 1941), pp. 93–96; Bulletin No. 644, *Family Income and Expenditure in Nine Cities of the East Central Region, 1935–36, Volume I, Family Income* (Washington, 1939), pp. 137–40; Bulletin No. 647, *Family Income and Expenditure in the Southeastern Region, 1935–36, Volume I, Family Income* (Washington, 1939), pp. 147–150.

Consumer Finances they must be derived by subtracting reported savings from reported income; the original data have been published in much fuller and more detailed form; data are available for individual cities and for rather narrowly defined occupational groups. On the other hand, these data have two serious disadvantages for our present purpose. (1) For independent business families, measured income is defined essentially as withdrawals from business.[32] This must have the effect of reducing the relative importance of transitory components of income. When measured income, including business income, is abnormally low, consumption is likely to be

[32] See, for example, Bureau of Labor Statistics, Bulletin No. 647, *Family Income and Expenditure in Southeastern Region, 1935–36*, Vol. I, Family Income, pp. 505, 506 and 509.

74

financed, at least in part, by withdrawals from the business in excess of current earnings, and, conversely, when measured income is abnormally high, some part tends to be retained in the business. The restriction of recorded income to withdrawals is also likely to make the recorded average propensity to consume higher than one based on the alternative concept of income, since it seems likely that a substantial part of the savings of businessmen takes the form of business investment. The same definition of income is used for independent professional families. However, its effect seems less serious for them, in view of the generally much smaller scope for direct investment in, or withdrawal of funds from, professional than business activities. (2) Income data were obtained for a representative sample of units, albeit with some eligibility requirements. Consumption data, on the other hand, were obtained for a much smaller and designedly nonrepresentative sample. The result is that the basic reports on the study do not give figures on average consumption for a group as a whole, covering all income classes. Computation of such an average requires constructing a weighted average of estimated consumption for individual income classes; and since some income classes were not covered at all in the expenditure sample, estimates for these require extrapolation from other classes.[33] The computations involved are so extensive that I have not attempted to compute average propensities for the Consumer Purchases Study. I have reported such propensities only when they had already been computed as part of another study.

The evidence from the Study of Consumer Purchases in Table 6 is for three cities: New York; Columbus, Ohio; and Atlanta, Georgia. The particular selection of cities is arbitrary; similar data can be obtained for a considerable number of other cities. The effect on the income elasticity of using withdrawals instead of net earnings from business as a measure of income for independent business families is clear. Whereas the elasticity is .70 for the 1948–50 nationwide data which use net earnings, it is .90 in Table 6 for the New York data, which measure income by withdrawals, and this value is higher than for any other occupational group except wage earners. For income measured by withdrawals, only about 10 per cent of the total variance is contributed by transitory factors. The elasticity is lower for independent professional families than for independent business, whereas the reverse relation seems more plausible for the net earnings concept of income. None of the other

---

[33] This is the method employed by the National Resources Planning Board in constructing their estimates, which we have mostly used above.

elasticities show any regularities deserving of note; this may be because the data are for just three cities. Perhaps if a larger number of cities were included, some regularities would emerge.

The estimated measures of relative dispersion are more illuminating than the income elasticities themselves. There seems no reason why the use of withdrawals should systematically affect the variance of the permanent component, and the figures in Table 6 conform with this expectation. In New York, the dispersion of the permanent component is decidedly higher for business families than for any of the nonentrepreneurial groups, and almost the same as for the independent professional group; for each of the other cities, the two entrepreneurial groups have a decidedly higher dispersion of permanent components than any of the other groups. The only striking inter-city differences in the dispersion of the permanent components is for salaried business and salaried professional; these display a higher dispersion in New York than in the other cities; a result that seems entirely consistent with the differences in the economic character of the cities. New York offers greater opportunities for managerial and professional specialization than either of the other cities; the range of activities included under "salaried business" and "salaried professional" might be expected to be correspondingly broader. There is little difference among any of the other groups: the dispersion of the permanent component is in the neighborhood of 50 per cent for all four nonentrepreneurial groups in Columbus and Atlanta, and for wage earners and clerical groups in New York as well, compared with some 60 to 70 per cent for salaried business and professional families in New York and some 80 per cent for independent groups in all cities.

These remarks about the economic character of New York also seem relevant in explaining why the dispersion of the permanent component should be larger for all groups combined for New York than for the other cities. It is striking that the dispersion of the transitory component is almost the same in all cities, a result that seems entirely plausible, for there is nothing about the wider range of activities in New York that gives any reason to expect more uncertainty to be attached to any given activity. These considerations also explain why the elasticity should be higher for New York than for the other cities.

The main effect of the use of withdrawals for independent business families shows up in the estimated dispersion of the transitory component of their incomes in New York. At about 26 per cent, the dispersion is of the same order of magnitude as for the nonentrepreneurial groups in the table and for all nonfarm families (see Table 4). The only differences that stand out in the table are: (1) the larger dispersion for independent professional families in New York and for the two independent groups combined in the other cities; this is in line with expectations and the numerical values are almost the same as those recorded in Table 4 for farm families; (2) the much lower dispersion for New York wage earner families than for other groups. I am inclined to view this result with suspicion, since the elasticity for this group seems out of line with other values.

To judge from the evidence of this and the preceding section, entrepreneurial families, whether farm or nonfarm, are alike in being subject to much uncertainty with respect to their income; the standard deviation of their transitory components of income appears to be something over 40 per cent of their mean income, or something like $1\frac{1}{2}$ to 2 times as large as for other families. The only substantial difference between farm and nonfarm entrepreneurs in the character of their income distributions is that the latter differ more widely than the former in respect of their permanent income status; the standard deviation of the permanent component is about 80 per cent of their mean income for nonfarm entrepreneurs, about 60 to 70 per cent for farm entrepreneurs.[34]

We saw in Table 1 that for nonfarm groups, consumption averaged about 90 per cent of income for studies ranging from 1888–90 to date. However, the earlier studies were restricted to wage-earner families, whereas the later studies covered a broader range of families, including in particular independent business families. If the figures could be taken at their face value, this would imply that the similarity in average propensity to consume concealed a significant change in wage earners' propensity to consume, since if independent business families were excluded from the later studies, the resulting average propensity would be higher than for the earlier studies. This possible conclusion is to some extent offset by the fact that the income figures for independent business families in most of the later studies are for withdrawals rather than net business earnings; and hence these studies doubtless understate the savings of these families. But this can hardly offset the conclusion completely, if only because, as we have seen, the use of withdrawals instead of net income has much less effect for independent professional families than for business families. In consequence, the apparent constancy of the average propensity must be regarded as concealing a secular rise. How this can be reconciled with time series data, which show no important secular

[34] This is for total income including nonmoney income.

change in the ratio of savings to income, is discussed in section 1b of the next chapter.

The substantial difference in the average ratio of consumption to income between entrepreneurial and other units, and between farm and nonfarm entrepreneurs, has important implications for the variables determining the k of our equation (2.6). We have already suggested that one variable accounting for the observed difference may be the larger dispersion of transitory components; if so, this is an important dimension of our portmanteau variable u. But it is clear that this is not the only variable. The dispersion of transitory components is of the same order of magnitude for farm and nonfarm entrepreneurs, yet nonfarm entrepreneurs apparently save a decidedly larger fraction of their income on the average. Another variable already mentioned is the rate of return that can be earned on savings—the i in our equation (2.6). It is likely that entrepreneurs are able to earn larger returns on the average through direct investment in their business—or at least expect to do so—than they or others can earn in other ways, if only because direct investment dispenses with the need for the services of brokers, financial institutions, and other intermediaries. Moreover, for the period spanned by Tables 3 and 5, farming was a declining source of income compared to independent business,[35] which suggests that the prospective earnings on capital were higher for nonfarm entrepreneurs. If, as seems plausible, this higher rate of return was a major factor accounting for the higher savings ratio of nonfarm than of farm entrepreneurs, this means that the rate of interest that can be earned on savings is an important determinant of the average ratio of savings to income, a conclusion that is entirely consistent with our earlier theoretical analysis but that runs counter to widely prevailing opinions about the effect of the interest rate on savings. Another factor that may help to explain the differences in the savings behavior of the various groups is a possible difference in tastes that accounts, on the one hand, for entry into independent business and, on the other, for high savings. The wide dispersion of permanent components in nonfarm independent business can be interpreted as meaning that this is a good route to high income status: people who place relatively great value on achieving high income status might thereby be attracted to it; by the same token they will place relatively great value on savings as another route to high income status. Still another factor, of a rather different sort, is the difference in the age and family composition of the entrepreneurial and other groups, a difference that might well be

[35] See *National Income, 1954 edition*, pp. 168–169.

designated a statistical bias. The clearest example is for people who are retired; these are necessarily excluded from the independent business group, yet are likely to have a relatively high ratio of consumption to income; this and similar exclusions of people who have not yet gone into business mean that the entrepreneurial group is likely to be rather heavily weighted with people or families that are in their peak earnings periods. These comments are, of course, purely suggestive. Detailed analysis for much finer groups would be required, and is highly to be desired, to support more precise and definitive conclusions.

e. NEGRO AND WHITE FAMILIES

The two panels of Figure 9 display the observed relation between the consumption and the income of white and Negro families for two cities. As in preceding charts, each point shows average consumption and income for a group of families in the same measured income class; the points are thus observations on the regressions of consumption on measured income. In both cities, the regressions for white and Negro families are roughly parallel and the regression for Negroes is below the regression for whites. At the same measured income, Negroes spend less on consumption than whites. As Table 7 shows, these results hold not only for the two cities covered by Figure 9 but also for other communities: in each of the six communities or group of communities covered by the table, the elasticity of consumption with respect to measured income is nearly the same for whites and Negroes—the minor differences show no consistency, the elasticity being higher for whites in two communities, higher for Negroes in three, and the same in one—and the regression for whites is above that for Negroes, as shown by the uniformly higher level of consumption for whites at a measured income of $1,000.[36]

[36] See Brady and Friedman, op. cit., pp. 262–265; Horst Mendershausen, "Differences in Family Savings between Cities of Different Size and Location, Whites and Negroes," Review of Economic Statistics, XXII (August, 1940), pp. 122–137, and Richard Sterner (in collaboration with Lenore A. Epstein and Ellen Winston), The Negro's Share (New York: Harper, 1943), pp. 91–94, for similar analyses of the 1935–36 data.

The 1934–36 wage-earner study also contains information on Negro and white families separately. For all cities combined, the data, like those summarized in Figure 9 and Table 7, show lower consumption for Negroes than for whites at each measured income level within the range covered by the data. Like them also, they show little difference in the average propensity to consume for all classes combined, which is .99 for white families, .98 for Negro families; however, this slight difference is in the opposite direction from that recorded in Table 7. The one striking difference in results is with respect to the elasticity of consumption, which is .87 for the white families, .96 for the Negro families, a wider difference than for any of the cities covered in Table 7. (These estimates are based on data in Williams and Hansen, op. cit., pp. 13, 14, 23, and 24.) I conjecture that the reason for this discrepancy between the two studies is the difference

These results are precisely those that, on our hypothesis, would be expected to follow from the decidedly higher average income of whites than of Negroes: the average income of whites is approximately 75 per cent higher than the average income of Negroes in the northern communities, and 140 to 235 per cent higher in the South. This higher average income means that a given measured income corresponds to a higher permanent income for whites than for Negroes, and therefore, on our hypothesis, to a higher level of consumption. In consequence, the higher consumption and lower savings of whites at each measured income level may reflect simply the inadequacy of measured income as an index of economic status.

We can come closer to a comparison of consumption habits proper by comparing not consumption at the same measured income but the ratio of mean consumption to mean measured income for all income classes combined. If mean transitory components of income and consumption were zero, these ratios would be estimates of our k. Unfortunately, such average propensities are readily available for only four of the six groups covered by Table 7 [column (5)]. To complete the picture, I have entered in Table 7, column (6), the ratio of consumption to income at the mean income of each group as computed from the regression of the logarithm of consumption on the logarithm of income.[37] As can be seen by comparing columns (5) and (6), as well as from other data for which we have both the ratio of averages and the ratio at the average income as computed from a regression between the logarithmic values, the ratio at the average income tends to

---

between them in eligibility requirements, which, as noted earlier, were more restrictive for the 1934–36 study. These requirements, which had the effect of excluding much of the variation in transitory components, disqualified a much larger fraction of Negro than of white families (*ibid.*, p. 30). By reducing the variance of the transitory component for Negroes more than for whites, they would tend to produce the observed difference in elasticities.

Results similar to those cited in the text are reported by Klein and Mooney for the North on the basis of data for 1947, 1948, 1949, and 1950 from the Surveys of Consumer Finances. However, for the South, they report a similar result only for lower incomes; for disposable incomes above about $2,000 they report higher consumption expenditures for Negroes than for whites. They suggest the possibility, and present some evidence to support it, that the different pattern for the South may arise from their inclusion of purchases of durable goods as consumption; while the Consumer Purchases Study also included durable goods as consumption, durable goods purchases may well have been more important for this group in 1947–50 than in 1935–36. See L. R. Klein and W. H. Mooney, "Negro-White Savings Differentials and the Consumption Function Problem," *Econometrica*, XXI (July, 1953) pp. 425–456, esp. pp. 425, 426, and 454.

[37] If the regression were a straight line between the arithmetic values of consumption and income, it would, of course, tend to go through the point corresponding to mean consumption and mean income.

FIGURE 9

Regressions of Consumption on Income for Native White and Negro Nonrelief Families, Columbus, Ohio, and Atlanta, Georgia, 1935–1936

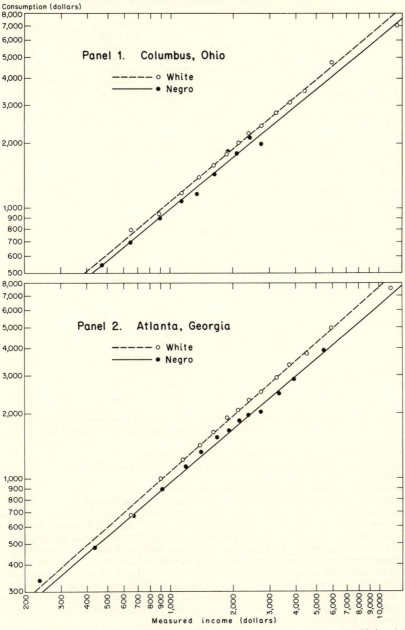

Consumption (dollars)

Panel 1. Columbus, Ohio

- - - - - o White
———— • Negro

Panel 2. Atlanta, Georgia

- - - - - o White
———— • Negro

Measured income (dollars)

Logarithmic scales

Source: Dept. of Labor, Bulletin No. 648, Vol. III, pp. 52-55.

TABLE 7

Relation between Consumption and Income, and Relative Dispersion of Measured
Income and Its Components, Native White and Negro Nonrelief
Complete Families in Selected Communities, 1935–1936

Community and Group (1)	Arithmetic Average Income[a] (2)	Income Elasticity of Consumption[b] (3)	Consumption at a Measured Income of $1,000[a,c] (4)	Average Propensity to Consume (5)	Ratio of Consumption to Income at Mean Income of Group[c] (6)	Measured Income (7)	Relative Dispersion[d] of: Permanent Component (8)	Transitory Component (9)
New York, N.Y.:								
White	$2,645	.89	$1,110	.98	1.00	.77	.73	.26
Negro	1,500	.89	1,050	.99	1.01	.52	.49	.17
Columbus, Ohio:								
White	2,058	.81	1,070		.94	.68	.61	.30
Negro	1,130	.80	978		.96	.61	.54	.27
Atlanta, Ga.:								
White	2,158	.84	1,080	.93	.96	.70	.64	.28
Negro	888	.81	960	.96	.98	.89	.80	.38
Southeast, middle-size cities:[e]								
White	2,086	.86	1,040		.94	.72	.67	.27
Negro	686	.88	930		.98	.82	.77	.29
Southeast, small cities:[f]								
White	1,683[h]	.92	1,025	.95	.97	.52	.49	.14
Negro	620[h]	.94	960	.99	.98	.53	.52	.13
Southeast, villages:[g]								
White	1,674[h]	.88	1,015	.92	.96	.57	.53	.19
Negro	500[h]	.93	970	1.00	1.02	.48	.47	.13

[a] Dollar figures are in current prices. To convert into 1935–39 prices requires division by .986.

[b] Slope of graphically fitted straight line regression of logarithm of consumption on logarithm of measured income.

[c] Computed from regressions described in preceding footnote.

[d] For meaning and method of computation see notes b, c, and d to Table 4.

[e] Columbia, S.C., and Mobile, Ala.

[f] Gastonia, N.C.; Sumter, S.C.; Albany, Ga.; Griffin, Ga.

[g] 34 villages in North Carolina, South Carolina, Georgia, and Mississippi.

[h] These averages are of somewhat more questionable accuracy than the others in this column. They are based on the data from the expenditure sample of the Consumer Purchases Study, whereas the others are based on data for the income sample. The expenditure sample was deliberately designed to be nonrepresentative, and the Bureau of Labor Statistics in its publications gives no averages for all income groups based on the expenditure sample. The Bureau of Home Economics does, saying that it found only minor differences between averages computed directly for the expenditure sample and those computed from it by weighting the observations in individual cells according to their relative frequency in the income sample. However, it warns explicitly that the least reliable averages are for all income classes combined, precisely the ones we use. I have used them nevertheless because of the labor involved in using the data for the income sample.

(cont. on next page)

TABLE 7 (cont.)

Source:

Arithmetic average incomes and frequency distributions used in computing relative dispersion of measured income: New York, N.Y.—Department of Labor, Bulletin No. 643, Vol. I, pp. 93, 99, 156, and 162; Columbus Ohio—Department of Labor, Bulletin No. 644, Vol. I, pp. 137, 143, 185, and 191; Atlanta, Ga.—Department of Labor, Bulletin No. 647, Vol. I, pp. 147, 153, 195, and 201; middle-size cities—*ibid.*, pp. 243, 249, 270, 275, 296, 301, 322, and 327; averages for Columbia and Mobile combined by weighting by estimated number of native complete families in a 100 per cent sample as given in *ibid.*, pp. 138 and 140; small cities and villages—Department of Agriculture, Miscellaneous Publication No. 464, *Changes in Assets and Liabilities of Families, Five Regions* (Washington, 1941), pp. 88, 93, 95, and 96.

Consumption and income by income classes, used to fit regressions: New York, Columbus, Atlanta, and middle-size cities—Department of Labor, Bulletin No. 648, Vol. VIII, pp. 46, 47, 52–55, 62, and 63; small cities and villages—Department of Agriculture, Miscellaneous Publication No. 464, pp. 88, 93, 95, and 96.

Average propensity to consume: New York and Atlanta—derived from data given by Richard Sterner, *The Negro's Share,* (New York, 1943) pp. 92, 96–98; small cities and villages: Department of Agriculture, Miscellaneous Publication No. 464, p. 88.

be some one to five percentage points higher than the ratio of the averages, which explains why the numbers in column (6) are systematically higher than most of the average propensities we have so far cited.

The ratios in columns (5) and (6) tell a very different story from the absolute values in column (4): in each of the ten comparisons, the ratio is higher for Negroes than for whites. According to this evidence, it is the whites who are on the average more thrifty.

I hasten to add that this result cannot itself be interpreted confidently as reflecting the effect of race per se. (1) In each community, a decidedly smaller fraction of Negro families than of white are independent business or professional families. As we saw in the preceding section, such families tend to save a larger fraction of their income than other families, so their smaller relative importance tends to make the average propensity higher for all Negro than for all white families. This tendency is not fully reflected in these data, due to the use of withdrawals as a measure of entrepreneurial income, but even so, rough calculations suggest that this factor alone would make the average propensity something like one percentage point higher for Negroes. (2) The limitation of the data to nonrelief families might work in the same direction. A decidedly smaller fraction of Negro than of white families were classified as nonrelief. At the lower measured income levels, nonrelief families are on the average highly likely to have a negative transitory component of income, and certain to have a higher average permanent income than the relief families at the same measured income. This may well affect the average for all measured income classes, making for a negative mean transitory component for all nonrelief families. If so, the effect would be greater for Negroes than for whites and would make the ratios in columns (5) and (6) even more of an overestimate of k for Negro than for white families.[38]

The final three columns of Table 7 give estimates of the relative dispersion of measured income and the permanent and transitory components. These show an interesting difference between the North and the South. In the two northern cities, the dispersion of both permanent and transitory components is wider for whites than for Negroes—only slightly wider in Columbus, decidedly wider in New York. In the Southern communities, the difference between Negroes and whites is generally in the opposite direction: for measured income and permanent components, in three of the four communities; for transitory components, in two. The differences are consistent for Atlanta and the middle-size cities and larger for these than for other southern communities. This result is most suggestive and not at all implausible—though again it must be regarded with some suspicion as possibly being simply a disguised reflection of the restriction of these data to nonrelief families. In the South, the whites and Negroes are more nearly two economically separated societies than in the North. The integration in the North means that the Negroes tend to be specialized; their lower average income reflects very largely the fact that they engage in lower paid occupations; they depend on the white community, as it were, for the services of the more highly paid occupations. In the South, being less fully integrated in this sense in the society, Negroes may tend to depend more on their own community for these more highly paid occupations; their lower average income reflects not only their concentration in lower paid occupations but also, to a much greater extent than in the North, a lower return for each activity separately. These effects would presumably tend

---

[38] It was noted in footnote 36 that for the 1934–36 wage-earner study the average propensity to consume is slightly higher for whites than for Negroes—.99 compared with .98. Two factors may explain this reversal from the pattern in Table 7: (1) The 1934–36 study covered only wage earners and lower salaried clerical workers, so point (1) in the text above does not apply. (2) Whereas the exclusion of families receiving relief might by itself tend to produce a negative mean transitory component of income, and to affect Negroes more than whites, the additional eligibility requirements in the 1934–36 study probably operated on balance in the opposite direction. In particular, the exclusion of all families with incomes under $500, which excluded a much larger fraction of Negro than of white families, clearly tended toward a positive mean transitory component. At the other end of the scale, the exclusion of families whose chief earner was a clerical worker earning more than $2,000 a year tended to introduce a negative mean transitory component and was much more important for whites than for Negroes. On balance, therefore, it seems not unlikely that the mean transitory component for Negroes in the sample is larger (in algebraic value) than for whites, just the opposite of the results conjectured for the Study of Consumer Purchases.

to be more marked in larger communities than in small cities or villages. A minor bit of evidence supporting this interpretation is that although the average income of nonrelief Negro families is more than 20 per cent lower in Atlanta than in Columbus, a slightly higher percentage of all Negro families, 10.3 compared with 9.8, are classified as business or professional families, independent or salaried.[39]

f. A DIGRESSION ON THE USE OF PARTIAL CORRELATION IN CONSUMPTION RESEARCH

One implication for consumption research follows so directly from the preceding analysis that it seems worth digressing briefly from our main path to consider it explicitly. A common method of analyzing the factors affecting consumption is to "hold income constant" while studying the effect of other variables. Income, it is argued, is the major factor affecting expenditures, so, unless its influence is first eliminated, the effect of other variables will be swamped. In this method, "income" is almost invariably taken to be what we have called "measured income" for a particular year, and it is "held constant" either by multiple correlation analysis in which income is one of the variables[40] or by a variant in which residuals from a consumption-income (or savings-income) regression are first calculated and then analyzed for the influence of other variables.[41]

If the preceding analysis is accepted, it is clear that these methods do not hold income constant in a sense that is meaningful for the determination of consumption behavior. What they hold constant is a mixture of income in such a sense—our permanent component— and accidental additions to or subtractions from current receipts that play little or no role in determining consumption behavior. And the particular mixture is likely to be related to the other variables being studied in a systematic way. Instead of eliminating the influence of income, these methods simply disguise its influence; it shows up as if it were the effect of other variables.

[39] Department of Labor, Bulletin No. 644, Vol. I, p. 122; Bulletin No. 647, Vol. I, p. 138. These percentages are for all families, relief and nonrelief, complete and incomplete. See also Gary S. Becker, "The Economics of Racial Discrimination," (1955) an unpublished Ph.D. dissertation at the University of Chicago; and Morton Zeman, "A Quantitative Analysis of White-Nonwhite Income Differentials in the United States," (1955), an unpublished Ph.D. dissertation at the University of Chicago.

[40] See, e.g., the equation set up by Lawrence Klein in Katona, Klein, Lansing, and Morgan, *Contributions of Survey Methods in Economics*, p. 203 and the subsequent analysis, as well as the various articles referred to in the bibliography appended to *ibid.*, especially those by Klein or by Klein and a collaborator.

[41] See, e.g., the two chapters by Morgan in *ibid.*

The Negro-white comparison perhaps brings this out most clearly. Let us hold measured income constant in analyzing the influence of color.[42] We shall then find that Negroes spend less on consumption and save more than whites. The reason, as we have seen, is simply that the same measured income systematically means a lower permanent income for Negroes than for whites. What this method leads us to call the effect of race for given income is predominantly the effect of the income differences which are concealed by a common measured income. As we have seen, when the comparison is made so as to eliminate this effect, namely, by comparing behavior at the means of groups at which transitory effects can be supposed roughly to cancel out, there is no evidence at all that Negroes are more "thrifty" than whites; on the contrary, such evidence as there is argues in the opposite direction. The appearance produced by holding measured income constant is an illusion attributable to the method of analysis.

The various earlier parts of this section are additional examples of the same point. The recent volume of the Michigan Survey Research Center, *Contributions of Survey Methods to Economics*, especially the chapters by Morgan and Klein, provides further examples that may be worth citing, particularly because these chapters are in the main such admirable pieces of work, revealing a high degree of sophistication and ingenuity in statistical technique and economic analysis, great care in examination of the basic material, and the loving and generous expenditure of time and effort in its analysis. Yet, if our hypothesis and its application along the lines of the earlier part of this section are accepted, their findings are rendered almost worthless because of the use of partial correlation techniques which hold measured income "constant."

Morgan first isolates groups that seem to differ appreciably in the slope of the regression of saving on income, and then computes a regression for each of these groups. For each consumer unit, he takes the difference between observed savings and savings estimated from the regression for the group to which it belongs as an estimate of the effect of variables other than (1) income and (2) those defining the groups, mostly home ownership status and size of liquid assets.[43]

[42] As Klein and Mooney do in their analysis of Negro-white savings differentials. See "Negro-White Savings Differentials and the Consumption Function Problem," esp. pp. 429–430.

[43] In Chapter III, he uses seven regressions: three for nonhomeowners, all for 1947 and 1948 combined, for three classes determined by liquid assets at beginning of year— 0 liquid assets, $1–$499, and $500 or more; four for homeowners—two for 1947 and 1948 combined, liquid asset classes 0–$199, and $200–$2,999, and two for liquid asset class $3,000 or more, one for 1947 and one for 1948. In Chapter IV, where he uses

He then examines the effect of other variables on the residuals. This same type of analysis is carried out twice, once using regressions based on data for essentially all units in his sample, a second time using so-called "normal" regressions based on only about half the units.

One of the first variables by which Morgan classifies the residuals from the first set of regressions is size of city. From the average value of the residuals for each size of city, he concludes that city size has a significant effect on savings, savings at a given income being lower, and expenditures higher, in "metropolitian areas" than in nonmetropolitan cities or towns, and in the latter than in "open country nonfarm areas." It so happens that this is one of the few points at which Morgan reports average income and average savings. Average income is decidedly higher in metropolitan areas than in any of the three groups into which he classifies non-metropolitan cities or towns—among which average income differs

---

"normal" regressions (see below), he uses sixteen regressions, all for 1947, 1948, and 1949 combined, for four liquid asset classes for each of four housing status classes.

Though it is aside from our own major point here, it is interesting to speculate on the differences he finds. He finds that the marginal propensity to consume (unity minus the marginal propensity to save that he computes) decreases as the size of liquid assets increases and is lower for homeowners than for nonhomeowners. The explanation of the liquid asset effect seems reasonably straightforward on our hypothesis. Units that are subject to a relatively large transitory component of income have more need for reserves against emergency than others; in consequence they might be expected to hold larger amounts of liquid assets on the average. As argued in our discussion of the effect of occupation, both k and P_y will tend to be relatively low for such units, and, in consequence, so will their product, which is the marginal propensity to consume.

Evidence supporting this interpretation is available from Survey of Consumer Finances data on the distribution of liquid assets by size for different occupational groups—[see "1950 Survey of Consumer Finances, Part V," *Federal Reserve Bulletin* (December 1950), Table 34, for 1949 and 1950, and "1952 Survey of Consumer Finances, Part III," *ibid.* (September 1952), Table 12, for 1951 and 1952]. For 1950, for example, if we use Morgan's liquid assets classes for nonhomeowners, the percentage of units with liquid assets of $500 or more was 67, 62, and 46 for professional and semiprofessional, managerial and self-employed, and farm operators, respectively; it was 48, 35, and 26 for clerical and sales, skilled and semiskilled, and unskilled and service, respectively. The former are clearly the groups subject to greater transitory variation. The one exception is for retired, for whom the corresponding percentage is 62; but this group is too small to affect the result significantly. We cannot duplicate from the tables cited the class intervals Morgan uses for homeowners. If we use instead liquid assets of $5,000 or more, the percentages for 1950 in the order just given are 18, 19, and 11; 7, 4, and 3; and 24 for retired. Much the same picture prevails for other years.

I have not thought of any equally plausible explanation for the difference between homeowners and nonhomeowners. Perhaps, as Morgan suggests, this difference reflects largely the omission of imputed income from housing as an item of income and consumption; like him, however, I doubt that this can be the whole story. It seems to me more likely that it is a disguised reflection of other variables; for example, homeowners seem to have larger liquid assets than nonhomeowners and presumably differ in age and family composition, etc. See Katona, Klein, Lansing and Morgan, *op. cit.*, pp.101–113; pp. 157–161.

little—and decidedly higher in these three groups than in open country nonfarm areas. The result is that the same measured income can be expected to correspond to a higher permanent income, and so to a higher consumption and lower savings, in the metropolitan areas than in the nonmetropolitan, and in these than in the open country. The average propensity to consume, as computed from the reported figures, is .84 in the metropolitan areas; .83, .84, and .84 in the three groups of nonmetropolitan cities and towns; and .83 in the open country nonfarm areas. These certainly give little sign of any city-size effect at all. The alleged city-size difference, like the Negro-white difference, is a figment of Morgan's procedure.

In his other analyses of residuals, Morgan does not report average income and average savings. But it is reasonably clear from other evidence that many of the effects he finds to be significant are, like the Negro-white and city-size effects, produced largely or wholly by differences in average income that make the same measured income correspond to different permanent incomes. To cite a few: (1) He finds "less saving by spending units with more than one earner."[44] We know that average family income tends to rise with number of earners, which could produce this pattern in observed residuals. (2) He finds "significantly lower saving for primary spending units and higher saving for secondaries."[45] Again we know that primary units tend to have higher average incomes than secondary units. (3) He finds "little difference in average residuals between different occupation groups, the only residual significantly different from zero being, strangely enough, that for unskilled and service workers,"[46] a group which has positive average savings residuals. It is also, of course, a group that has a relatively low average income, so this finding is not at all strange on our interpretation of it.

Morgan uses "normal" regressions at the second stage of his analysis in an attempt to solve the problem raised by transitory components of income, a problem of which he is aware though he does not, of course, use our terminology. He derives these regressions from data for "groups of people in reasonably 'normal' circumstances,"[47] the groups being obtained by excluding units with a head over 65 years of age, unemployed, or retired, and units that received large gifts or inheritances or experienced an increase in income of 25 per cent or more or a decrease of 5 per cent or more. He then uses

[44] *Ibid.*, p. 129.
[45] *Ibid.*, p. 129.
[46] *Ibid.*, p. 132.
[47] *Ibid.*, p. 157.

these regressions to compute residuals for both "normal" and other units. Unfortunately, despite its good intentions, this technique is either useless or makes matters worse. In the first place, the "normal" regressions cannot be regarded as relations between "permanent" components. The variance of transitory components for the included units is doubtless smaller than for all units but can hardly be zero; in any event, the variance of permanent components must also be smaller, though probably not so much so.[48] The result is some kind of hybrid that is difficult to interpret at all precisely. In the second place, suppose that the "normal" regressions could be regarded as relations between permanent components. They could then be used to eliminate the effect of the differences in permanent income only if some estimate of permanent income were available for the individual consumer unit. But no such estimate is available. Morgan simply uses measured income and thereby introduces an additional source of error into his residuals.

The crucial fallacy is the assumption that permanent, or, as Morgan would phrase it, "normal," consumption or savings is the same for the same measured income, provided other variables affecting saving behavior are held constant. Given this fallacy, it makes little difference what relation between savings and income is used to estimate "normal" savings; insofar as the same measured income corresponds to different permanent incomes, the residuals have not been freed from the effect of income.

I am not, of course, arguing that the variables Morgan considers may not affect spending behavior, or even that their effects may not be in the direction that he finds. My point is only that it is impossible

---

[48] As noted in footnote 43, Morgan uses data for 1947, 1948, and 1949 combined for his "normal regressions;" for 1947 and 1948 only, for his initial regressions; in addition, rather than 7 he uses 16 groups, of which it is not clear that any match precisely in definition. For these reasons it is not possible to make a valid comparison between the parameters of his two sets of regressions and so to test this conjecture directly or to estimate by how much more the variance of the transitory components is reduced than the variance of the permanent components. Somewhat more satisfactory evidence is furnished by a comparison of the regression coefficients for the included and excluded groups, though this too is blurred by differences in the classifications for which separate regression coefficients are reported. Crude calculations from these data support the conjecture that the variance of transitory components is reduced by somewhat more than the variance of permanent components. They suggest, however, that the differential effect is small in magnitude, so that the fraction of the variance of income accounted for by transitory components is about 75 per cent as large for the included as for the excluded groups (*ibid.*, pp. 159 and 160).

The liquid asset effect discussed in footnote 43 above is about as marked in the "normal" regressions as in the initial regressions. If the interpretation of this effect offered in that footnote is correct, this is a further bit of evidence that the "normal" regressions are not much closer to regressions between permanent components than the initial regressions.

to know from his analysis whether they affect spending behavior or in what direction.

Klein, in the first of his chapters in the *Contributions* volume, follows a method similar to Morgan's, except that he uses regression equations involving a number of variables simultaneously, and so multiple correlation rather than simple correlation, in getting his residuals; he uses as his independent variable the ratio of savings to income rather than savings alone; and he devotes much more of his attention to the equations themselves, and less to the residuals. In practically every equation, Klein includes income (or the logarithm of income) and liquid assets at the beginning of the year (usually as a ratio to income). One of his most consistent findings is that for given income (which means, of course, given measured income) savings decrease as liquid assets increase, which means that consumption increases. Now this finding, which has been pointed out in other studies of the effect of liquid assets, may, so far as this evidence goes, be simply another example of the bias introduced by the partial correlation technique. For there is ample evidence that income is on the average higher, the higher the level of liquid assets; in consequence, a given measured income tends to correspond to a higher permanent component, and so to higher consumption and lower savings, the higher the level of liquid assets. These correlations, therefore, give no usable evidence on the effect of liquid assets in their own right.

One incidental calculation which Klein makes is a correlation using income and savings for a two-year time unit rather than the usual one year. As he points out, lengthening the time period produces results that are consistent with our hypothesis: the ratio of savings to income is less highly correlated with other variables and the estimated marginal propensities to consume are higher.[49]

3. *Savings and Age*

There is an apparent discrepancy between our hypothesis and some results reported by Janet Fisher in a study based on data from the Survey of Consumer Finances. The first four columns of Table 8 are from this study. The income mean ratios in column (3) are estimates of the ratio of the average measured income of the age group in question to the average measured income of all spending units; and the savings mean ratios in column (2) are estimates of the corresponding ratios for savings. From the figures in column (3), it seems plausible to interpret the income ratios as estimates of—or at any rate as correlated with—the ratio of measured income to permanent

[49] See *ibid.*, pp. 220–221.

TABLE 8

Relation of Savings and Income to Age of Head of Spending Unit,
United States, 1946

Age of Head of Spending Unit (1)	Savings Mean Ratio (2)	Income Mean Ratio (3)	Mean Savings as a % of Mean Income (4)	Assumed Mean Age (5)	Estimated Mean Lifetime Income Ratio (6)	Adjusted Income Mean Ratio (3) ÷ (6) (7)
18–24	−15	57	−3	21.5	144	40
25–34	57	95	6	30	122	78
35–44	136	118	12	40	100	118
45–64	149	116	13	55	74	157
65 and over	55	57	10	70	55	104
All ages	100	100	10		100	100

Source:
Columns (1) to (4) reproduced from Table 10, p. 92 of Janet A. Fisher, "Income, Spending, and Saving Patterns of Consumer Units in Different Age Groups," *Studies in Income and Wealth*, XV (New York: National Bureau of Economic Research, 1952), pp. 77–102. They are based on a reported total of 3,058 cases collected in the Survey of Consumer Finances.

The income " 'mean ratio' was derived by dividing the percentage of total income received by spending units in a particular group by the percentage of the total spending unit population in that age group" (*ibid.*, p. 81). The savings mean ratio was derived in the same way. Savings are here defined to exclude purchases of durable goods, such expenditures being counted as consumption expenditures.

income; measured income might be expected to be less than permanent income in the early and late years of a working lifetime, and to be greater than permanent income in the middle years. On our hypothesis, we would then expect the income ratios in column (3) to be closely correlated with the ratios of measured savings to measured income in column (4). Since consumption is related to permanent rather than measured income, it should be high relative to measured income when measured income is lower than permanent income, and conversely. This relation would be reversed for measured savings, so columns (3) and (4) should be positively correlated. To some extent, the figures correspond with this expectation; the ratio of savings to income is lower for the terminal than for the middle classes. But the correlation is very loose indeed; the income ratio for the terminal class is the same as for the initial class; yet savings are 10 per cent of income for the one and −3 per cent for the other.

The apparent discrepancy between these results and our hypothesis is readily explained. Column (3) shows mean income ratios in a single year for spending units differing in age of head; it cannot be interpreted as showing directly the prospective lifetime income of a single spending unit unless the absolute real income of spending units of a given age can be expected to remain constant over time. But per capita real income in the United States has risen over at least the past half century at a rate of about 2 per cent per year, and there seems no reason why it should not continue to rise in the future. If it does, the mean lifetime earnings which the youngest group can anticipate is decidedly higher than the average for the whole group covered in the table—the average that is set equal to 100. If, more or less arbitrarily, we assign this average of 100 to age 40, and assume per capita income to continue to rise at the same rate as in the past, the expected mean lifetime earnings of the youngest group would be 144, the figure entered in column (6) of the table. Similarly, the oldest group received a mean average lifetime earnings well below the mean for the whole group; we have estimated its mean as 55, by arbitrarily setting the mean age of the group at 70. The estimates in column (6) provide a rough basis for correcting the ratios in column (3) for the discrepancy that can be expected to arise in a progressive society between the pattern of contemporaneous incomes of units with heads of different age and the lifetime income pattern of a single unit.[50] The resulting rough estimate of the pattern of lifetime earnings is given in column (7).

The percentage of income saved is much more closely correlated with the adjusted income mean ratio than with the original income mean ratio. The consumption expenditures of an age group are adjusted to its own permanent income expectations, not to the average permanent income of a heterogeneous collection of age classes. While the close correlation between columns (4) and (7) is therefore in accord with our hypothesis, the numerical magnitudes of mean savings are not consistent with an interpretation of the hypothesis that would regard the figures in column (6) as the permanent component of income to which expenditures are adjusted. If k is approximately .9, as the average ratio of savings for all ages suggests, if 144 is the permanent component of income for the youngest class, then .9 × 144 or 130 would be permanent expenditures, so savings would be −90, or −225 per cent of measured income, instead of −3 per cent, and similarly with the other classes. The explanation—or rationalization—is the one referred to at an

[50] The adjustment is crude on many scores. (1) The 2 per cent figure is a rough estimate; (2) the assumed mean ages in column (5) are chosen arbitrarily; they probably should be lower for the two oldest classes and perhaps higher for the two youngest; (3) the assignment of the average income of the group to age 40 is arbitrary; (4) the average of this group is not really the relevant average for lifetime incomes; it is a weighted average of the averages for separate age groups, the weights being the actual percentage of units in an age group at a point of time, whereas the weights should be the fraction of units that can be expected to survive to a particular age. And there are doubtless other crudities as well.

earlier point. The permanent income component is not to be regarded as expected lifetime earnings; it can itself be regarded as varying with age. It is to be interpreted as the mean income at any age regarded as permanent by the consumer unit in question, which in turn depends on its horizon and foresightedness.[51] Accordingly, the entries in column (7) are to be regarded solely as indexes of the ratios of measured income to permanent income; they differ from unity in the same direction as the latter but not necessarily by the same magnitude.

The general consistency of these figures with other evidence from budget studies can be roughly checked by comparing the relation of column (4) to column (7) with corresponding relations for consumer units classified not by age but simply by the ratio of their actual incomes to the mean income of the group. Brady and Friedman plot the ratio of savings to money income against the ratio of measured income to average income for urban families, as computed from budget studies for 1901, 1917–19, 1941, and 1935–36.[52] The points defined by columns (4) and (7) fall closely in line with the results from these budget studies. Even more striking, they come closest to the points for 1917–19, almost precisely duplicating the relation for that year. And of the years plotted, 1917–19 seem most nearly comparable to 1946 in terms of the importance of mean transitory components of income and expenditure; both are at the end of or immediately following a major war and in the midst of a war or postwar inflation.

Further evidence is available from a study by Dorothy Brady based on budget data for a wide range of years in which she derived a relation between consumption expenditures, family income, and the average income of the community in which the family resides. If we interpret the ratio between family income and average income of the community as comparable with the entries in column (7), and modify Brady's function so that it gives the same average percentage saved of 10 per cent, the function yields the following estimates of the percentage of income saved for the successive values in column (7): —8,

[51] See Friedman and Kuznets, *op. cit.*, pp. 355–362. To justify changing permanent incomes with age in a rather different fashion, the expected lifetime income of the youngest class is the discounted value of expected future receipts, not the simple sum of them. If the capital market were perfect, the lifetime income so computed could be regarded as constant over the lifetime by proper positive and negative charges to the depreciation account. But the capital market is imperfect, so that—from the point of view of sums available for expenditures—the rate of interest that must be used is larger for borrowing than for lending and larger for borrowing over a longer term than over a shorter term. The result is that a pattern of actual receipts like that in column (7) would yield a pattern of permanent income components of the same shape but smaller amplitude, even if individual units calculated permanent income on a lifetime basis. A shorter horizon would not change the pattern but would increase the amplitude.

[52] *Op. cit.* p. 261.

+5, +13, +18, +11. The agreement between these estimates and the figures in column (4) is striking, in view of the crudeness of the estimates in column (9) of our table, as well as of the complete independence of the two sources of data.[53]

More recently, data similar to those in Table 8 have been published for Great Britain (Table 9). These data are derived from the Surveys

TABLE 9

Relation of Savings and Income to Age of Head of Income Unit,
Great Britain, 1953

	1952		1953	
Age of Head of Income Unit (1)	Income Mean Ratio (2)	Mean Savings as a % of Mean Income (3)	Income Mean Ratio (4)	Mean Savings as a % of Mean Income (5)
18–24	64	0	62	1.2
25–34	112	1.3	114	.9
35–44	125	0	134	2.9
45–54	130	5.7	126	1.2
55–64	98	1.9	93	2.2
65 and over	57	−9.4	55	−6.0
All ages	100	1.0	100	1.0

Source:

Harold Lydall, "The Life Cycle in Income, Saving, and Asset Ownership," *Econometrica*, XXIII (April, 1955), pp. 131–50, esp. Tables III, XI, XII. Income is net income (i.e. after personal taxes) throughout. Savings exclude expenditures on durable goods which are treated as consumption expenditures. Column (3) is copied from Lydall's Table XII. Column (4) is computed directly from his Table III, and column (5) from figures on savings in his Table XI and on income in Table III. Column (2) is computed indirectly, since Lydall does not give income figures for 1952. In Table XII, he gives "durable consumption plus total saving" both in absolute amounts and as a percentage of net income. Net income was estimated from the ratio of the former to the latter.

[53] See Dorothy S. Brady, "Family Savings in Relation to Changes in the Level and Distribution of Income," *Studies in Income and Wealth*, XV (New York: National Bureau of Economic Research, 1952), p. 114, where she gives the formula: $\log y = -0.0295 + 0.8 \log x + 0.2 \log z$, where y is consumption expenditures, x is family income, z community income, and the logarithms are to the base 10. If we subtract $\log x$ from both sides, this becomes

$$\log \frac{y}{x} = -0.0295 - 0.2 \log \frac{x}{z}.$$

The constant term implies consumption expenditures of .93 of income when $x/z = 1$. To convert this to .90, the constant term must be −.0458, which gives as the equation from which the figures cited in the text were computed:

$$\log \frac{y}{x} = -.0458 - 0.2 \log \frac{x}{z}.$$

of Personal Income and Savings made by the Oxford Institute of Statistics, some of the results of which were used above in the comparison between Britain and the United States.[54] I have not made as detailed an analysis for these data as for the American data, partly because the difference in secular experience in Britain and the United States, particularly in war and postwar years, makes it uncertain how to correct for the secular effect. The British data show the same income pattern as the American data, though with a somewhat larger amplitude. The savings figures are much less regular than the American, though they show the same general tendency for savings to be higher in the middle than in the terminal years. The chief difference from the American figures is the tilt of the age pattern: in the American data, savings are decidedly higher relative to measured income for the oldest spending units than for the youngest; in the British data, they are decidedly higher for the youngest income units than for the oldest; in the American data, the only group with negative savings is the youngest, in the British, the oldest.

I can suggest three possible explanations for this difference, though, unfortunately, the data are not readily available to test their validity or relative importance.

(1) The difference in tilt may in part simply reflect the difference in the dating of the two bodies of data. The American table is for 1946, only one year after the end of the war, the British table, for 1953. Wartime shortages, particularly of durable goods, affected younger units more than older, and the data in Table 8 treat expenditures on durable goods as consumption expenditures. Perhaps a corresponding American table for 1953 would conform more closely to the British pattern.[55]

(2) The difference in tilt may reflect the difference in secular experience. The secular growth in real income per capita has been both larger and more regular in the United States than in Great Britain, particularly in recent decades that might be expected to count for most in forming expectations. In consequence, less of a correction to the income mean ratios, or even no correction at all, may be required for the secular effect. But this cannot be the whole explanation, since the uncorrected income mean ratios for the first and last classes are too close together to explain the difference between a zero or positive savings percentage and a sizable negative percentage.

(3) The difference in tilt may also reflect a difference in definition of

[54] See Harold Lydall, "The Life Cycle in Income, Saving, and Asset Ownership," *Econometrica*, XXIII (April 1955), pp. 131–150.
[55] I am indebted to John Frechtling for this possible explanation.

units. The American spending unit includes all related persons in a household who are regarded as "pooling" their income; in the British data, "each single person of 18 years or over and each married couple is a separate income unit, children of under 18 being attached to the income unit of their parents or guardians," except that, "in the few cases in which an individual was found to have an income of less than £50 and was living with relatives, he or she was 'amalgamated' . . . into his relations' income unit."[56] As a result, the youngest age group in the British data presumably contains, as separate units, individuals or even young married couples, living with relatives and largely supported by them, who would have been counted as parts of other units in the American data. These units might be expected to have relatively high ratios of savings to measured income: they all have at least £50 of measured income; the recorded measured income presumably does not include the money value of the consumption in kind provided by the relatives with whom they live; what is counted as measured income and their own assets are therefore not the only, and, indeed, not the major means of financing consumption. By contrast, the units in this age group in the American data are mostly living separately and are mainly dependent on their measured income or their own assets to finance consumption. This difference in definition may account not only for the relatively higher saving in the youngest age group shown by the British data but also for the relatively lower saving in the oldest age group. For here the definitional difference may work in the opposite direction: the older units who are counted separately in the British data but as part of other units in the American data may be those who cannot afford to live alone and have moved in with their relatives as an economy move to reduce the drain they are making on their assets. That these definitional effects can be of significant magnitude is shown by the difference between the American and British data in the average size of the units classified in the different age groups: in the middle age group, the number of persons per unit is only slightly larger in the American data, in the younger and older age groups, decidedly larger.[57] It should be noted that the wider amplitude of the income ratios in the British data may reflect this same effect of the difference in definition.

[56] *Ibid.*, p. 134.

[57] Fisher does not give the average number of persons per spending unit in each age group but does give the percentage distributions by number in each spending unit. Janet A. Fisher, "Income, Spending, and Saving Pattern of Consumer Units in Different Age Groups," *Studies in Income and Wealth*, XV (New York: National Bureau of Economic Research, 1952), Table 7, p. 88. The estimates in the following comparisons were computed by treating the class "Five or more" as if it averaged six persons:

4. *The Effect of Change in Income*

It has frequently been suggested that the consumption behavior of consumer units is related to the change in measured income experienced by them in the recent past. Two very different lines of reasoning have been adduced in support of this expectation. One, which is very much in the spirit of our hypothesis, is that the change in income is evidence of the inadequacy of measured income as an index of income status; that a large rise or a large fall in income may imply that current income is "abnormal," whereas a stable income is evidence that current income is "normal." The second implicitly accepts measured income as an adequate index of income status, but supposes that there is a lag in the adjustment of consumption to a change in income status, so that units that have just risen to a given measured income are not adapted to it as fully as those who have been there for some time. The two lines of reasoning lead to similar empirical expectations. Units that have just risen to a given measured income will tend to spend less on consumption than units that have remained at that measured income, and these, in turn, less than units that have fallen to this measured income. But the two lines of reasoning imply rather different hypotheses of consumption behavior and suggest different directions of research into the effect of change in income.

On the permanent income hypothesis, the effect of change in income is to be sought entirely in its implications for the meaning of measured income. A simple example will serve to show that our hypothesis has such implications, and that they lead to fairly precise inferences about the effect of change in income. Consider a group of consumer units which has the same average measured income in two years; suppose that transitory components of income average out to zero in each year, so that average permanent income is equal to average measured income and is also the same in the two years. Let

Age of Head of Unit	Average Number of Persons Per Unit	
	U.S.	Great Britain (1953)
18–24	1.68	1.24
25–34	3.14	2.80
35–44	3.67	3.52
45–54⎱ 55–64⎰	2.86	2.67 2.09
65 and over	2.24	1.44
All ages	2.85	2.36

us classify these consumer units by the change in income from the earlier year to the later and for each such class determine the regression of consumption in the later year on measured income in the same year. What, if anything, can we say on our hypothesis about these regressions and their relation to one another and to a regression computed for the group as a whole?

For simplicity, suppose the permanent component to be the same in the two years for each unit separately as well as for the group as a whole.[58] Any changes in income are then attributable to changes in transitory components. But these transitory components are supposed uncorrelated with the permanent components. Hence groups classified by change in income will not differ systematically with respect to the distribution of permanent components of income; they will all tend to have the same mean permanent component and the same dispersion of the permanent component. But, on our hypothesis, consumption depends only on the permanent component of income, not on the transitory component. Consequently, our hypothesis implies that mean consumption is the same for all income-change classes.

Mean measured income is not, however, the same. The units that experienced a decline in income must have had a smaller transitory component in the second year than in the first; we have just seen that their mean permanent component is the same; accordingly, their mean measured income must be lower in the second year than in the first. Similarly, units experiencing a rise in income must have a larger transitory component in the second year and so a higher mean measured income. Given the same mean measured income for all groups combined in the two years, and symmetry between the two years, measured income in the second year is on the average lower for the units experiencing a decline in income than for those experiencing a rise. Since average consumption is the same, it follows that the regressions of consumption on measured income must differ in height for the different income-change classes, being lower, the larger the algebraic change in income.

What of the slope of the regression? The considerations just adduced make it clear that the members of an income-change group are more alike with respect to transitory components than is the group as a whole. For example, the group experiencing the largest increase in income can have hardly any members who have a large negative

---

[58] This is not required by the definition of the permanent component. For example, it is noted above that the permanent component may be systematically related to the age of the head of the unit. The inability to take account of such differences in age is one source of error in the empirical examples that follow.

transitory component in the second year. It follows that the variance of the transitory component is smaller for an income-change class than for the group as a whole; but the variance of the permanent component is the same; hence, P_y is greater for an income-change class than for the group as a whole. Our hypothesis therefore implies that the consumption-income regression tends to be steeper for a group of units that have experienced the same income change than for all units.

FIGURE 10

Hypothetical Regressions for Groups Classified by Change in Income
(average change assumed zero for group as a whole)

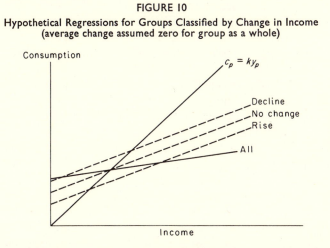

Figure 10 displays the relations among the regressions to which our hypothesis leads. This figure does not show the common average consumption for the different groups.

The preceding discussion has been deliberately phrased so as to apply to either the arithmetic or logarithmic variant of our hypothesis. For the arithmetic variant, the units are to be regarded as classified by the absolute amount of the change in income; for the logarithmic variant, by the percentage change in income.

The Appendix to this chapter presents a more detailed analysis of the implications of these two variants of our hypothesis. This analysis is, in one respect, more general than that given above: it allows for a change in the average permanent component between the two years, provided the change is of the same absolute amount (arithmetic variant) or the same percentage amount (logarithmic variant) for each consumer unit; and it does not assume transitory components to average out to zero. In another respect it is less general: it makes special assumptions about the distribution of the transitory components in the two years (that they are jointly normally distributed with the same variance in the two years). This analysis confirms and

99

extends the preceding conclusions. Perhaps the most interesting general extension is that the slope of the regression for a given change in income is the same whatever may be the magnitude of the change in income; i.e. that if regressions like the dashed lines in Figure 10 were computed for a series of values of the change in income (or for equally broad income-change classes) they would be parallel. This is the justification for making them parallel in Figure 10. The analysis leads also to specific formulas expressing the slope and intercept of the regression for a particular income-change class in terms of parameters for the group as a whole, the size of the income change, and a characteristic of the income structure. We shall use these formulas in interpreting available data on the effect of change in income.

I have examined in some detail the consistency of our hypothesis with two bodies of data: (1) Data for something over 600 farm families which have been used by Ruth Mack to analyze the effect of change in income.[59] These data were collected by the Farm Security Administration and are for the years 1940 to 1942.[60] (2) Data for nearly 5,000 spending units collected in the Survey of Consumer Finances and used by James N. Morgan to analyze the effect of change in income.[61] These data are for 1948 and 1949.

In addition, I have examined rather more casually the consistency of the hypothesis with data for nearly 400 farm families in Tennessee for 1943 and 1944. Like the other two bodies of data, these conform reasonably closely to the implications of the hypothesis, though they differ from it in one respect.[62]

[59] Ruth P. Mack, "The Direction of Change in Income and the Consumption Function," *Review of Economics and Statistics*, XXX, No. 4 (November 1948), pp. 239–258.

[60] See Willard W. Cochrane and Mary D. Grigg, *The Changing Composition of Family Budgets for Selected Groups of Corn Belt Farmers*, Department of Agriculture, Bureau of Agricultural Economics (Washington, October 1946).

[61] See Katona, Klein, Lansing, Morgan, *op. cit.*, pp. 153–154.

[62] See Jean L. Pennock and Elisabeth L. Speer, *Changes in Rural Family Income and Spending in Tennessee, 1943–1944*, Miscellaneous Publication No. 666, Department of Agriculture (March 1949).

The chart on page 8 of this publication is like Figures 11 and 12 that follow except that it is for only three income-change groups (decreased, constant, increased), and does not contain any relation for all combined. The plotted values for the three groups would clearly yield three very nearly parallel regressions, steeper than the regression for all groups and less steep than a relation between permanent components. The one respect in which there is a discrepancy from the predictions of our hypothesis is that the regression for the constant income group, instead of being between the other two, is to the right of the regression of the increased income group. A possible explanation is that this discrepancy reflects the use of a definition of consumption that includes expenditures on durable consumer goods. Perhaps the higher expenditures at each measured income level of the families that experienced an increase in income than of the families that had constant income simply reflect greater expenditure on consumer durables. Unfortunately, the published data are not adequate to test this explanation, though the small bits of relevant information in Table 7, page 9, are consistent with it.

a. THE FSA DATA

Figure 11 is reproduced from Ruth Mack's article, except that I have added a line through the mean of the sample and the origin to represent $c_p = ky_p$ or the relation between the permanent components.[63] It will be seen that Figure 11 corresponds closely with our hypothetical Figure 10, if allowance is made for the difference between them in the average change in income for which they are drawn. Figure 10 was drawn for a group that had the same average

FIGURE 11

Regression of Family Consumption on Income for Farm Families,
Five Income-Change Groups, 1942
(income change from 1940 to 1942)

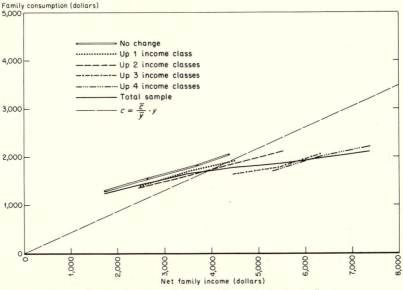

Source: Ruth P. Mack, "The Direction of Change in Income and the Consumption Function,"
Review of Economic Statistics, November 1948, p. 242.

income in the two years, so it is the "no change" line that goes through the intersection of the regression for all units and the relation between permanent components. Figure 11 is for a group that had an increase in average income of $1,618. The "up two income classes" subgroup comes closest to having the same average change—the average change for it is $1,910—so the regression for it corresponds to the "no change" line in Figure 10 and goes through the intersection of the two relations for the group as a whole. As our hypothesis predicts, the

[63] I am indebted to Ruth Mack for making her worksheets available to me.

regressions for individual income-change classes are roughly parallel, steeper than the regression for the group as a whole, and less steep than a line through the origin and the mean point of the group.

Table 10 gives a more exacting comparison between the observed data and predictions derived from our hypothesis. Because the units

TABLE 10

Comparison of Observed and Predicted Results for Income-Change Classes, Farm Security Administration Sample of Farm Families
(*dollar figures in thousands*)

Income-Change Class	Slope of Regression		Income at Intersection of Regression for Class and for All Families		Average Consumption[d]
	Observed[a]	Predicted[b]	Observed[a]	Predicted[c]	
No change	.29	.23	$1.9	$1.6	$1.5
Up 1 income class	.27	.23	2.7	2.8	1.6
Up 2 income classes	.25	.23	3.1	4.2	1.7
Up 3 income classes	.23	.23	5.9	5.8	1.7
Up 4 income classes	.24	.23	6.7	7.3	1.9
All classes	.15				1.6

[a] Computed from graphic fit to points plotted in Figure 11.

[b] Computed from equation (4.26) in the Appendix, with $r_{tt'}$ set equal to zero. The observed ratio of mean consumption to mean income was used for k, and the slope of the graphically fitted regression to all families for b.

[c] Computed from equation (4.27) in the Appendix, using the numerical values in the preceding note, together with values of $(d - \bar{d})$ computed from Willard W. Cochrane and Mary D. Grigg, *The Changing Composition of Family Budgets for Selected Groups of Corn Belt Farmers*, Department of Agriculture, Bureau of Agricultural Economics (Washington; October 1946).

[d] Computed from data in *ibid.*

Note: Regressions are for 1942 and income change is from 1940 to 1942. Income class is $1,000 in width, except for top open-end class.

are classified by the absolute change in income, we have had to use the arithmetic variant of our hypothesis in making predictions. Again, the general agreement is excellent: our hypothesis predicts a slope of .23 for the separate income-change-class regressions; the actual slope varies from .23 to .29; there is a very close family resemblance between the observed and predicted incomes at the intersection of the separate and the over-all regressions.

Yet there are also some minor differences in detail. (1) The formula from which the predicted slope is computed is for a hypothetical class all members of which have precisely the same income change; the actual classes include a range of income changes approximately $1,000 wide; the effect should be to make the observed slope lower than the predicted slope; yet the observed slopes are uniformly higher. (2) The observed intersection incomes differ systematically from the predicted, being less widely dispersed. (3) Another reflection of the same phenomenon is the final column showing average consumption. If the arithmetic model as developed in the Appendix applied fully to these data, these averages would be identical; yet they display a decided upward trend.

Deviations (2) and (3) reflect a shortcoming in a supplementary assumption we found it necessary to incorporate in our model, rather than a real deviation from the basic hypothesis. The group as a whole experienced a substantial increase in income from 1940 to 1942—an increase of over $1,600 or nearly 75 per cent of the 1940 level. Our arithmetic model assumes that any change in permanent income is the same *absolute* amount for all units. This might not be a bad approximation for a small change in average income and so presumably also in permanent income. For a change as large as 75 per cent in average income, and presumably of a similar order of magnitude in permanent income, it would be preferable to regard the change in permanent income as the same *percentage* for all units—this is clearly so for the something like 20 per cent increase that must be attributed simply to a rise in prices, and seems reasonable for the rest as well. But on this interpretation, the absolute amount of income change is not uncorrelated with the size of the permanent income; the larger the absolute change in income, the larger on the average the absolute change in permanent income, and hence the larger the average permanent income. The rising average consumption in the final column of Table 10 presumably reflects this rising average permanent income; so also does the lesser dispersion of the observed points of intersection than of the predicted points, for the effect of the rising average permanent income is to bring the several regressions closer together.

One factor that may partly account for deviation (1) is that the mean transitory component of consumption is probably negative. One of the parameters used in computing the predicted slope is k, the ratio of mean permanent consumption to mean permanent income. I have used the observed ratio of average consumption to average income for the group as a whole as an estimate of k. It seems clear that this is too low. 1942 was a wartime year when consumption restrictions were beginning to be felt; the mean transitory component of consumption was almost certainly negative, and of income, almost certainly positive. In another connection, an estimate is made below (see Chapter VI, section 4) of the mean transitory component of consumption for this group. Use of the corresponding k raises the predicted slope, but from .23 only to .24, so this factor accounts for only part of deviation (1).

b. THE SURVEY OF CONSUMER FINANCES DATA

The Consumer Finances data are for a much larger sample—nearly 5,000 units, approximately half of whom reported for 1947, the rest for 1948. The data are mostly for urban spending units but presumably include some farm units.[64] Data for the two years are pooled in the analysis. For each year, the income-change class is determined by the reported income change from the preceding year. These data have one advantage over the FSA data in addition to the larger sample: the units are classified by percentage change in income, and so we can use the logarithmic variant of our hypothesis, the variant that in general we have found to fit the data rather better. But they also have one serious disadvantage: the basic data are nowhere published in anything like the same fullness. The analysis that follows is based mainly on some unpublished data kindly made available to me by James Morgan; unfortunately, even these are not extensive enough for our purposes, so I have had to resort to rather arbitrary measures to shape the data to the needs of our analysis.

Figure 12 is an adaptation of a chart published by Morgan.[65] As on his chart, points for the final income class, $7,500 and over, are omitted. The reason is that the values used for income are midpoints of class intervals (except for the class $5,000 to $7,500 for which $6,000 is used), computed averages apparently not being available, and the use of any single value for the upper open-end class would be arbitrary and subject to undue error. I have added to the chart the two lines for all classes combined: the line labeled A, which is the assumed relation between permanent components, the value of k being taken as the ratio of average consumption to average income for the sample as a whole; and the line labeled B, which is an estimated regression of the logarithm of consumption on the logarithm of income.[66] It will be seen that Figure 12, like Figure 11, corresponds

[64] Morgan does not specify the exact coverage of the sample or its relation to the samples he used earlier in the same chapter, but I infer from the numbers involved that it must include farm and business units.

[65] Op. cit., chart IV, p. 154. Morgan devotes considerable attention to the effect of income change. But most of his analysis uses the residuals from consumption-income regressions, and so, as noted in section 2f above, is of little value. He does give some regressions between savings and income for income-change classes (pp. 155 and 160). But these are for subgroups classified by amount of liquid assets. The analysis of the Appendix clearly does not apply directly to such subgroups, and I have not been able to construct a plausible variant that would. This is why I do not discuss these results.

[66] Since I did not have data for all families on mean income and mean consumption for individual income classes, this regression was determined by a roundabout process. Among the data Morgan made available were the sums, sums of squares, and sums of cross-products of the arithmetic values of income and savings. From these was computed the least-squares straight line between the arithmetic values of income and consumption and the elasticity of this regression at the arithmetic mean income; this was used as the

very closely with our hypothetical Figure 10. The one exception is for the class whose income fell more than 25 per cent; the regression for this class is abnormally high and flat.

Table 11 presents a numerical comparison between observed and

FIGURE 12

Regressions of Consumption on Income for Five Income-Change Groups, Based on Survey of Consumer Finances Data, 1947 and 1948
(income change from preceding year)

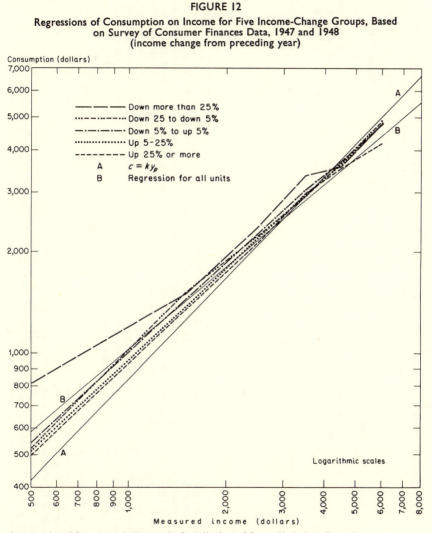

Source: Adapted from James N. Morgan, in *Contributions of Survey Methods to Economics*, Columbia University Press, 1954, Chart IV, p. 154.

slope of *B*. The geometric mean of consumption and income was approximated from these data and the intercept of *B* determined so that the line *B* would pass through the corresponding point.

105

TABLE 11

Comparison of Observed and Predicted Results for Income-Change Classes, Based on Survey of Consumer Finances Data, 1947 and 1948

(dollar figures in thousands)

Income-Change Class (1)	Measured Income Elasticity of Consumption		Income at Intersection of Regression for Class and for All Families		Arithmetic Average Consumption[d] (6)	Standard Deviation of		
	Observed[a] (2)	Predicted[b] (3)	Observed[a] (4)	Predicted[c] (5)		Measured Income[e] (7)	Permanent Component of Income[f] (8)	Transitory Component of Income[g] (9)
Down more than 25%	.77	.89	$19.6	$ .1	$1.9	$1.42	$1.25	$.68
Down 25% to down 5%	.87	.89	1.6	.6	2.5	2.36	2.20	.85
Down 5% to up 5%	.88	.89	1.4	1.6	2.4	2.26	2.11	.80
Up 5% to up 25%	.89	.89	2.3	3.5	2.8	2.15	2.03	.71
Up 25% or more	.87	.89	5.3	8.9	2.5	2.55	2.37	.93
All classes	.82				2.5	2.28	2.06	.98

[a] For income-change groups, elasticity is slope of log-log straight line fitted graphically to points plotted in Figure 12; for all classes, elasticity at arithmetic mean income of arithmetic straight line fitted to original data by least squares. I am grateful to James Morgan, of the Michigan Survey Research Center, for making available the basic data for this computation and the others referred to in these notes. This elasticity is used because the data for a graphic log-log fit were not available to me. As a check, corresponding elasticities were computed for the several income-change classes; the results, in the order in which the classes are listed in the above table, were: .77, .88, .86, .81, .77. The regression for all classes used in computing the points of intersection and plotted in Figure 12 is a log-log straight line with slope equal to .82 and going through a point corresponding to the geometric mean income and consumption. These in turn were estimated from the corresponding arithmetic means and variances.

[b] Computed from formula (4.20) in the Appendix to this chapter. r_{YY} was set equal to .828, the correlation between the logarithms of incomes in 1947 and 1948 for urban spending units of 2 or more persons in the Survey of Consumer Finances reinterview sample (see below, Table 18, item 8).

[c] Computed from formula (4.23'). The values of D were taken, rather arbitrarily, as the logarithms of .65, .85, 1.00, 1.15, and 1.35 for the several income-change classes, and of $\bar{D}$ as the weighted average of these values, the weights being the number of units in each class.

[d] Computed from the data made available by Morgan.

[e] Computed from sums and sums of squares of absolute incomes made available by Morgan.

[f] Square root of product of entry in column (2) and square of standard deviation of measured income.

[g] Square root of product of complement of entry in column (2) and square of standard deviation of measured income.

Note: Sample combines observations for 1947 and 1948, so regressions are for average of 1947 and 1948. Income change is from preceding year (1946 to 1947 or 1947 to 1948). Regressions are logarithmic.

predicted values. Except for the income-change class just referred to, observed elasticities are very close to the predicted, and even the deviations conform to expectation. The observed elasticity should be lower than the predicted because the predicted is for a single value of income change, the observed, for a class containing a range of values. For the same reason, the observed elasticity should fall below the predicted by a larger amount, the broader the income-change class, as, with one exception, it does.

The observed and predicted incomes at the intersection of the regressions for each class and for all classes combined agree much less well. Again, the only very large deviation is for the group whose income fell more than 25 per cent, but the remaining values are considerably more discrepant than the corresponding values for the FSA sample. I have not been able to construct any plausible explanation for this discrepancy.

The average consumption of the income-change classes, given in Column (6), conforms more closely to expectation than the corresponding column for the FSA sample. Except for the first class, which is a deviant throughout, average consumption is much the same for the various income-change classes and shows no systematic relation to income-change.

For these data, we can extend the test to the estimated dispersion of the components of income for the separate income-change classes, the estimates of absolute dispersion in columns (8) and (9) being derived from the observed elasticities in column (2) and the computed standard deviations of measured income in column (7). We have seen that, on the permanent income hypothesis, the dispersion of the permanent component of income should be roughly the same for the separate income-change classes, and the same for each as for the group as a whole; whereas the dispersion of the transitory component should be less for each income-change class than for the group as a whole. The data clearly conform closely to these predictions, except again for the deviant class, "down more than 25 per cent," which has an unusually low dispersion both in total and for each component separately.

Why should the "down more than 25 per cent" class be so consistently a deviant? I have no fully satisfactory answer. But, in part, this deviant behavior reflects a defect of the analysis enforced by the absence of data, namely, failure to take into account the age of the heads of the consumer units. For a group of the same age it is reasonable to suppose, as our analysis does, that the members of the group retain the same relative permanent income status from one year to the next. This is much less reasonable for a group differing in age; those not yet at their peak income period are climbing the relative income status ladder, those past their peak are descending. Data are available for 1948 on the age distribution of the heads of units in the various income-change classes. These show a disproportionately large number of heads 65 years of age or older in two income-change classes: "down 5 per cent to up 5 per cent" and "down more than 25 per cent."[67] Presumably the former retired some time ago and in the survey year were receiving a stable retirement income; they did not experience any significant change in permanent income status and so cause no difficulty in the analysis. The older heads in the "down more than 25 per cent" class, on the other hand, must mostly have retired or partly retired during or just prior to the survey year; the decline in their income is in substantial part a decline in permanent income. The effect is to make the average permanent income for the "down more than 25 per cent" class lower than for the other classes, and so to make average consumption lower, as it is according to column (4). It seems unlikely, however, that this effect can account for the whole difference between average consumption for this class and the other classes. The difference is of the order of 20 per cent, which implies a difference of the same magnitude in average permanent income, yet units with heads of 65 or over account for only about 18 per cent of all units in this income-change class in 1948 and units with heads of 55 or over for only 35 per cent. Similarly, while this effect may help to explain why the measures of dispersion in columns (7), (8), and (9) are so low for this class, it seems unlikely that it can account for it in full.

Expressed as percentages of mean income, the standard deviations for all classes are 75 per cent, 68 per cent, and 32 per cent, for measured income, permanent component, and transitory component, respectively. These estimates are very close to those for all nonfarm or urban families in 1935–36 and 1941 in Table 4 above. I have not computed similar figures for the separate income-change classes because mean measured income for such a class cannot be regarded as an approximation to mean permanent income.

C. THE SIGNIFICANCE OF THE COMPARISONS

There is clearly a very close correspondence between the observed effect of classifying consumer units by change in income and the effect predicted by the permanent income hypothesis. This correspondence goes beyond general features and carries over to rather

[67] "1950 Survey of Consumer Finances, Part III," *Federal Reserve Bulletin* (August 1950), Table 3.

precise numerical characteristics. Two points need to be emphasized in judging the significance of these results.

(1) The correspondence, particularly in numerical characteristics, is in some ways the most striking bit of evidence for our hypothesis that has so far been adduced. It is so partly because the comparisons between observation and prediction are for fairly precise implications of the hypothesis that could readily have been contradicted; partly, because these implications have not heretofore been drawn from other hypotheses and some had not even been established as empirical generalizations. These comparisons therefore both demonstrate the fecundity of the hypothesis in generating implications and provide new fields on which to try out the hypothesis.

(2) The acceptance of our hypothesis in interpreting these data does not mean that change in income is not an important variable for consumption analysis. Our hypothesis explains why it should be an important variable and what effect it can be expected to have. The consistency of the data with our hypothesis means that the effect of change in income need not be regarded as evidence of any meaningful "lag" in the reaction of consumer units to changes in circumstances; on the contrary, change in income can be regarded as having an effect precisely because it cannot be taken as a valid change in circumstances, because a large change in income is—on the average— a sign that measured income is affected to an unusual extent by transitory factors.

Appendix to Section 4:

The Effect of Change in Income on the Regression of Consumption on Income

Consumption data classified by change in income generally take one of two forms: (1) like the FSA data, they are classified by the *absolute amount* of the change in income; (2) like the Survey of Consumer Finances data, they are classified by the *percentage* change in income. It turns out to be convenient to make slightly different assumptions in deriving the implications of our hypothesis for these two types of data: to assume for (1) that any change in permanent income between the years for which the income change is recorded is of the same absolute amount for every consumer unit in the group considered; to assume for (2) that it is of the same percentage.

1. PERMANENT INCOME CHANGE OF SAME ABSOLUTE AMOUNT

Let y = measured income in the year in question

y' = measured income in the earlier year from which the change in income is calculated

$d = y - y' =$ change in income
$c =$ measured consumption in year in question
$a =$ intercept of regression of c on y for all units
$b =$ slope of regression of c on y for all units

Let a subscript d to any of these symbols (other than d itself) represent the corresponding variable for a group of units for which d is the same, i.e. for an income-change class.

The problem is to determine the values of a_d and b_d.

From our earlier analysis,

$$(4.1) \qquad\qquad b = kP_y$$

$$(4.2) \qquad\qquad a = \bar{c} - b\bar{y} .$$

By strictly similar reasoning,

$$(4.3) \qquad\qquad b_d = k_d P_{yd}$$

$$(4.4) \qquad\qquad a_d = \bar{c}_d - b_d \bar{y}_d .$$

By assumption, the relation between permanent components is the same for every unit, so

$$(4.5) \qquad\qquad k_d = k .$$

Given that the change in the permanent component of income is the same absolute amount for all units, any differences among units in the value of d are accounted for by differences in the transitory component of income. But, on our hypothesis, the transitory component of income is uncorrelated with the permanent component of income and hence of consumption and also with the transitory component of consumption. It follows that consumption is uncorrelated with the value of d, whence

$$(4.6) \qquad\qquad \bar{c}_d = \bar{c} .$$

We can thus restrict attention to evaluating P_{yd}, and $\bar{y}_d$, or features of the income distribution. Now

$$(4.7) \qquad\qquad P_y = \frac{\sigma_p^2}{\sigma_y^2} ,$$

where σ_p^2 is the variance of the permanent component of income and σ_y^2 is the variance of measured income. Similarly

$$(4.8) \qquad\qquad P_{yd} = \frac{\sigma_{pd}^2}{\sigma_{yd}^2} .$$

But under our assumptions,

$$(4.9) \qquad\qquad \sigma_{pd}^2 = \sigma_p^2 ,$$

since differences in d reflect only differences in transitory components, which are assumed uncorrelated with permanent components. The distribution of permanent components, like the distribution of consumption, is the same for a group of units with the same d for all values of d and the same as for all units together. It follows that

$$(4.10) \qquad P_{yd} = \frac{\sigma_y^2}{\sigma_{yd}^2} \cdot P_y \,,$$

so our problem reduces to determine $\bar{y}_d$ and σ_{yd}^2.

For simplicity, assume that y and y' are jointly normally distributed. Then y and $d = y - y'$ are also jointly normally distributed. Hence, $\bar{y}_d$ is a linear function of d, say

$$(4.11) \qquad \bar{y}_d = e + f(d - \bar{d}).$$

The parameters are given by

$$(4.12) \qquad f = \frac{E(y - \bar{y})(d - \bar{d})}{E(d - \bar{d})^2} \,,$$

$$(4.13) \qquad e = \bar{y} \,.$$

But since $(d - \bar{d}) = (y - \bar{y}) - (y' - \bar{y}')$,

$$(4.14) \qquad f = \frac{\sigma_y^2 - r_{yy'}\sigma_y\sigma_y}{\sigma_y^2 - 2r_{yy'}\sigma_y\sigma_{y'} + \sigma_{y'}^2} \,.$$

Assume that $\sigma_y = \sigma_{y'}$. Then

$$(4.15) \qquad f = \tfrac{1}{2} \,,$$

so

$$(4.16) \qquad \bar{y}_d = \bar{y} + \tfrac{1}{2}(d - \bar{d}).$$

We now want to compute

(4.17)

$$\sigma_{yd}^2 = E(y - \bar{y}_d)^2 = E[(y - \bar{y}) - \tfrac{1}{2}(d - \bar{d})]^2$$
$$= E[\tfrac{1}{2}(y - \bar{y}) + \tfrac{1}{2}(y' - \bar{y}')]^2 = \tfrac{1}{4}(\sigma_y^2 + 2r_{yy'}\sigma_y\sigma_{y'} + \sigma_{y'}^2) \,.$$

Again assuming $\sigma_y = \sigma_{y'}$

$$(4.18) \qquad \sigma_{yd}^2 = \tfrac{1}{2}\sigma_y^2(1 + r_{yy'}) \,.$$

Substituting in (4.10),

$$(4.19) \qquad P_{yd} = \frac{2P_y}{1 + r_{yy'}} \,.$$

Substituting (4.5) and (4.19) in (4.3), and using (4.1),

$$(4.20) \qquad b_d = \frac{2k \cdot P_y}{1 + r_{yy'}} = \frac{2b}{1 + r_{yy'}} .$$

Substituting (4.6) and (4.16) into (4.4) and using (4.2),

$$(4.21) \qquad \begin{aligned} a_d &= \bar{c} - b_d\bar{y} - {}^1/_2 b_d(d - \bar{d}) \\ &= a + \bar{y}(b - b_d) - {}^1/_2 b_d(d - \bar{d}) . \end{aligned}$$

In application, a_d is likely to be subject to a very large sampling error, so it is better to use some index of height which is nearer the middle of the range of incomes observed. This could be consumption at the mean income which is simply

$$(4.22) \qquad c(\text{at } \bar{y}) = \bar{c} - {}^1/_2 b_d(d - \bar{d}) .$$

Another alternative is to determine the value of y at which the regression for a given value of d intersects the regression for the group as a whole. This intersection value of y is given by

$$(4.23) \qquad y = \frac{a_d - a}{b - b_d} = \bar{y} - \frac{1}{2}\left(\frac{b_d}{b - b_d}\right)(d - \bar{d}) .$$

We can convert (4.20) into a somewhat different form by getting a different expression for $r_{yy'}$. Let p' stand for the deviation of the permanent component in year 1 from its mean value, t' for the corresponding deviation of the transitory component, and p and t for the same variables in year 2. By our assumptions, $p = p'$. Then

$$(4.24) \qquad r_{yy'} = \frac{E(p + t')(p + t)}{\sigma_y \sigma_{y'}} = \frac{\sigma_p^2 + r_{tt'}\sigma_t\sigma_{t'}}{\sigma_y \sigma_{y'}} ,$$

taking into account the zero correlation between p and t and p and t'. Again, assume $\sigma_y = \sigma_{y'}$. Also assume $\sigma_t = \sigma_{t'}$. We then have

$$(4.25) \qquad r_{yy'} = P_y + (1 - P_y)r_{tt'} .$$

Substitute (4.25) into (4.20) and also replace P_y by its equivalent b/k. The result is

$$(4.26) \qquad b_d = \frac{2kb}{k + b + (k - b)r_{tt'}} .$$

Substitute (4.26) into (4.23). The resulting intersection value of y is

$$(4.27) \qquad y = \bar{y} + \frac{k}{(k - b)(1 - r_{tt'})}(d - \bar{d}) .$$

Although t and t' are taken as uncorrelated with p, there is nothing

112

in our hypothesis that requires them to be uncorrelated with one another. Whether they are depends on the length of the horizon implicit in permanent income and on the lapse of time between the two years considered. If the horizon were two years in length, t and t' would be uncorrelated even if the years considered were adjacent; if it is three years, they would not be uncorrelated for adjacent years because the unit would regard some effects lasting more than one year as transitory, but they would be uncorrelated for years separated by one year. And so on.

For the FSA data covered by Figure 11, the change in income is between two years with one year intervening. Evidence is presented later which suggests that a horizon of three years is a good approximation. If this is so, for these data $r_{tt'}$ can be taken to equal zero, which puts (4.26) and (4.27) into particularly simple form.

One important implication of (4.20) or (4.26) which is independent of the precise numerical value it yields is that the slopes of the regressions for given values of d are independent of d—i.e. that the regressions are parallel. Another implication is that if $k > b$, then $k > b_d > b$, i.e. that the regression for a given value of d is steeper than for the group as a whole and less steep than the relation between the permanent components.

It should be emphasized that our analysis is for a given value of d. The effect of grouping units for which d is between two values will be to give a result intermediate between b and b_d, so that in general (4.20) or (4.26) may be expected to overestimate the observed slopes.

2. PERMANENT INCOME CHANGE OF SAME PERCENTAGE

The preceding case was constructed to correspond with the FSA data, which are classified by the absolute change in income. This case is constructed to correspond with the Consumer Finances data, which are classified by the percentage change in income.

Accordingly, let

$$(4.28) \qquad y_p = m y'_p .$$

Take logarithms of both sides, letting capital letters stand for logarithms of corresponding lower case letters:

$$(4.29) \qquad Y_p = M + Y'_p .$$

Let

$$(4.30) \qquad D = Y - Y' .$$

Consider now the logarithmic variant of our hypothesis, for which

$$(4.1') \qquad B = P_Y$$

$$(4.2') \qquad A = \bar{C} - B\bar{Y} = K + \bar{C}_t - \bar{Y}_t P_Y + \bar{Y}_p(1 - P_Y) .$$

Correspondingly

(4.3′) $$B_D = P_{YD}$$

(4.4′) $$A_D = \bar{C}_D - B_D \bar{Y}_D .$$

As before,

(4.6′) $$\bar{C}_D = \bar{C}.$$

If we suppose Y and Y' to be jointly normally distributed, this case reduces to the preceding case and we can write down directly:

(4.16′) $$\bar{Y}_D = \bar{Y} + {}^1/_2(D - \bar{D}) ,$$

(4.20′) $$B_D = P_{YD} = \frac{2P_Y}{1 + r_{YY'}} = \frac{2B}{1 + r_{YY'}},$$

(4.21′) $$A_D = A + \bar{Y}(B - B_D) - {}^1/_2 B_D(D - \bar{D}) ,$$

(4.22′) $$C(\text{at } \bar{Y}) = \bar{C} - {}^1/_2 B_D(D - \bar{D}).$$

The intersection value of Y is

(4.23′) $$Y = \bar{Y} - \frac{1}{2}\left(\frac{B_D}{B - B_D}\right)(D - \bar{D}) .$$

Once again

(4.25′) $$r_{YY'} = P_Y + (1 - P_Y) r_{TT'} ,$$

so

(4.26′) $$B_D = \frac{2B}{1 + B + (1 - B) r_{TT'}}$$

and the intersection value of Y is

(4.27′) $$Y = \bar{Y} + \frac{1}{(1 - B)(1 - r_{TT'})}(D - \bar{D}) .$$

CHAPTER V

Consistency of the Permanent Income Hypothesis with Existing Evidence on the Relation between Consumption and Income : Time Series Data

IN Chapter II, we saw that the permanent income hypothesis implied, under certain conditions, a relation between the aggregate permanent components for a group of consumer units of the same form as the relation between the permanent components for a single consumer unit. That is,

$$(2.10) \qquad c_p^* = k^*(\qquad)\cdot y_p^* ,$$

where c_p^* and y_p^* are aggregate, or per capita, permanent consumption and income, respectively, for a group of consumer units, and k^* depends on the form of the function k for a single consumer unit as well as on the distribution of consumer units by the variables entering into k, in particular, i, w, and u.

Suppose that the conditions required to justify (2.10) can be regarded as satisfied for a particular set of data on the aggregate or per capita measured income and consumption of a group of consumer units in each of a series of time units. Suppose, further, that the numerical value of k^* can be taken as roughly the same for the different years or other time units covered, so that the variables that belong in the empty parenthesis of (2.10) need not be specified and can be neglected. Under these conditions, the applications of our hypothesis to hypothetical family budget data that were made in Chapter III, and to actual family budget data in Chapter IV, carry over directly to time series data. It is only necessary to reword the results to allow for the fact that the individual observation is on aggregate or per capita measured consumption and measured income rather than on measured consumption and measured income of a single consumer unit. In particular, the regression of measured consumption on measured income computed from time series will yield a marginal propensity less than the average propensity and an income elasticity of consumption approximately equal to P_{y^*}, where this symbol as before means the fraction of the variance of measured income attributable to variation in the permanent component of income.

This chapter examines the consistency of this simple model with existing time series data. The first topic is the general characteristics of the long-period savings estimates for the United States recently constructed by Raymond Goldsmith. These are the main justification for regarding k^* as numerically constant over this period. Section 2 covers more detailed features of regressions of consumption on contemporaneous incomes—in particular, the effect of the period covered and the form of data on observed elasticities, and the differences between time series and budget study elasticities. Section 3 interprets a number of regressions computed by other writers in which consumption is expressed as a function not only of contemporaneous but also of past income, and reports on a consumption function of a similar kind suggested by our hypothesis. While the data considered cover a fair span of time and a variety of features of consumption behavior, they are, like the budget data, much more limited geographically than would be desirable, being almost entirely for the United States.

1. *Recent Long-period Estimates of Aggregate Savings for the United States*

a. THEIR GENERAL PATTERN

Figure 13 plots per capita personal consumption expenditures in the United States against per capita personal disposable income, both expressed in 1929 prices, for the period 1897–1949; it is based on Raymond Goldsmith's comprehensive study of savings, the first study to estimate savings directly year by year for so long a period. The figures plotted treat expenditures on major consumer durable goods in excess of the use value of services rendered by them as savings, and include in consumption only the estimated use value of their services. Personal disposable income measures income received by consumer units after the payment of direct taxes; the variant used here includes increases in government pension and retirement funds, that is, treats social security on an accrued rather than cost basis; it excludes undistributed income of corporations as well as increases in private pension rights and similar income items. It is by no means clear that this concept of income is best for our purposes, since consumer units may take account of accrued but not distributed changes in their capital position other than social security. However, it is certainly fairly close to the desired concept.

Even a cursory examination shows that the general pattern of these

116

data fits our hypothesis remarkably well. On our hypothesis, the ratio of planned or permanent consumption to permanent income depends on factors other than the level of income. If these other factors had been roughly constant, or offsetting, for the period 1897–1949, the ratio of permanent consumption to permanent income would have

FIGURE 13

Relation of Personal Consumption Expenditures per Capita to Personal
Disposable Income per Capita, 1897–1949
(1929 prices)

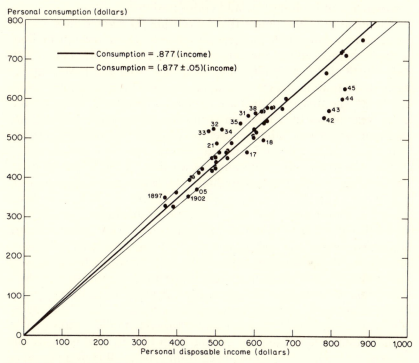

Source: Data made available by Raymond Goldsmith.

been a constant during this period, which means that points in Figure 13 representing permanent consumption and permanent income would all be on a single straight line through the origin. The heavy line on the diagram is such a line, drawn for a consumption ratio of .877, the ratio of average consumption for 1897–1949 to average income for the same period (see line 14 of Table 12). The two lighter lines on either side of the heavy line are for consumption ratios 5 percentage points higher and lower.[1] The fan of three lines

[1] The figure of 5 percentage points was chosen rather arbitrarily, so no special significance should be attached to it. See the next footnote.

117

contains more than two-thirds of the points, and describes the pattern of the points reasonably well. More detailed study of the dates of the plotted points indicates no marked temporal pattern of the deviations from the central line. Some of the early years lie below, some above, and so on, except for the 1930's, which lie mostly above the line, and the 1940's, which lie mostly below, a phenomenon that is commented on further below. Clearly, on this superficial level, the scatter is not inconsistent with the hypothesis that the observed points were generated from points on the central line by the addition of transitory components of both income and consumption.

The identity of the points that lie outside the lighter lines is even more illuminating than the general consistency of the fan of lines with the points. The points below the lines are for 1942, 1943, 1944, 1945, 1918, 1917, and 1905, in that order from the lowest to the highest fraction of income consumed, and 1902 is only a trifle inside the line.[2] The first six points are all years of wartime inflation; and every year of wartime inflation is included among them. These are years in which one might expect both a positive mean transitory component of income and a negative mean transitory component of consumption: the former, because the wartime incomes were regarded as abnormally and temporarily high; the latter, because of unavailability of goods and patriotic drives to restrict consumption. Both would make for an abnormally low ratio of measured consumption to measured income. The other two points listed, 1902 and 1905, are for years of relatively high prosperity. Business annals record one of the deepest depressions on record in the 1890's, with a business cycle trough in 1894, an incomplete recovery to a submerged peak in 1895, and a relapse to another trough in 1897. A vigorous recovery, one of the sharpest on record, then occurred to a peak in 1899, followed by a mild and brief decline to 1900, and renewed but mild expansion to a peak in 1902. The subsequent decline from 1902 to 1904 is one of the mildest on record and was followed from 1904 to 1907 by a period of continued expansion. All told, the period from 1897 to 1907 was a period of expansion, punctuated by only brief and mild recessions. The year 1902 was a relative peak year in this expansion, the year 1905 a good year, though not a relative peak. In both years it is not

[2] There is a decided break between 1902 and the next higher observation (1899) in the array of points by fraction of income consumed. The fraction is .829 for 1902 and .843 for 1899, a difference of .014. So large a difference does not appear again as we proceed upwards in the array until we come to 1938, the first point above the upper line. The fraction for 1938 is .942, for 1911, the next lower observation, it is .924, a difference of .018. The largest difference between any two neighboring observations falling within the two light lines is .007. The existence of these gaps in the array was a major reason for choosing to locate the light lines ±5 percentage points from the center line.

unreasonable to suppose that the transitory component of income was positive and that this is the reason why recorded consumption was an abnormally low ratio of measured income.

The points above the upper light line are for 1933, 1932, 1934, 1921, 1931, 1935, 1897, and 1938, in that order from the highest ratio of consumption to income to the lowest. Every year is a year of deep depression; and there is no year that clearly deserves to be so designated that is excluded from the list. These are all, therefore, years in which the transitory component of income was negative: income was lower than it could be expected to be over the long pull. It is not surprising that consumption, being on our hypothesis adjusted to permanent income, was an abnormally high ratio of measured income.

As noted above, all points for the decade of the 1930's are above the heavy line, all but one of the points for the decade of the 1940's below the line. Considerations like those adduced in the preceding two paragraphs make it highly plausible that the transitory component of income was generally negative for the 1930's and positive for the 1940's. This seems a more satisfactory explanation than the sudden emergence of a secular trend.

The consistency of our hypothesis with the general pattern of Figure 13 is not, of course, very strong evidence for the hypothesis. All that has so far been shown is that the hypothesis can explain some of the more striking features of the behavior of savings in this country over the past half-century or so. The later sections of this chapter submit the hypothesis to the much more stringent test of its ability to explain detailed quantitative features of the behavior of these and similar data. But before proceeding to this test, it is interesting to speculate on possible reasons for the rather surprising secular constancy of the ratio of consumption to income revealed by these data, as well as by the various budget studies presented in the preceding chapter.

b. THE CONSTANCY OF k^*

The secular constancy of k^*, while consistent with the permanent income hypothesis, is not in any way required by it. Our hypothesis only says that k for the single consumer unit is a function of variables other than the current level of income; it does not say that k is a numerical constant for each unit, let alone the same constant for different units. Even if the function k were the same over time for each unit or each relevant kind of unit—to avoid the problem of aging—separately, its numerical value could change because of changes in the variables determining k; and even if its numerical value were the same, either because these variables were unchanged or offset one another or because the function was insensitive to their values, the value of k^* for the aggregate could vary because of changes in the relative number of units of various kinds. So the observed rough constancy of k^* is about as much of a puzzle as substantial variations in it would be.

Anything like an exhaustive investigation into this phenomenon is a study in itself; my purpose here is only to speculate about some of the major factors such a study would have to examine in detail.[3] Of the variables entering into k, two—the rate of interest and the ratio of wealth to income, or the ratio of nonhuman to human wealth—have probably affected savings in opposite directions. The rate of interest— i.e. some kind of an average rate of interest—apparently rose from the turn of the century to about 1920 and then declined over the next three decades, ending at a lower level than that at which it began.[4] However, the interpretation of these changes, recorded most fully in bond yields, is clouded by changes in price levels which make the nominal interest rates imperfect measures of "real" rates of return and by frequently divergent movements of rates of return on fixed dollar obligations and on equities. Taken at face value, the initial rise in the rate of return would have tended to lower k^* and the subsequent fall to raise it by an even larger amount. On the other hand, to judge by the fraction of the national income estimated to have been derived from property, the ratio of nonhuman to human wealth appears to have declined, though again the evidence is by no means unambiguous. Any such decline would, other things the same, tend to reduce k^*.

I turn from these movements to three others that are plainer to the naked eye and that, perhaps for that reason alone, I am inclined to regard as of more consequence for the behavior of k^*. These are (1) the sharp reduction in the fraction of the population on farms, (2) the changing distribution of consumer units by size, and (3) the altered role of the state in the provision of security.

Since the turn of the century, there has been a sharp decline in the fraction of consumer units deriving most of their income from the operation of a farm. There seems to have been no comparable change in either direction in the fraction engaged in other entrepreneurial activities. We saw in the preceding chapter that entrepreneurs, including farmers, tend to save a relatively high percentage of permanent

---

[3] Compare Goldsmith, *A Study of Saving*, I, pp. 6–8, 11–19.

[4] See, for example, W. Braddock Hickman, *The Volume of Corporate Bond Financing since 1900* (Princeton University Press for National Bureau of Economic Research, 1953), p. 129.

income. In consequence, the reduction in the relative number of farm families is a factor making for a reduction in the fraction of income saved or an increase in k^*. Very rough calculations suffice to give an idea of the possible order of magnitude of this effect. Farm operator families apparently receive currently something in excess of one-tenth of total personal disposable income.[5] To judge from changes in the number of farm families, the corresponding fraction could hardly have exceeded one-third in 1900. Suppose farmers then and now saved on the average 20 per cent of their income, a figure that if anything seems too high on the evidence of the preceding chapter; and nonfarmers, 11 per cent. These numbers would imply average savings for both groups combined of 14 per cent in 1900, and of 12 per cent (approximately the observed percentage) currently, or a decline of 2 percentage points in the fraction of income saved. This is surely the maximum possible effect that can be attributed to this factor.

Since the turn of the century, there has been a sharp decline in the average size of the family, from nearly 5 persons per census family to approximately 3.5 persons, or a decline of about 30 per cent. In addition, there has been a change in the distribution of families by size; the extremely large families have become relatively less numerous so that the reduction in average size has been associated with, and in a measure produced by, a greater homogeneity of families by size. It has frequently been argued that the ratio of savings to income decreases as size of family increases. Unfortunately, the statistical evidence for this proposition is marred by the use of an inappropriate technique in deriving it. The studies that I know about have all examined the influence of size of family while holding measured income constant; they have used, that is, the partial correlation technique discussed above in section 2f of Chapter IV. But average income, and presumably average permanent income, tend to increase with size of family. In consequence, even though permanent consumption were the same fraction of permanent income for families of different size, measured consumption for a given measured income would tend to increase with size of family, and so produce the observed statistical results.

It is my impression from rather unsystematic but somewhat more than casual examination of the evidence that this deficiency of analysis does not account for the whole of the observed effect of size of family, that even if comparisons were made at the mean incomes of the several sizes of family, consumption would be found to be a larger

[5] See, for example, Department of Commerce, Office of Business Economics, *Income Distribution in the United States by Size, 1944–1950*, (Washington, 1953), pp. 8–11.

fraction of income, the larger the family.[6] And this statistical impression is consistent with a priori expectations. Children are, after all, a way of achieving security for old age; indeed in many cultures, the primary way. The raising of children can be viewed as a form of capital accumulation, only of human rather than nonhuman capital.[7] One might expect a reduction of savings in this form to be accompanied by an increase in other forms, and our statistics treat as savings only these other forms, so such a shift of form would show up in our data as an increase in savings. At any given time, those families that have fewer children than their neighbors and so are not providing as fully for their security in this form, might be expected to provide more fully in other ways. Over time, the changes in customs that are reducing the extent of reliance on one's children for security in old age—changes which are themselves both a cause and a consequence of the changing size of family—tend to promote accumulation of nonhuman capital. On both grounds, the reduction in the average size of family in the United States is a factor that, by itself, would have produced an increase in the fraction of income recorded as saved and hence a decrease in the observed value of k.

A rough idea of the possible order of magnitude of this effect can be obtained by disregarding the bias in the statistical measurement of the size of family effect. Dorothy Brady has estimated that, for a given measured income, consumption expenditures are proportional to the sixth root of the number of members of the family.[8] This implies that a family of 5 members spends 6 per cent more on consumption than a family of 3.5, or that if consumption of a family of 3.5 is 88 per cent of its income (the approximate average propensity according to Goldsmith's data), the consumption of a family of 5 would be almost 93 per cent of its income. Now this doubtless overestimates the effect of the change in family size, both because of the statistical bias that we have neglected and because it disregards the increased homogeneity of families by size, allowance for which would reduce the amount of correction called for.[9] Yet it makes clear that

[6] This statement oversimplifies the comparison required, since account would have to be taken of any factors that might make average measured income and consumption for a given family size differ from average permanent income and consumption.

[7] Size of family as measured by the Census at any given time is not the same thing as size of family in the sense relevant to this argument, for which the number of children who survive, whether or not they live with their parents, would perhaps be the best measure. A census family may be small because the children have set up separate families. My language is therefore inexact since I use size of families in these two different senses. I believe, however, that this inexactness is not a source of error; there tends to be a high correlation between size of family in the two senses.

[8] See Dorothy Brady, in Goldsmith, Brady, and Mendershausen, *A Study of Saving in the United States*, III, p. 211.

[9] Strictly speaking, the adjustment should be computed not for the arithmetic means

this effect is potentially of substantial magnitude. Perhaps it would not, by itself, have produced the rise of 5 percentage points in the fraction of income saved that these calculations suggest; but it might easily have offset or more than offset the decline of 2 percentage points that we estimated as the maximum possible effect of the decline in the relative number of farmers. This effect of changing size of family is hardly ever mentioned in discussions of the secular trend of savings;[10] yet it may be one of the major factors at work.

Over the period covered by these data, a drastic change has occurred in the responsibilities undertaken by the state to provide assistance to the aged, unemployed, and otherwise dependent. This change has had divergent results on the particular data under discussion. The availability of assistance from the state would clearly tend to reduce the need for private reserves and so to reduce private saving—it is equivalent, in terms of our hypothesis, to a reduction in the variance of transitory components. However, the data under discussion include as personal savings the increases in government pension and retirement funds. If these fully matched the corresponding increase in the present value of accumulated benefits, the combined result might be expected to be an increase in recorded savings: a dollar in the form of a reserve held by the government and available to the individual only under narrowly specified circumstances is worth less to him than a dollar in privately held reserves that he can dispose of at will; in consequence, each dollar increase in government held reserve would tend to produce less than a dollar decrease in private savings. In fact, however, social security obligations are not fully funded; the increase in accumulated benefits exceeds the increase in government pension and retirement funds. It may well be, therefore. that the increase in these funds has been less than the decrease in private savings that the existence of the corresponding benefit programs has produced. The conclusion is that, without much more detailed analysis, it is not possible to say whether the net effect of governmental social security and other programs has been to increase or to decrease recorded savings as a fraction of income, let alone by how much.[11]

These speculations are highly inconclusive, and a fuller and more

---

alone but for the whole distribution, or, what comes to the same thing, for the geometric means of the distribution.

[10] The discussion by Brady, *ibid.*, is a notable exception.

[11] Another factor similar in kind to the emergence of savings through government is saving through corporations, either in the form of undistributed corporate profits or pension rights. I have neglected these; the first, because Goldsmith's figures show it to have been a roughly constant fraction of savings over the period covered; the second, because it has started to become quantitatively important after the period in question.

satisfactory analysis is much to be desired, but perhaps they suffice to show that there have been offsetting forces at work on the ratio of consumption to income. If these forces had all been in one direction, particularly if they had all been working in the direction of reduced saving, the observed constancy would tell against our hypothesis and for the more usual absolute income hypothesis, since it would be tempting to call in the rising average real income as a counterweight to the other factors. The fact that the forces here mentioned have been in different directions is hardly strong evidence for our hypothesis, but at least it raises no disturbing questions about the consistency of the hypothesis with the observed constancy of k^*.

We noted in the preceding chapter that the average propensity computed from United States budget studies was remarkably constant over a period of some six decades. Three major points have to be allowed for before the apparent agreement between this finding and the constancy shown by Goldsmith's data can be regarded as additional evidence that k^* has been roughly constant. (1) As noted in section 2d of Chapter IV, the earlier budget studies were for wage earners alone, the later studies, for a broader group. The use of withdrawals as a measure of income for entrepreneurial groups lessens the resulting noncomparability of the figures but probably does not eliminate it entirely. If the figures were corrected for this difference in coverage, presumably they would show a secular increase in the ratio of consumption to income or decrease in the savings ratio. (2) Goldsmith's savings figures include the value of the increase in the stock of durable goods; the budget data do not. Goldsmith points out that consumer durable goods account for an increasing fraction of savings and that the ratio of savings excluding consumer durable goods to income has declined over the period covered.[12] The decline is of the order of 2 percentage points. Adjustment of the budget study data to exclude the value of the increase in the stock of consumer durable goods from consumption and to include it in savings would therefore make for a secular decrease in the ratio of consumption to income or increase in the savings ratio. (3) The consumer budget data do not include the increase in government pension and retirement funds as savings. Inclusion of these items would make for a secular decrease in the ratio of consumption to income or increase in the savings ratio.

The consistency of the budget data and the time series data presumably means that points (2) and (3) just about offset point (1). In view of the likely size of these effects, such a result seems not at all implausible.

[12] See Goldsmith, *A Study of Saving in the United States*, I, p. 7.

2. *Regressions of Consumption on Current Income*

Table 12 summarizes some of the consumption-income relations that have been computed for the United States both by Goldsmith, from the data considered in the preceding section, and by Ferber, from related data compiled by him. As for the budget studies summarized in Table 1 of the preceding chapter, the computed marginal propensity is below the computed average propensity for every relation in Table 12, so that the elasticity of consumption with respect to measured income is uniformly less than unity. We have noted repeatedly how this is required by our hypothesis and how, in light of the highly stable average propensity, it makes it impossible to regard the computed functions as stable relations between consumption and income.

The marginal propensities to consume recorded in Table 12 vary much more widely than the average propensities; in consequence, so do the income elasticities of consumption, which are the ratios of the marginal propensities to the average propensities. The recorded marginal propensities vary from .45 to .93; the recorded elasticities, from .48 to 1.00. In small part, these differences reflect differences in the definition of consumption and in the basic data (section b below). For the most part, however, they reflect differences in the periods covered by the series from which they were computed. The marginal propensity and elasticity tend to be relatively low when the period covered is short, and especially when it includes the Great Depression; they tend to be higher, the longer the period covered. How this result fits our hypothesis is considered in section a below. These marginal propensities and income elasticities vary much more widely than the corresponding values for the United States computed from budget studies and recorded in Table 1. Why this should be so is considered in section c below.

a. EFFECT OF PERIOD COVERED

On the simple model under consideration, two features of the period covered can be expected to affect the observed income elasticity: its length, and its particular historical characteristics.

The length of the period is important because, other things the same, P_{y^*}, and so the observed income elasticity, can be expected to be higher, the longer the period covered, provided that the society in question is undergoing a systematic secular change in income. The total variance of income equals the variance contributed by the transitory component plus the variance contributed by the permanent component, given our assumption that the two components are

TABLE 12

Relation between Consumption and Income Based on Time Series Data for the United States,
for Different Periods and Concepts of Consumption

Period Covered	Concept of Consumption Expenditure	Average Disposable Income per Capita (1929 prices)	Average Propensity to Consume[a]	Marginal Propensity to Consume[b]	Income Elasticity of Consumption[c]
A. Based on Data and Computations of Robert Ferber					
1. 1929 through 1940	D	$489	.97	.78	.80
2. 1923 through 1940	D	490	.97	.79	.82
3. 1923 through 1930, 1935 through 1940	D	510	.96	.93	.97
B. Based on Data and Computations of Raymond Goldsmith					
4. 1897 through 1949, excl. 1917, 1918, 1930 through 1933, 1942 through 1945	D	$559	.91	.91	.996
5. 1897 through 1949	D	578	.89	.74	.83
6. 1897 through 1906	ND	420	.89	.72	.81
7. 1907 through 1916	ND	495	.89	.65	.73
8. 1919 through 1929	ND	591	.88	.60	.68
9. 1929 through 1941	ND	607	.94	.45	.48
10. 1897 through 1914	ND	451	.89	.87	.97
11. 1915 through 1929	ND	581	.87	.69	.80
12. 1930 through 1949	ND	691	.87	.46	.53
13. 1897 through 1949, excl. 1917, 1918, 1942 through 1945	ND	558	.90	.82	.91
14. 1897 through 1949	ND	578	.88	.70	.80

D = Consumption includes expenditure on consumer durable goods.

ND = Consumption excludes expenditure on consumer durable goods; includes estimated value of services rendered by durable goods.

[a] Ratio of average consumption expenditure for indicated period to average income for same period.

[b] Throughout the value of b in a regression of the form $c = a + by$, where c = personal consumption expenditure per capita in constant prices, y = personal disposable income per capita in constant prices.

[c] Ratio of the marginal propensity to consume to the average propensity to consume, as defined in notes a and b. It is therefore the elasticity of the regression at the point corresponding to mean income and mean consumption.

Source:

Part A, Robert Ferber, *A Study of Aggregate Consumption Functions*, National Bureau of Economic Research, Technical Paper 8, 1953. Part B, average disposable income and average consumption computed from annual data for 1897 to 1949 made available by Raymond W. Goldsmith and based on his *A Study of Saving in the United States*, Princeton University Press, 1956, Vol. I, Table T-1, col. 2, and Table T-6, col. 1 minus col. 5; Vol. III, Part V, Table N-2, col. 5. Marginal propensity to consume equal to 1 minus marginal propensity to save in Vol. III, Part IV, Table Y-1, p. 393, and Table Y-4, p. 400.

uncorrelated. The variance contributed by the transitory component is not systematically affected by lengthening the period; by definition, the transitory components are largely random and short-lived. True, the variance may be larger at one time than another—this is why the historical characteristics of the period are important—but there is no reason why it should be systematically larger or smaller for a long than for a short period.[13] The variance contributed by the permanent component, on the other hand, tends to be systematically larger, the longer the period covered; the more widely separated two dates are, the larger the secular difference in income between them tends to be. As between two neighboring years, the change in the permanent component may well be small relative to the change in the transitory component. On the other hand, between 1900 and 1950, say, any transitory effect is almost certain to be swamped by the secular change in the permanent component. P_{y*}, the ratio of the variance contributed by the permanent component to the total variance, will therefore tend to be higher, the longer the period, and to approach unity as the period is indefinitely lengthened. If secular change were the only source of variation in the permanent component, the lower limit of P_{y*} would be zero and this limit would tend to be approached as the length of the period covered approached zero. Since there are other sources of variation in the permanent component, all one can say is that P_{y*} tends to approach some lower limit greater than zero as the length of the period approaches zero.

The figures in Table 12 conform to this expectation very well indeed. In almost every case, the elasticity for a longer period is higher than for the shorter periods contained within it, if the data are otherwise comparable—note that lines 3, 4, and 13 do not refer to shorter periods than lines 2, 5, and 14, respectively, but to regressions computed on the basis of only some of the years within periods of the same length; these comparisons are considered separately below. For Ferber's data, only one comparison is possible, between lines 1 and 2. The elasticity for line 2, the longer period, is higher than for line 1. For Goldsmith's data, the calculations shown on page 128 summarize the results.

If a steady secular trend were the only factor producing differences in permanent income, it would be possible to predict the quantitative as well as the qualitative effect of lengthening the period. For example, if the income elasticity were .675 for each 11 year period, it would be .974 for a 47 year period; if it were .765 for each 18 year

---

[13] This statement should be taken as referring to the variance of logarithmic components, or the ratio of the variance to the square of the mean income, or else the mean income should be impounded in *caeteris paribus*.

Lines	Average Length of Period (years)	Years Included	Average Income Elasticity
6, 7, 8, 9	10.75	1897 through 1941, excl. 1917, 1918	.675
13	47	1897 through 1949, excl. 1917, 1918, 1942 through 1945	.912
10, 11, 12	17.67	1897 through 1949	.765
14	53	1897 through 1949	.798

period, it would be .965 for a 53 year period.[14] As these examples show, the effect of lengthening the period, when computed in this way, is uniformly greater than the effect revealed by Table 12. And this is as it should be. For factors other than secular trend produce differences in permanent income so that the computed figures are estimates of the maximum effect to be expected, on our hypothesis, from lengthening the period. It would be most disturbing if the observed effects exceeded these maxima; the fact that they do not lends some minor additional support to our hypothesis.

Comparison of line 2 with line 3, line 4 with line 5, and line 13 with line 14 testifies to the effect of the character of the period covered. In each case, the two regressions in a pair are for data covering the same time span; however, one is based on data for fewer years within that time span. In each case, the years excluded are not an arbitrarily chosen set of years at the beginning or end of the period but years regarded as "abnormal." These years are bunched and come somewhere inside the period, so they do not reduce the range of variation in the permanent component introduced by secular factors. Their exclusion may reduce the variance contributed by the permanent component, but if so, by a much smaller amount than if the corresponding number of years were taken from one end or the other of the period; it is even possible that their exclusion increases the variance

---

[14] Let $y_p = a + xt$ be the permanent component, where x is the constant increment per time unit and t stands for time. The variance of the permanent component for any period is then $x^2(n^2 - 1)/12$, where n is the number of time units in the period. Let σ^2 stand for the variance contributed by the transitory component. Then

$$P_y = \frac{x^2 \left(\dfrac{n^2 - 1}{12} \right)}{x^2 \left(\dfrac{n^2 - 1}{12} \right) + \sigma^2} = \frac{\dfrac{n^2 - 1}{12}}{\dfrac{n^2 - 1}{12} + \dfrac{\sigma^2}{x^2}}.$$

Given P_y and n, one can compute σ^2/x^2; given σ^2/x^2 and n, one can compute P_y, which is how the figures in the text were obtained.

contributed by the permanent component. On the other hand, the "abnormal" years are clearly characterized by relatively high transitory components of income, so their exclusion lowers the variance contributed by the transitory component much more than the exclusion of the same number of years chosen at random. The exclusion of "abnormal" years might therefore be expected to *raise* rather than lower P_{y^*} and so to have an effect precisely the opposite of that produced by dropping years from the beginning or end of the period. The systematic increase in the computed elasticity in Table 12 when "abnormal" years are eliminated is therefore fully consistent with, and indeed predicted by, our hypothesis.

There is a strong tendency in Table 12 for elasticities for short periods that include the Great Depression to be low: the elasticity in line 9 is less than in lines 6, 7, or 8; in line 12, than in lines 10 or 11. The explanation is presumably the large variation in the transitory component of income during this period and the resultant relatively low value of P_{y^*}.

b. EFFECT OF FORM OF DATA

The relations summarized in Table 12 are all between figures on consumption and income expressed per capita and deflated to correct for price changes. Similar relations have been computed between per capita figures in current prices and between aggregates, both deflated and in current prices. How, on our hypothesis, would one expect the form of the data to affect the results?

Consider, first, correction for population. Since the population of the United States has been growing secularly along with income, the secular rate of rise of aggregate real income has been decidedly higher than of per capita real income—approximately 3 per cent per year rather than 2 per cent. Along the lines of the analysis of the preceding section, this increases the variance in the permanent component contributed by secular factors. On the other hand, there seems little reason why the variance of the transitory component should be any larger, and some why it should be smaller, in aggregate figures than in per capita figures (provided, of course, allowance is made for the difference in the absolute level of the two series). Population change proceeds smoothly and so is not likely to be an important source of random or transitory movements in either aggregate or per capita income.

To put the point in another way, our aggregate function is the summation of functions for individual consumer units. The aggregate permanent component is the sum of the permanent components for the separate consumer units; the aggregate transitory component, the sum of the transitory components. The consumer unit can be viewed as reacting to a permanent component expressed either per capita or as a total for the consumer unit. Long-run changes in number or size of consumer units, or short-run changes that are anticipated, introduce transitory elements into neither total nor per capita income. They simply change either the number of units for which permanent components are aggregated or the relation between total and per capita components. Their effect on the variance of the permanent components depends on the facts of the situation.

If it so happened that population growth was accompanied by a decline in per capita income, aggregate income might vary less over time than per capita income. In fact, of course, in the United States population growth has been accompanied by a rise in per capita income, so the (relative) variance of the permanent component clearly tends to be greater for aggregate than for per capita income. Unanticipated short-run changes in either the number of consumer units or their size do not affect the permanent components; they do introduce transitory elements. Whether the effect is larger for aggregate or per capita income depends again on the particular circumstances. It may be conjectured that the most frequent source of such unanticipated changes is the birth of children, which might be expected in general to have no effect on the total income of the consumer unit while introducing a transitory component into per capita income. If this is so, unanticipated population changes would increase the (relative) variance of transitory components more for per capita than for aggregate income. The effects of population changes on the permanent and transitory components thus reinforce one another: both make for a larger value of P_{y^*} for aggregate than for per capita figures. On our hypothesis, we are therefore led to expect income elasticities to be higher when computed from aggregate than from per capita data.

Long-run or anticipated short-run changes in prices have much the same effect as corresponding changes in population: they introduce no transitory elements into either current or deflated income. Again, their effect on the variance of the permanent component depends on the facts. If prices tended to be high when output was low, and low when output was high, current income would vary less than deflated income. Again, the facts are the reverse. Over the past fifty years, prices have on the average displayed a secular rise and so has output; within the period, prices and output have generally tended to move together during cyclical swings. The relation is much the same during the two wartime periods.[15]

[15] A minor qualification is required for these periods: prices and aggregate output

In consequence, the variance of the permanent component can clearly be expected to be greater for current than for deflated income. It is much more difficult to make a firm judgment about the effect of unanticipated short-run changes in prices. They introduce transitory elements into both current and deflated income; and, in the short run, movements in prices and output are more likely to be negatively related than over rather longer periods. Nonetheless, it seems not implausible that even in short-run periods, unanticipated changes in prices introduce larger transitory changes into current than into deflated income. On this analysis, the variance of both the permanent and transitory components is larger for current than for deflated income, so that an unambiguous conclusion cannot be reached about the size of P_{y^*}, though there is perhaps some presumption that the effect on the permanent components, being clearer, also tends to be larger and hence that P_{y^*} is generally larger for current than for deflated income. This very weak result can be sharpened by taking account of the length of the period. Along the lines of the preceding section, the effect on the transitory component is independent of the length of period covered; the effect on the permanent component increases with the length of the period. We are therefore led to expect, on our hypothesis, that income elasticities will generally tend to be higher for the United States when computed from current than from deflated income; that this tendency will be strongest when the period covered is fairly long, and that it may be weak or non-existent for short periods.

These predictions about the effect of correcting for population and price changes correspond closely to the available evidence. Table 13 gives marginal propensities to consume computed by Ferber and Goldsmith from time series data in different forms and for various periods. Our predictions are, it is true, in terms of income elasticities rather than marginal propensities. However, since the average propensity to consume is likely to differ only negligibly with the form of the data, the marginal propensities on any one line are approximately in the same proportion as the elasticities, so it did not seem worth computing the elasticities.[16]

---

moved together, but at times prices and the fraction of output corresponding to disposable consumer income may have moved in opposite directions.

[16] For each year separately, of course, the ratio of consumption to income is identically the same regardless of the form of the data, provided the same population and price series are used to deflate both consumption and income. For any period of years, however, the ratio of average consumption to average income need not be the same, since this is a weighted average of the ratios for the individual years and the weights are different for the different forms of the data. However, these differences in weights are hardly likely to lead to sizable changes in the ratio of the averages.

TABLE 13

Marginal Propensities to Consume Computed from Four Different Forms of
Time Series Data for the United States

| Period Covered | Concept of Consumption Expenditure | Marginal Propensity to Consume | | | |
| | | Current Prices | | Deflated | |
		Aggregate	Per Capita	Aggregate	Per Capita
		A. Computed by Robert Ferber			
1. 1929 through 1940	D	.848	.853	.800	.777
2. 1923 through 1940	D	.864	.870	.858	.792
3. 1923 through 1930, 1935 through 1940	D	.965	.947	.964	.934
		B. Computed by Raymond Goldsmith			
4. 1897 through 1929	D	.89			.82
5. 1897 through 1949, excl. 1917, 1918, 1930 through 1933, 1942 through 1945	D	.913			.907
6. 1897 through 1949	D	.84			.74
7. 1897 through 1906	ND	.80	.78	.77	.72
8. 1907 through 1916	ND	.77	.72	.65	.65
9. 1919 through 1929	ND	.72	.67	.74	.60
10. 1929 through 1941	ND	.60	.60	.52	.45
11. 1897 through 1914	ND	.90	.89	.89	.87
12. 1915 through 1929	ND	.89	.89	.84	.69
13. 1930 through 1949	ND	.75	.72	.58	.46
14. 1923 through 1940	ND	.57	.60	.60	.36
15. 1915 through 1929, excl. 1917, 1918	ND	.87	.88	.82	.73
16. 1930 through 1949, excl. 1942 through 1945	ND	.81	.80	.69	.61
17. 1897 through 1929	ND	.86	.86	.84	.78
18. 1897 through 1941	ND	.88	.86	.89	.82
19. 1897 through 1949, excl. 1917, 1918, 1942 through 1945	ND	.86	.86	.86	.82
20. 1897 through 1949	ND	.81	.80	.79	.70

D = Consumption includes expenditure on consumer durable goods.
ND = Consumption excludes expenditure on consumer durable goods; includes estimated value of services rendered by durable goods.
Source:
Lines 1 to 3, Robert Ferber, *A Study of Aggregate Consumption Functions*, National Bureau of Economic Research, Technical Paper 8, 1953. Lines 4 to 20, Raymond W. Goldsmith, *A Study of Saving in the United States*, Princeton University Press, 1956, Vol. III, Table Y-1, p. 393, Table Y-4, p. 400.

The effect of using per capita rather than aggregate data is as follows:

Marginal Propensity for Aggregate Data	Number of Entries for:		
	Current Data	Deflated Data	Total
Greater than for per capita	9	16	25
Same	4	1	5
Less than for per capita	4	0	4
Total	17	17	34

There are only four clear exceptions to the predicted tendency for marginal propensies to be greater when computed from aggregate than from per capita data, and even these are illuminated by the preceding analysis. All four are for current data. Two are for the period 1923 through 1940, the other two for 1929 through 1940, and 1915 through 1929 (excluding 1917 and 1918). Because of the Great Depression, the correlation for 1923 through 1940 between changes in population and in real output is probably negative; and between changes in population and money income in current dollars—which is what is relevant—almost certainly negative; much the same is true for 1929 through 1940 though to a smaller extent; for 1915 through 1929, the real output correlation is positive, but the sharp drop in prices in 1921 and the generally lower level in the 1920's may well have made the money-income correlation negative. These cases are, therefore, exceptions to the explicit prediction but not to the analysis leading to it.

The effect of using deflated rather than current data is as follows:

Marginal Propensity for Current Data	Number of Entries for:		
	Aggregate Data	Per Capita Data	Total
Greater than for deflated	13	17	30
Same	1	0	1
Less than for deflated	3	0	3
Total	17	17	34

The general tendency is again as predicted; indeed, even more clearly than for the preceding comparison. This result is a bit disturbing, since our analysis leads to a more unambiguous conclusion about the effect of adjusting for population change than for prices. Presumably, the explanation is to be found in a factor neglected in our earlier

133

analysis: the relative size of the longer-term movements in population and prices. Population roughly doubled from 1900 to 1950; consumer prices considerably more than doubled from 1900 to 1920, fell by well over a third from 1920 to 1933, and then nearly doubled by 1948, so that by 1950, prices were about triple their level in 1900, and there had been a substantial additional movement within the period. Both the larger secular movement in prices than in population and the tendency for prices and output to move together during many of the shorter swings enhanced the effect of correcting for price changes on the variance of the permanent component.

The exceptions to the general tendency are less illuminating for prices than for population. They are for aggregate data and 1919 through 1929, 1923 through 1940, and 1897 through 1941. Only one is for the kind of brief period for which our analysis suggests exceptions, and there is not much all three have in common which distinguishes them from the rest of the observations.

The three comparisons in Table 13 not included in the preceding summaries, lines 4, 5, and 6, all conform to expectation: the marginal propensity is larger when computed from current aggregate data than from deflated per capita data, both adjustments working in the same direction.

The entries in Table 13 are by no means all independent. The Ferber and Goldsmith data have common roots; many of the relations computed by each are for periods that overlap or that differ only by the inclusion or exclusion of a few years. The number of comparisons listed in the preceding summary tables therefore greatly overstates the number of independent observations, a consideration that reduces the significance to be attached to this agreement between experience and the implications of our hypothesis.

C. THE RELATION BETWEEN TIME SERIES AND BUDGET ELASTICITIES

On our hypothesis, income elasticities of consumption computed from time series data and from budget data are estimates of different things. Neither tells anything directly about consumption behavior—or rather adds anything to what is incorporated in our hypothesis. Both measure instead a feature of the income structure, and they measure different features. The budget elasticity measures the fraction of the variance of the incomes of a group of consumer units *at a point in time* contributed by differences in permanent components. The time series elasticity measures the fraction of the variance of aggregate or per capita incomes of a *series of time units* contributed by differences in permanent components. These two features of the income structure are not entirely unrelated. If, for example, all differences among consumer units were attributable to permanent components, the transitory component, being zero for each unit, would be zero for all taken together. In consequence, all differences among years (or other time units) would also be attributable to differences in permanent components, so the income elasticity would, on our hypothesis, be unity whether computed from budget data or time series data. At the other extreme, the connection is much looser. Even if all differences among consumer units were transitory, so that all had the same permanent component, this common permanent component might, and presumably would, change from year to year; on our hypothesis, the elasticity computed from budget data would be zero; the elasticity computed from time series data would be greater than zero and, indeed, might be close to unity, since the transitory component could average out nearly to zero for each time unit separately. The relation is equally loose for the intermediate cases. The influence of the first extreme gives some reason to expect that if, say, the elasticity computed from budget data is systematically higher for comparable groups for country A than for country B, the elasticity computed from time series data for periods of equal length will also be higher for country A. But I have not been able to find any way to predict the quantitative relation between the two.

We have seen that time series elasticities depend critically on the length and character of the period covered: they tend to be low for short periods, and to increase with the length of the period covered, at least for communities experiencing a secular change in income. Budget elasticities depend primarily on the characteristics of the group covered. Consider a fairly broad group within which there are substantial differences in permanent income so that the elasticity is reasonably high—say urban or all families in the United States for whom the elasticity is about .8. The time series elasticity might then be expected to be less than this elasticity when computed from data for a short period, and to exceed it when computed from data for a long period. The length of period for which the two are equal cannot be expected to be a constant; it depends critically on the characteristics of the period, being relatively short for a period characterized by rapid and smooth secular progress, relatively long for a period characterized by stagnation and violent short-period movements, For example, for the 10 year period, 1897 through 1906, which was just such a period of rather smooth and rapid growth, the elasticity computed by Goldsmith (.81) about equals the budget elasticity; for the 12 year period, 1929 through 1941, which was a period of stagnation and sharp short-period movements, the elasticity computed by Goldsmith (.48) is decidedly less than the budget elasticity; for the whole 53 year period, 1897 through 1949, which is very much of a mixture of periods of smooth, rapid growth and periods of violent short-term movements, the elasticity (.80) is about equal to the budget elasticity. The relevant period is thus in the one case 10 years, in the other, over 50 years.

One other feature brought out in our earlier discussion of Table 12 deserves attention: the apparently greater variability among time series elasticities than among budget elasticities for similar groups. One reason why this is to be expected on our hypothesis is explicit in the preceding discussion: the effect of length of period covered means that the time series elasticities in Table 12 are estimates of different things, and consequently vary for a reason that does not apply to budget elasticities for similar groups. Another reason is implicit in the discussion of the character of the period covered: the time series elasticities are computed for very small effective samples—at most, 53 items; such samples can therefore be expected to differ widely among themselves, and so to yield widely differing estimates of the value of P_{y^*}, even if, in some sense, P_{y^*} is not subject to long-run secular change. The budget elasticities, on the other hand, are computed from very much larger samples, generally numbering in the thousands. Put differently, both types of elasticities vary for two reasons: underlying differences from time to time in the characteristics of the income structure that they estimate, and sampling errors. Both sources of variation can be expected to be larger for time series elasticities: the first, because of the importance of length of period; the second, because of the drastically smaller size of sample.

A number of attempts have been made in recent years to combine budget and time series data in computing statistical demand functions for particular commodities.[17] The procedure is generally to compute from budget data an income elasticity of expenditures on the particular commodity or category of consumption for which the demand function is being computed. This income elasticity is taken to apply more or less directly to aggregate data reported in time series. The remaining parameters in the desired demand function are then estimated from time series data.

It is clear that, on our hypothesis, this procedure is erroneous. Though stated in terms of the elasticity of total expenditures, our conclusion that elasticities computed from budget data and from time

[17] See, for example, James Tobin, "A Statistical Demand Function for Food in the U.S.A.," *Journal of the Royal Statistical Society*, Series A, CXIII (1950), pp. 113–140; Herman Wold, *op. cit.*, pp. 228–234, and Richard Stone (assisted by D. A. Rowe and W. J. Cortlett, Renée Hurstfield, Muriel Potter), *The Measurement of Consumers' Expenditure and Behaviour in the United Kingdom 1920–1938*, I (The University Press, Cambridge, 1954), pp. 275–278.

series are estimates of different magnitudes applies also to the elasticity for a particular category (for a fuller discussion, see Chapter VIII, section 2). The income elasticity computed from budget data cannot be expected to be the same (on the average) as that computed from time series data for a particular span of years unless transitory components of income have the same importance for the two bodies of data. There is no reason to expect the transitory components to have the same importance, and, as we have seen, if they do for one span of years, they will not for a longer or shorter span. (See Chapter VIII, section 2, for some suggestions about other ways of combining budget and time series data.)

3. Regressions of Consumption on Current and Past Income

The lack of success in predicting consumption by means of simple regressions of consumption on income like those considered in the preceding section led to experiments with more complicated functions. In connection with their emphasis on relative income position, Modigliani and Duesenberry expressed consumption as a function of the ratio of current income to the highest level of income previously experienced. Ruth Mack, in connection with her emphasis on changes in income, expressed consumption as a function of income in the current year and the change in income from the preceding year. These equations readily lend themselves to interpretation in terms of our hypothesis, and this interpretation in turn suggests an extension of them.

a. FUNCTIONS BY MODIGLIANI, DUESENBERRY, AND MACK

The relations computed by Modigliani and Duesenberry are of the form

$$(5.1) \qquad \frac{c^*}{y^*} = f\left(\frac{y^*}{y_0^*}\right),$$

where y_0^* is the highest income experienced prior to the year in question, and all the variables are deflated and expressed per capita. If this relation is computed from a regression of the consumption ratio (or equally the savings ratio) on the income ratio,—or from the regression of consumption (or savings) on y^* and y_0^*,—and if the transitory component of consumption can be regarded as having a mean of zero, then, on our assumptions, c^* on the left hand side of the computed regression can be replaced by c_p^*, just as in the corresponding regressions from family budget data.

In our simple model,

$$(2.10) \qquad c_p^* = k^* y_p^*,$$

or

(5.2) $$\frac{c_p^*}{y^*} = k^* \frac{y_p^*}{y^*},$$

so the righthand side of (5.1) is to be interpreted as an estimate of the righthand side of (5.2). A plausible way to do so is to regard the introduction of y_0^* as a means of estimating the permanent component. It hardly seems reasonable to regard y_0^* itself as an estimate of the permanent component since this would mean that the estimated permanent component would remain unchanged during a decline and subsequent recovery to a new peak. It seems more reasonable to regard a weighted average of y_0^* and y^* as an estimate of y_p^*, say:

(5.3) $$\text{Estimate of } y_p^* = w_1 y_0^* + w_2 y^*,$$

where

(5.4) $$w_1 + w_2 = 1.$$

In some of his regressions, Modigliani introduces the income of the preceding year, say y_{-1}^*, as a variable. In these cases we can expand (5.3) to

(5.5) $$\text{Estimate of } y_p^* = w_1 y_0^* + w_2 y^* + w_3 y_{-1}^*,$$

where

(5.6) $$w_1 + w_2 + w_3 = 1.$$

Inserting (5.5) in (5.2), and replacing c_p^* by c^*, gives

(5.7) $$\frac{c^*}{y^*} = \frac{k^*(w_1 y_0^* + w_2 y^* + w_3 y_{-1}^*)}{y^*}$$

$$= k^* w_1 \frac{y_0^*}{y^*} + k^* w_2 + k^* w_3 \frac{y_{-1}^*}{y^*}.$$

This is precisely the form of some of the regressions computed by Modigliani, though for the regressions for which he uses this form he omits y_{-1}^*, i.e. takes $w_3 = 0$. The form that Modigliani uses for the rest of his regressions can be obtained by multiplying both sides of (5.7) by y^* and adding a constant term to the righthand side to give:

(5.8) $$c^* = a + k^* w_1 y_0^* + k^* w_2 y^* + k^* w_3 y_{-1}^*,$$

though of course in neither case does he use our notation. With one exception—his regressions for Sweden—Modigliani finds that the constant term is not statistically significant, so that, with this one exception, his numerical regressions are essentially in the form (5.7).

Duesenberry uses a form slightly different from (5.7), namely,

$$\frac{c^*}{y^*} = a + b\frac{y^*}{y_0^*}.$$

This can be converted into the form (5.7) by replacing y^*/y_0^* by its approximation by a Taylor series in y_0^*/y^*.

Mack uses the function

(5.9)
$$c^* = a + by^* + c\,\Delta y^*$$
$$= a + by^* + c(y^* - y_{-1}^*),$$

which requires only minor rearrangement to be put into the same form as (5.8), with $w_1 = 0$.

The values of k^* and w_1, w_2, and w_3 implied by the various functions calculated by Modigliani, Duesenberry, and Mack can be determined readily by using equations (5.6), (5.7), and (5.8); the results are summarized in the upper half of Table 14.

The differences among the values of k^* reflect at least in part, and perhaps in major part, differences in definition. The lowest value, for Canada, is for the ratio of consumption not to income but to gross national product, which is necessarily larger than income. For Sweden, the computed regression, which is of the form described by (5.8) has a significant constant term. This is consistent neither with our hypothesis nor with the results for the remaining regressions, and means that the unbracketed value of k^* in the table, computed by neglecting the constant term, understates the average ratio of consumption to income. Allowance for this understatement raises k^* to about .93, more nearly in line with the other values in the table.

There is some similarity, though it is not marked, in the weights assigned to the different incomes. In all cases, the highest previous income receives a weight decidedly less than one-half; it is as low as one-seventh in two cases. Considerably greater similarity emerges in the lower half of the table, which presents the recomputations of these relations by Ferber using the same data and comparable periods for all the relations. However, the appearance of increased homogeneity in the lower half of the table reflects mainly the exclusion of the Canadian and Swedish results rather than the greater comparability of the data and periods.

The practical identity of Ferber's recomputations of the Modigliani and Duesenberry equations is a purely arithmetic result: the two equations, as our earlier discussion shows, are algebraic transformations of one another and so can yield different results only because they imply different statistical methods of estimating the parameters

TABLE 14

Selected Measures Derived from Regressions of Consumption on Current and
Past Income Computed by Modigliani, Duesenberry, and Mack, and
Recomputed by Ferber

Country, Years Covered, Income Variable	Ratio of Permanent Consumption to Permanent Income (k^*)	Weight Attached, in Computing Permanent Income, to:		
		Highest Previous Income (w_1)	Current Income (w_2)	Preceding Year's Income (w_3)
Modigliani				
1. United States, 1921–40, disposable income	.90	.14	.86	
2. United States, 1921–40, income = disposable income plus corporate savings	.90	.14	.56	.30
3. Canada, 1923–39, gross national product	.79	.32	.17	.51
4. Sweden, 1896–1913, 1919–1934, national income	.85 (.93)[a]	.41	.59	
Duesenberry				
1. United States, 1929–40, disposable income	.95	.20	.80	
Mack				
1. United States, 1929–40, disposable income	.86(.97)[a]		.93	.07
Ferber Recomputations (All United States, disposable income)				
1. Following Modigliani				
a. 1923–1940	.96	.16	.84	
b. 1923–30, 1935–40	.96	.10	.90	
2. Following Duesenberry				
a. 1923–1940	.96	.16	.84	
b. 1923–30, 1935–40	.96	.10	.90	
3. Following Mack				
a. 1929–1940	.79(.97)[a]		.96	.04
b. 1923–1940	.82(.97)[a]		.90	.10
c. 1923–1930, 1935–1940	.96		.87	.13

[a] Value allowing for significant constant term.

Source:

Franco Modigliani, "Fluctuations in the Saving-Income Ratio: A Problem in Economic Forecasting," *Studies in Income and Wealth*, XI (New York: National Bureau of Economic Research, 1949).

1. Equation III-1, *ibid.*, p. 381. The dependent variable is the ratio of personal savings (or consumption) to disposable income; the independent, the ratio of the difference between current and previous peak income to current income, with all variables deflated by a price index and expressed per capita.

2. Equation XII-3, *ibid.*, p. 423. The dependent variable is individual plus corporate saving; the independent variables, disposable income plus corporate savings in the current year, the preceding year, and the preceding peak year, with all variables deflated by a price index and expressed per capita. A constant term was computed but did not differ significantly from zero.

(cont. on next page)

TABLE 14 (cont.)

3. Equation VI-1a, *ibid.*, p. 394. Dependent variable is personal consumption, excluding expenditures on consumer durables except motor cars, plus government expenditure; independent variables, gross national product for current, preceding, and previous peak year, all variables deflated by a price index, but apparently expressed as aggregates rather than per capita. The computed constant term was not significantly different from zero.

4. Equation VI-2, *ibid.*, p. 396. Dependent variable, personal consumption plus government expenditures on goods and services; independent variables, national income (including taxes and corporate savings) for current and previous peak year, all variables deflated by a price index and expressed per consumption unit. The computed constant term was significantly different from zero, which throws some doubt on our interpretation, which treats it as zero.

James S. Duesenberry, *Income, Saving and the Theory of Consumer Behavior*, Harvard University Press, 1952, pp. 90–91.

(a) Dependent variable, ratio of personal savings to disposable income; independent variable, ratio of disposable income in current year to highest previous disposable income. All variables on a per capita basis and deflated by a price index. (b) Duesenberry gives the constant term of his linear equation as .196; this is presumably a typographical error, since internal evidence indicates that it is −.196. The slope is .25. In converting his equation to the form described by (5 .7), his y^*/y_0^* was replaced by $1.754 - .769y_0^*/y^*$, which are the first two terms of a Taylor's expansion around a value of $y_0^*/y^* = 1.14$, the approximate average for the period covered.

Ruth P. Mack, "The Direction of Change in Income and the Consumption Function," *Review of Economics and Statistics*, XXX (1948), p. 256.

The dependent variable is consumption; the independent variables are disposable income and the change in disposable income. All variables are national aggregates in current dollars.

Robert Ferber, *A Study of Aggregate Consumption Functions*, National Bureau of Economic Research, Technical Paper 8, 1953.

1. a, b, *ibid.*, p. 69, equations (2.21b) and (2.21c) respectively. Dependent variable is ratio of personal savings to disposable income; the independent, the ratio of the difference between current and previous peak income to current income, with all variables deflated by a price index and expressed per capita.

2. a, b, *ibid.*, p. 69, equations (2.22b) and (2.22c) respectively. Dependent variable is ratio of personal savings to disposable income; the independent, the ratio of current income to previous peak income, with all variables deflated by a price index and expressed per capita. In converting these equations to the form described by (5.7), y^*/y_0^* was replaced by $1.84 - .846y_0^*/y^*$ for 2a, and by $1.963 - .963y_0^*/y^*$ for 2b. These are the first two terms of Taylor's expansion around values of y_0^*/y^* of 1.087 and 1.019 respectively, the means for the relevant periods.

3. a, b, c, *ibid.*, p. 66, equations (2.8a), (2.8b), and (2.8c) respectively. Dependent variable is personal savings; independent variables are current and previous year's disposable income, with all variables deflated by a price index and expressed per capita.

from the available data.[18] For the Mack recomputations, the constant term is significantly different from zero for two out of the three relations. Apparently, the inclusion of only the preceding year's income is not as successful as the inclusion of the highest previous income in rendering the equation homogeneous.

[18] The Modigliani function fitted by Ferber is

$$\frac{c^*}{y^*} = a + b\frac{y^* - y_0^*}{y^*} = (a + b) - b\frac{y_0^*}{y^*}.$$

Perhaps the most interesting result, common to all three sets of equations is the dominant weight attached to current income in computing permanent income. However, this result, as we shall see in the next section, is partly accounted for by the brevity of the time series from which the equations are computed.

b. ALTERNATIVE FUNCTIONS FITTED TO DATA FOR A LONG PERIOD

The computations summarized in Table 14 are all for the interwar period or parts thereof. It is possible to fit comparable functions to Goldsmith's data for a much longer period. This section records the results of doing so, and, in addition, of an experiment in fitting a related function suggested by our interpretation of the functions covered by Table 14.

On this interpretation, the incomes of prior years enter into the functions as a means of estimating permanent income. Judged from this point of view, the Modigliani-Duesenberry and Mack functions are questionable in several respects. In the first place, they estimate permanent income as the average of two or at most three years, yet it seems plausible that permanent income should be estimated from a longer period. More important, this is not an issue that should be decided a priori; the data themselves should dictate the appropriate number of years. In the second place, the use of the highest previous income seems rather arbitrary. For example, it might lead to use of a different year according to the form of the data—one year, say, for per capita deflated data, another for aggregates in current prices. It seems rather arbitrary, too, that the same weight should be attached to the highest previous income regardless of how many years separate it from the current year.

One alternative is to construct a weighted average of a longer series of years, allowing both the weights and the number of years to be determined by the data; the weights, by multiple correlation, the number of years, by adding years until an additional year produces no significant increase in the correlation. Unpleasantly complex in theory, this alternative also has the statistical defect that it uses up an undue number of degrees of freedom in application. But it does indicate a direction along which to proceed.

One way to proceed in this direction is to limit the characteristics of the weighting pattern to be determined from the data by expressing the weights as a function of the elapsed time between any given time

The Duesenberry function is

$$\frac{c^*}{y^*} = a + b\frac{y^*}{y_0^*}.$$

The only difference is that the independent variable in the one equation is the reciprocal of the independent variable in the other.

unit and the time unit for which permanent income is being estimated. Given the relatively heavy weight of current income revealed by Table 14, it seems appropriate to use a weighting pattern that gives most weight to current income and successively declining weights to earlier incomes. To state the procedure in its most general form, free from an arbitrary time unit, let us regard measured income as a continuous function of time and denote it by

(5.10) $$y^*(t) .$$

We might then construct an estimate of the permanent component at time T as

(5.11) $$\text{Estimate of } y_p^*(T) = \int_{-\infty}^{T} w(t - T) y^*(t) \, dt ,$$

where

(5.12) $$\int_{-\infty}^{T} w(t - T) \, dt = 1 .$$

One simple weighting pattern that has acceptable characteristics is an exponential, declining as one goes backward in time, say

(5.13) $$w(t - T) = \beta e^{\beta(t - T)} .$$

This weighting pattern has been used for a rather similar problem by Phillip Cagan, namely, to estimate the expected rate of change of prices during hyper-inflations from the time series of past rates of change.[19] The model that led him to his weighting pattern can be readily adapted to the present problem and may perhaps make the use of this pattern seem somewhat less arbitrary than the strictly empirical approach that I have so far followed.

For this purpose, tentatively regard y_p^* as the "expected" or predicted value of current measured income. Suppose this expected value is revised over time at a rate that is proportional to the difference between expected and actual income, or

(5.14) $$\frac{dy_p^*}{dT} = \beta[y^*(T) - y_p^*(T)] .$$

The solution of this differential equation with suitable initial conditions to make the constant term zero, is

(5.15) $$y_p^*(T) = \beta \int_{-\infty}^{T} e^{\beta(t - T)} y^*(t) \, dt ,$$

or the estimate stated earlier.[20]

[19] See Phillip Cagan, "The Monetary Dynamics of Hyperinflation," in Milton Friedman (ed.), *Studies in the Quantity Theory of Money* (University of Chicago Press, 1956), pp. 25–117.

[20] Note that, to first order terms, the same estimate is valid if the adjustment equation is expressed in logarithmic terms, or

(5.14′) $$\frac{dY_p^*}{dT} = \beta[Y^*(T) - Y_p^*(T)] .$$

One obvious defect of this approach is that it does not allow for predicted secular growth. Being an average of earlier observations, the estimated y_p^* is necessarily between the lowest and the highest, so that this method of estimation applied to a steadily growing series yields estimated values systematically below the observed values. To allow for this, we can suppose y_p^* to be estimated in two parts: first, a trend value which is taken to grow at a constant percentage rate, and second, a weighted average of adjusted deviations of past values from the trend, the adjustment being made to allow for the trend change itself, and thus to put all deviations at the same level as the present deviation. This would give:

$$(5.16) \quad y_p^*(T) = y_0 e^{\alpha T} + \beta \int_{-\infty}^{T} e^{\beta(t-T)}[y^*(t) - y_0 e^{\alpha t}]e^{\alpha(T-t)} \, dt,$$

where α is the estimated rate of growth and y_0, the value of income at the time taken as zero. This expression reduces to the much simpler form:

$$(5.17) \quad y_p^*(T) = \beta \int_{-\infty}^{T} e^{(\beta-\alpha)(t-T)} y^*(t) \, dt \, ,$$

and this is the form that we shall use. If we combine (5.17) with our basic consumption equation (2.10), and recall that measured consumption on the average equals permanent consumption for any given value of measured income, we have as a consumption function to be fitted to aggregate data:[21]

$$(5.18) \quad c^*(T) = k^* \beta \int_{-\infty}^{T} e^{(\beta-\alpha)(t-T)} y^*(t) \, dt \, .$$

This equation has three parameters: β, α, and k^*. One of these, however, which we take to be α, must be determined in some way other than by getting the best fitting approximation to (5.18), so in effect there are only two parameters to be determined from the set of data on measured consumption and measured income.[22] Yet, in principle, the equation estimates permanent income from the whole set of observed values of measured income.

In fact, of course, the earlier years get rapidly diminishing weights in determining y_p^*, so that beyond some point in time the observations have a negligible effect on the estimate. The span of time that matters depends on the size of β, the adjustment coefficient. The larger β, the larger the adaptation to any existing discrepancy between measured and expected income, and hence the more rapid the adjustment and

---

[21] It is interesting that Robert Solow suggested precisely this form of consumption function in "A Note on Dynamic Multipliers," *Econometrica*, XIX (July, 1951), p. 308.

[22] The fitting process makes it possible to determine only $(\beta - \alpha)$ and $k^*\beta$. Any triplet of values of β, α, and k^* which yield the same values of $\beta - \alpha$ and $k^*\beta$ will necessarily lead to the same prediction of consumption from a given series of observations on $y^*(t)$.

the shorter the retrospective time span that matters. One way of measuring the effective time span is by computing the weighted average time span between the observations that are weighted and the present or

$$(5.19) \qquad T - \bar{t} = \beta \int_{-\infty}^{T} e^{\beta(t-T)}(T - t)\, dt = \frac{1}{\beta}.$$

This is the average time lag between the estimated permanent income and the observations from which it is estimated; twice this time lag may be called the "effective weighting period."[23]

Of course, equation (5.18) cannot be fitted directly to data for discrete time units, such as years. For application, $y^*(t)$ is treated as a step function having the same value throughout each year. This is equivalent to converting the integral in (5.18) into a summation of annual terms, the weight for each year being the integral of the weight function over the corresponding period. Only a limited number of terms are retained, the number depending on the value of β and being determined so that the retained terms account for the great bulk of the weight. In this form, the equation has been fitted to the data in Figure 13, namely, real disposable income per capita and real consumption per capita based on Goldsmith's savings estimates. A number of details about the fitting process deserve explicit mention: (1) The method of fitting involved successive approximations and was worked out by Phillip Cagan in connection with the study mentioned earlier.[24] (2) The necessity of using incomes for prior years made it necessary to drop the earlier values of c^* available. The number that had to be dropped depends itself on the value of β. After preliminary experimentation the final function was fitted to data for 1905–51. This same period was used for comparability for the other functions covered in Table 15.[25] (3) In the final computation

---

[23] An alternative way of measuring the lag is to determine how far back one has to go to account for half the weights. This median time lag is $.69/\beta$.

[24] Cagan supervised the present statistical computations, and I am deeply indebted to him for his help, which has affected most of what follows in this section even where I make no explicit mention of his contribution. See Cagan, *op. cit.*, pp. 92–93.

[25] After this work was done and the description in the present section written, I discovered that the data used to fit the function were not comparable for the whole period. The data for the final two years, 1950 and 1951, are rough-and-ready extrapolations of estimates constructed in great detail for the period through 1949. Moreover, more extensive data that have become available since these extrapolations were made show them to be wide of the mark. It would have been better not to have used them. At the same time, since their omission could hardly affect the results substantially, I have not thought it worth the cost that would be involved to recompute the results, especially since it is likely that more nearly comparable figures for these and still later years will become available in the near future and so permit recomputation not only to correct this defect but also to cover a longer period. I have therefore contented myself with omitting 1950 and 1951 from Figure 14.

17 terms were retained in computing expected income; with this number, the weights, when rounded to three decimal places, sum to unity. The use of this number of terms for the earlier period made it necessary to extend the data back in time. This was done by extrapolating the 1897 figure backward along an exponential growth trend rising at the rate of 2 per cent per year. Since the sum of the weights applied to these hypothetical figures never exceeds .027, this expedient cannot introduce serious error and has the great virtue of enabling us to use a longer period for estimation.[26] (4) The value of α was taken as .02 on the basis of the secular rate of growth of c^*. This did not affect the fitting process but only the interpretation of the computed constants. (5) The war years, 1917, 1918, 1942 through 1945, were excluded on the grounds that special circumstances of those years made it rather absurd to use a formula like (5.15) to estimate permanent income and that the consumption data had abnormal transitory elements. For similar reasons, in computing permanent income in postwar years, the actual measured income in the war years was replaced by expected income in the last prewar year (1916 and 1941 respectively) plus 2 per cent per year to allow for secular growth.[27]

Table 15 summarizes the results of this computation and compares it with the results of fitting to the same data functions like those used by Modigliani and Duesenberry, and by Mack. The Modigliani-Duesenberry function used is

$$(5.20) \qquad c^* = k^*(w_1 y_0^* + w_2 y^*) .$$

The Mack function used is

$$(5.21) \qquad c^* = k^*(w_2 y^* + w_3 y_{-1}^*) .$$

All three functions involve determining two parameters from the set of data on consumption and income, and so they are all strictly comparable in this respect. In addition to the estimates in the table, based on fitting (5.18), (5.20), and (5.21) to the data, we also computed corresponding equations with a constant term added, in order to check the homogeneity of the equations. The constant term was smallest for the expected income equation and decidedly larger for the other two; in all three, however, forcing it to equal zero had relatively little effect on the estimates of the other parameters.[28]

---

[26] The retention of as many as 17 terms is doubtless an excess of precision. It is dubious that the results would be appreciably affected by retaining, say, only 9 terms and adjusting the weights for them to sum to unity.

[27] It may be worth recording that this device was decided on before the computations were made and was in no way altered in light of the results.

[28] The numerical value of the constant term was -4.0 for the expected income equation, $+52.8$ for the preceding year's income equation, and $+98$ for the highest previous

TABLE 15

Three Consumption Functions for the United States: Regressions of Consumption on Current and Past Incomes, Nonwar Years 1905 through 1951[a]

| Regression | Ratio of Permanent Consumption to Permanent Income (k*) | Weight Attached, in Computing Permanent Income, to: | | | | Square of Multiple Correlation Coefficient (R²) | Standard Error of Estimate as a % of Average Value of Measured Consumption |
		Highest Previous Income	Current Income	Preceding Year's Income	All Prior Years Combined		
Highest previous income[b]	.88	.45	.55			.98	2.8
Preceding year's income[b]	.90		.64	.36		.94	5.0
Expected income[c]	.88		.33	.22	.45	.96	4.0

[a] Excluded years are 1917–18, 1942 through 1945.

[b] Although the war years 1942 through 1945 were excluded from current income in computing these regressions, 1945 was used as the highest preceding income and as the preceding year's income for the 1946 current income observation, since 1941 was so far out of line. For World War I, since no break was introduced, 1917–18 was omitted for the other variables as well.

[c] The estimated value of β, on which the weights are based, is .4. The weights for 17 individual years to three decimals are as follows, starting with the current year and going backward in time: .330, .221, .148, .099, .067, .045, .030, .020, .013, .009, .006, .004, .003, .002, .001, .001, .001.

Note: Consumption = real consumption per capita. Income = real disposable income per capita.

Figure 14 presents the results graphically, plotting the time series of measured income, measured consumption, and consumption as predicted by each of the three equations. As both the table and the figure show, all three of the equations fit the observed data extremely well: the squares of the multiple correlation coefficient range from .94 to .98; the standard errors of estimate, from about 3 to 5 per cent of the average level of consumption.

The squares of the multiple correlation coefficient and standard errors of estimate entered in Table 15 are, however, somewhat misleading for two rather different reasons. In the first place, as is evident from the graph, both measured income and measured consumption have common and fairly steady upward trends of about 2 per cent per year. This common trend accounts for a large part of the high multiple correlation. Predicting consumption from its own trend yields a standard error of estimate of 6.6 per cent, and a value comparable to the squares of the multiple correlation coefficient in Table 15 of .90, so that 90 per cent of the variance of consumption over the period in question is accounted for simply by its own trend,

year's income equation. These are respectively approximately .24, .6, and 2.7 times their approximate standard errors.

and hence by the similar trend of income. Of course, the common trend of income and consumption is itself evidence in favor of the hypothesis that the permanent components of income and consumption are proportional; however, it is evidence from one observation, as it were, not from 41, the number from which the estimates in the table are supposedly computed.

FIGURE 14

Measured Disposable Income per Capita, and Consumption per Capita Measured and as Estimated from Three Regressions, 1905–1949

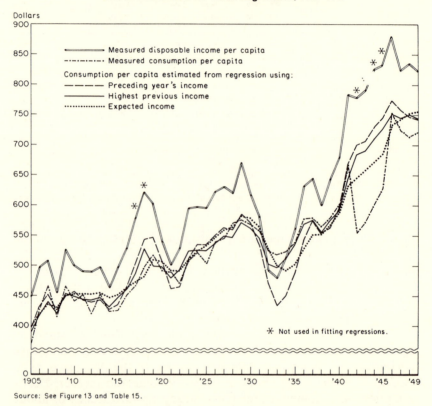

Source: See Figure 13 and Table 15.

In light of this common trend, a more meaningful way to interpret the squares of the correlation coefficient may be to regard the preceding year's income equation as explaining 40 per cent of the variance not accounted for by the common trend; the expected income equation, as explaining 60 per cent; and the highest previous income equation, as explaining 80 per cent. Viewed in this way, the differences among the equations seem much larger and more important. But even these need further examination. Instead of predicting

148

consumption from its own trend, suppose we were to predict it as a constant multiple of measured income in the same year. The result is a standard error of 5.7 per cent, and a value comparable to the square of the multiple correlation coefficient of .92. The terms other than current income can therefore be regarded as accounting for one-quarter, one-half, and three-quarters of the remaining variance for the preceding year's income, the expected income, and the highest previous income equation, respectively. Finally, we might predict consumption as a linear function of current income rather than a simple multiple of it—this is the absolute income hypothesis itself, and unlike the preceding comparison involves computing from the data the same number of constants as for the three equations in Table 15. The result is a standard error of estimate of 4.9 per cent and a squared correlation coefficient of .94. The preceding year's income equation makes no improvement compared with this alternative; the expected income equation accounts for one-third of the remaining variance; the highest previous income equation for two-thirds.

The importance of current income gives rise to the second reason why the standard errors of estimate and the squares of the multiple correlation coefficient in Table 15 are somewhat misleading, particularly in respect of the comparative success of the expected income and the highest previous income equations in predicting current consumption. The figures on consumption used in fitting these equations were computed as the difference between Goldsmith's estimates of savings and his separately derived estimates of disposable income. There is no reason to suppose that these two series have any important common sources of statistical error. But this means that the difference between them has the statistical errors of both. What is crucial for our present purpose, any statistical error in the estimate of disposable income means a statistical error of the same size and sign in the estimate of consumption. This common statistical error is a source of spurious correlation between measured consumption and measured current income which makes all of the correlation coefficients we have been citing too high.[29] To put it differently: given these statistical counterparts of our theoretical constructs, measured income can successfully predict in part the statistical errors in consumption. The result is the same as, and statistically indistinguishable from, a positive correlation between the transitory components of consumption and income. This bias in our estimated correlation coefficients is more important the higher the weight attached to current income. For this reason, the preceding year's income equation

[29] I owe this point to Phillip Cagan.

must be regarded as somewhat superior to the simple absolute income equation even though both yield the same correlation, because it gives a weight of 64 per cent rather than 100 per cent to current income. By the same token, both the other equations must be regarded as superior to the preceding year's income equation by an even wider margin than our earlier comparisons suggested.

The effect of the spurious correlation on the comparison between the expected income and highest previous income equations is much more difficult to evaluate. For the spurious correlation works in the same direction as the difference in the observed correlation. The highest previous income equation gives the higher correlation; it also gives greater weight to current income; the common error in consumption and income therefore raises its correlation by more than it raises the correlation for the expected income equation. Can the whole of the difference between the observed correlations be accounted for in this way? This question is examined in the Appendix to this Chapter. The conclusion reached is that it can be, though it is by no means clear that it is.

On statistical grounds alone, therefore, there is little basis for choosing between the highest previous income equation and the expected income equation. Despite what seem to me the theoretical defects of the highest previous income equation, it fits the data better than the aesthetically more appealing expected income equation, though both fit the data extremely well, and the difference in fit is of an order of magnitude that can be explained on purely statistical grounds of spurious correlation.

The estimates in Table 15 in all cases assign a much lower relative weight to current income than the estimates in Table 14 for equations fitted to shorter periods. In the highest previous income and preceding year's income equations, current income still gets more than half the weight; in the expected income equation, it gets only one-third the weight.

The expected income equation gives evidence on a feature of the consumption relation largely assumed in the other equations, namely, the average lag. The value of β turned out to be .4, implying an average lag of $2^1/_2$ years, or an "effective weighting period" of 5 years.[30] In terms of our hypothesis, this period is presumably related to the horizon implicit in judgments of permanent income by individual consumer units. It seems plausible that this period would be longer for aggregate data than the corresponding horizon for individual units, due to the averaging out of random factors.

In Cagan's study of hyper-inflations, he derived values of β strictly

[30] The "median" lag is 1.72 years.

comparable with ours, except that his relate to the lag in adjusting expected rates of price change to actual rates of price change. Under comparable circumstances, there seems no reason why men's horizons or speed of adjustment should be any different in adjusting expected income to measured income than in adjusting the expected rate of price change to the actual rate of price change. Indeed, insofar as we regard men as estimating both expected money and expected real income, expectations about price changes enter into expectations about income. Periods of rapid change might be expected to produce a shortening of horizons, or a speeding up of adjustment with respect to both variables. The average lag might therefore be expected to be shorter—that is, the value of β to be higher—for hyper-inflation periods like those studied by Cagan than for the less erratic peacetime period of our calculations. The results conform to expectation: Cagan finds values of β between .6 and 4.2 compared with our estimate of .4, or an average lag between $1/_4$ of a year and $1^2/_3$ years compared with our $2^1/_2$ years.[31] The consistency of these estimates for different countries, periods, and phenomena is both striking and highly relevant to the plausibility of our procedure. Certainly, if the computed value of β had turned out to be smaller for hyper-inflations than for other periods, it would have been necessary to reject the interpretation offered for one or the other set of data.

A number of segments of Figure 14 sharpen the impression derived from the summary parameters in Table 15. One is for the two wars. For 1917 and 1918, neither of which was used in fitting the functions, the preceding year and previously highest year functions both decidedly overestimate measured consumption. The expected income function gives very close estimates. For the excluded years of the second world war, 1942 through 1945, all three functions decidedly overestimate consumption, though the expected income function does so less than the others. These results are consistent with the interpretation that measured income contains a significant positive transitory component in both wars, while measured consumption was largely free from any transitory component in World War I, and contained a sizable negative transitory component in World War II. The estimates for the expected income function, as they were constructed, are not affected at all by the transitory component of income, whereas the others are, and none of the estimates takes into account any transitory component of consumption. This interpretation is

[31] The numbers cited in Cagan are on a per month basis. I have multiplied them by 12 to make them comparable with the value of β for the annual consumption data. *Ibid.*, p. 43.

eminently plausible in light of other information for the two periods. Certainly, there was a decided negative transitory component in consumption during World War II, caused by the unavailability of some goods and the explicit rationing of others. It is very much less clear that a similar situation existed during World War I, which was shorter, which drew upon a smaller fraction of aggregate resources, and which involved no explicit rationing and little direct control over production.

Another segment of Figure 14 worth attention is the Great Depression. In 1933, 1934, and 1935, consumption was higher than predicted by any of the functions and in 1931 and 1932, higher than predicted by either the preceding year or previously highest year function. Further, the expected income function continued to underestimate consumption substantially in 1936 and 1937. The interpretation seems reasonably straightforward. Human beings are more flexible than the particular mathematical equations we used to summarize their behavior; they recognized, as these equations could not, that the Great Depression was something exceptional and special, to be taken into account in a different way than the run-of-the-mill up and down of economic activity. Accordingly, they attributed a much larger part of the decline in income to a negative transitory component of income than do the various devices for estimating permanent income embodied in our equations. They therefore maintained a higher level of consumption than these equations predicted during much of the depression. The expected income function, having, as it were, the longest memory, went astray later than the others, but, having gone astray, stayed astray well after the others had come back into line.[32] This deviation from our functions during the Great Depression tells against the specific equations used to describe consumer behavior but seems, if anything, to support our general interpretation of consumer behavior.

Appendix to Section 3:

Effect on Multiple Correlation of Common Errors in Measured Consumption and Current Income

In what follows, I shall use the following notation:

[32] This interpretation of consumer behavior during the Great Depression, if accepted, has obvious and important implications for the cyclical interpretation of the period. It implies that expectations, far from being destabilizing as has so often been asserted, were, at least on the part of consumers, a stabilizing factor, which means that the extraordinary depth of the depression would have to be explained in some other way, as produced by some pressure on the system, such as the rapid decline in the stock of money from 1929 to 1933, particularly from 1931 to 1933.

| Variable | Symbol for the: | | |
	Measured Value	Error of Measurement	"Correct" Value
Income	y	δy	η
Savings	s	δs	Σ
Consumption	c	δc	γ

In addition, let the subscript t denote a current value of a variable; the subscript l, a lagged value; the subscript p, a "permanent" value.

All variables are taken to have means of zero; that is, they are expressed as deviations from the means of the corresponding unadjusted variables.

Both the expected income and the highest previous income equation can be interpreted as setting

$$(5.22) \qquad y_p = \alpha y_l + \beta y_t ,$$

$$(5.23) \qquad \eta_p = \alpha \eta_l + \beta \eta_t ,$$

$$(5.24) \qquad \alpha + \beta = 1 .$$

In the expected income equation, y_l is to be interpreted as a weighted average of incomes in all years preceding the current year; in the highest previous income equation, as the income of the highest previous year. So both equations can be interpreted as correlating c_t with y_p, and our problem reduces to determining the effect of the value of β on the correlation between c_t and $y_p(r_{c_t y_p})$ given common errors in c_t and y_t.

We take c to be computed as $y - s$, where y and s are independently measured, so

$$(5.25) \qquad \delta c = \delta y - \delta s .$$

Assume that

$$(5.26) \qquad r_{\delta y \delta s} = r_{\eta \delta y} = r_{\Sigma \delta s} = r_{\eta \delta s} = r_{\Sigma \delta y} = r_{\gamma \delta y} = r_{\gamma \delta s} = 0 ,$$

whether the variables refer to the same or different years, and also that

$$(5.27) \qquad r_{\delta y_t \delta y_l} = r_{\delta s_t \delta s_l} = 0 .$$

The value of $r_{c_t y_p}$, the effect on which of the size of β is our goal, is

$$(5.28) \qquad r_{c_t y_p} = \frac{E c_t(\alpha y_l + \beta y_t)}{[E c_t^2]^{1/2} [E(\alpha y_l + \beta y_t)^2]^{1/2}} .$$

Now

$$(5.29) \qquad E c_t(\alpha y_l + \beta y_t) = E(\gamma_t + \delta c_t)(\alpha \eta_l + \beta \eta_t + \alpha \delta y_l + \beta \delta y_t)$$

$$(5.30) \qquad = E \gamma_t \eta_p + \beta E \delta c_t \delta y_t ,$$

153

all other cross-products being zero by virtue of (5.26) and (5.27),

$$(5.31) \qquad = r_{\gamma_t \eta_p} \sigma_{\gamma_t} \sigma_{\eta_p} + \beta E(\delta y_t - \delta s_t) \delta y_t = r_{\gamma_t \eta_p} \sigma_{\gamma_t} \sigma_{\eta_p} + \beta \sigma_{\delta y_t}^2 ,$$

where σ stands for the standard deviation of the variable designated by its subscript.

$$(5.32) \quad Ec_t^2 = E(\gamma_t + \delta c_t)^2 = E(\gamma_t + \delta y_t - \delta s_t)^2 = \sigma_{\gamma_t}^2 + \sigma_{\delta y_t}^2 + \sigma_{\delta s_t}^2 ,$$

$$(5.33) \quad Ey_p^2 = E(\eta_p + \alpha \delta y_t + \beta \delta y_t)^2 = \sigma_{\eta_p}^2 + \alpha^2 \sigma_{\delta y_t}^2 + \beta^2 \sigma_{\delta y}^2 .$$

Let us assume that

$$(5.34) \qquad \sigma_{\delta y_t}^2 = \sigma_{\delta y_t}^2 = \sigma_{\delta y}^2 ,$$

so

$$(5.35) \qquad \sigma_{y_p}^2 = \sigma_{\eta_p}^2 + (\alpha^2 + \beta^2) \sigma_{\delta y}^2 .$$

Substituting in (5.28), we have

$$(5.36) \qquad r_{c_t y_p} = \frac{r_{\gamma_t \eta_p} \sigma_{\gamma_t} \sigma_{\eta_p} + \beta \sigma_{\delta y}^2}{[\sigma_{\gamma_t}^2 + \sigma_{\delta y}^2 + \sigma_{\delta s_t}^2]^{1/2} [\sigma_{\eta_p}^2 + (\alpha^2 + \beta^2) \sigma_{\delta y}^2]^{1/2}}$$

$$(5.37) \qquad = \frac{r_{\gamma_t \eta_p} + \dfrac{\beta \sigma_{\delta y}^2}{\sigma_{\gamma_t} \sigma_{\eta_p}}}{\left[1 + \dfrac{\sigma_{\delta y}^2 + \sigma_{\delta s_t}^2}{\sigma_{\gamma_t}^2}\right]^{1/2} \left[1 + (\alpha^2 + \beta^2) \dfrac{\sigma_{\delta y}^2}{\sigma_{\eta_p}^2}\right]^{1/2}} .$$

We have the following numerical values from our computations:

	Expected Income Equation	Highest Previous Income Equation
$r_{c_t y_p}^2$	·96	·98
$r_{c_t y_p}$	·98	·99
α	·67	·455
β	·33	·545
$\alpha^2 + \beta^2$	·5578	·5040

In order to use formula (5.37) we must have estimates of

$$\frac{\sigma_{\delta y}}{\sigma_{\gamma_t}}, \quad \frac{\sigma_{\delta s}}{\sigma_{\gamma_t}}, \quad \frac{\sigma_{\delta y}}{\sigma_{\eta_p}} .$$

Call these R, S, and T respectively.

Now we know that, approximately,

$$(5.38) \qquad \gamma = .9 \eta_p$$

$$(5.39) \qquad \text{so} \quad \sigma_\gamma = .9 \sigma_{\eta_p} ,$$

$$(5.40) \qquad R = \frac{1}{.9} T = 1.11 T .$$

To get an estimate of S, assume that

(5.41)
$$\frac{\sigma_{\delta s}}{\sigma_{\Sigma}} = \frac{\sigma_{\delta y}}{\sigma_y}$$

from which

(5.42)
$$S = \frac{\sigma_{\delta s}}{\sigma_y} = \frac{\sigma_{\Sigma}}{\sigma_y} \cdot \frac{\sigma_{\delta y}}{\sigma_y} = \frac{\sigma_{\Sigma}}{\sigma_y} \cdot R .$$

Now σ_{Σ}/σ_y is approximately equal to σ_s/σ_c which by computation from the data, equals .36. So that

(5.43)
$$\sigma_{\Sigma} = .36\sigma_y = .36(.9)\sigma_{\eta_p} .$$

But, on our hypothesis, the elasticity of the regression of consumption on income is an estimate of the fraction of the variation in y that is attributable to η_p. For the period in question, the computed elasticity is .87. It follows that

(5.44)
$$\sigma_{\eta_p}^2 = .87\sigma_y^2$$

so

(5.45)
$$\sigma_{\Sigma} = (.36)(.9)(.87)^{1/2}\sigma_y, \quad \text{or}$$

(5.46)
$$S = \frac{\sigma_{\Sigma}}{\sigma_y} \cdot R = (.36)(.9)(.87)^{1/2}(1.11)T = .33T .$$

Suppose, now, that we insert the expressions for R and S in terms of T from (5.40) and (5.46) into (5.37) as well as the computed value of $r_{c_l y_p}$ from the highest previous income equation, the corresponding value of $\beta(\beta = .545)$, and finally, assume that $r_{y_t \eta_p} = 1$ so that only statistical measurement errors account for correlations less than unity. This gives an equation in T, from which we can compute its value as
$$T = (.0397)^{1/2} .$$

Let us now use this value of T, together with the values of R and S as computed from (5.40) and (5.46), a value of $\beta = .33$, and again assume that $r_{y_t \eta_p} = 1$, and compute the value of $r_{c_l y_p}$ implied by (5.37). This is then an estimate of the correlation coefficient for the expected income equation on the assumption that the only reason why it differs from that for the highest previous income equation is because of the smaller value of β. The resulting answer is
$$r_{c_l y_p}^2 = .957 ,$$

or a number slightly less than the observed .960. It follows, that, under our assumptions, the whole of the difference between the two observed correlations can be accounted for by the difference in β.

One test of the reasonableness of our assumptions is to see whether they imply reasonable values for the various standard deviations. We have that

$$T^2 = .04 = \frac{\sigma^2_{\delta y}}{\sigma^2_{\eta_p}}$$

or

$$\sigma^2_{\delta y} = .04\sigma^2_{\eta_p} = (.04)(.87)\sigma^2_y = (.0348)\sigma^2_y \ .$$

But σ^2_y can be computed from the data. The resulting value of $\sigma_{\delta y}$ is about \$25, or about 4 per cent of mean measured income. In similar fashion, the computed value of $\sigma_{\delta s}$ turns out to be about 13 per cent of mean saving. These figures seem not unreasonable. If anything, they imply rather smaller errors in saving and income than I would have expected.

As another check on the reasonableness of these results, I made a similar computation for what seem two extreme assumptions:

Assumption 1: $R = S = T$

Assumption 1A: $R = T; S = 0$.

It seems plausible that these would be extremes, because savings are so much smaller on the average than consumption or income that one might expect the measurement error in savings to be smaller in absolute size than in income, though very likely much larger as a percentage of the magnitude being estimated. The results were as follows:

Hypothetical value of $r^2_{c_i y_p}$ for $\beta = .33$

Assumption 1:   .973

Assumption 1A: .956

These two values are on either side of the observed value of .96. Similarly, the value earlier computed of .957 is between them as well.

CHAPTER VI

The Relation Between the Permanent Income and Relative Income Hypotheses

THE preceding two chapters demonstrate that the permanent income hypothesis is consistent with a wide variety of empirical evidence on consumption behavior. It offers a simple interpretation of the rough constancy of the average propensity to consume both among budget studies made at widely separated dates and over time as recorded in aggregate time series data spanning more than half a century. It gives plausible explanations of (1) differences in the observed consumption-income regressions among consumer units living in different countries, deriving their livelihood from different pursuits, and differing in race; and of (2) different ratios of savings to income for consumer units headed by persons differing in age. It predicts correctly the effect on budget study consumption-income regressions of classifying families by the change in their measured income from an earlier period and on similar regressions computed from aggregate time series data, of the length of the period covered and the form in which the data are expressed. It accounts for both the major characteristics of the long-period time series data and many of their details, and it suggests an aggregate consumption function that gives strikingly good results when fitted to these long-period data.

This is impressive evidence for our hypothesis. But, as is always the case in empirical work, there must be numerous other hypotheses with which this same evidence would be consistent; insofar as we choose ours, it is because we regard it as simpler and more fruitful than others that have come to our notice, or because we can find additional evidence consistent with ours but not with some of these others. In particular, much of the evidence cited as consistent with our hypothesis has also been cited as evidence for a specific alternative hypothesis: the relative income hypothesis proposed by Brady and Friedman, Modigliani, and Duesenberry. Indeed, the literature bearing on that hypothesis has been an important source of the data cited in the two preceding chapters. The purpose of this chapter is to explore the relationship between the permanent income hypothesis and the relative income hypothesis. Both of these are offered as alternatives to what I shall call the absolute income hypothesis—that consumption is a function of the absolute value of current measured real income—so we shall have occasion to consider it as well.

The relative income hypothesis asserts that the ratio of measured consumption to measured income is a function of the relative position of consumer units in the income distribution. Now it is intuitively clear that there is at least a family connection between this hypothesis and our own. Suppose that transitory components of income and expenditure average out to zero for any one group as a whole. The measured income of consumer units whose measured income is equal to the average for their group then equals their permanent component of income, and their average consumption is, on our hypothesis, equal to k times their income. For units at this position in the measured income scale, the ratio of consumption to income varies from group to group only because of differences in k; there are no differences in the ratio of permanent to measured income to introduce additional variation. Similarly, the mean transitory component of income is positive for incomes above the average and negative for incomes below the average, so that classifying units by their relative position rather than their absolute income at least makes the sign of the transitory component the same for units in the same relative income class but in different groups. Under certain conditions, then, our hypothesis predicts that the ratio of measured consumption to measured income is a function of relative income position.

Though closely related in this way, the two hypotheses are not identical. In order to examine the relation between them more thoroughly, we must consider separately two variants of the relative income hypothesis that have been used in the literature: (1) the basic variant measures relative income position by the percentile position of the consumer unit in the income distribution of the group to which it is regarded as belonging; (2) because data frequently do not permit satisfactory estimates of percentile position, a secondary variant uses the ratio of the income of the unit to the average income of the group as an approximation to the relative income position. These two variants give the same results—in the sense that regressions of the consumption ratio on relative income position computed for different groups diverge to the same extent—if, and only if, the income distributions of the several groups differ only by a scale factor, which is equivalent to their all having the same Lorenz curve. Although variant (1) is regarded as the basic variant, it is simpler to show the relation of variant (2) to our hypothesis; accordingly, we shall consider it first.

It is well to be explicit in advance about the question to be asked in comparing the two hypotheses. For any one group of consumer units taken by itself, there is no possibility of conflict between the two hypotheses: the regression of consumption on measured income of the kind that we have been interpreting in terms of our hypothesis (call this a relation of Type A) can be converted to a relation between the ratio of measured consumption to measured income and the ratio of measured income to mean income (call this a relation of Type R) by algebraic manipulation, including a change of scale. The relative income hypothesis says nothing about the size of the parameters, and hence says nothing about one group of consumer units taken by itself. Our hypothesis says that the parameters of the regression depend on k and P_y. Insofar as these can be independently estimated, our hypothesis does say something about a single group and in this way is more fruitful than the relative income hypothesis. The essential content of the relative income hypothesis is for a comparison among groups. It says, first, that relations of Type A can be expected to differ significantly among groups that have different income distributions; and, second, that these differences are reduced or eliminated if the relations are converted into Type R. It predicts, that is, that groups whose consumption behavior must be regarded as heterogeneous if judged by relations of Type A will be found to be homogeneous if judged by relations of Type R. Now our hypothesis can be used to predict when relations of Type R will be the same, and here a possibility of conflict arises. The question to be asked of our hypothesis is therefore the conditions under which, according to it, relations of Type R are the same for different groups and the conditions under which they diverge. For the first set of conditions, the two hypotheses agree; evidence for one is equally evidence for the other. For the second set of conditions, the two hypotheses disagree; if these conditions can be identified empirically, they offer the possibility of discriminating between the two hypotheses.

On either variant, one reason why, on our hypothesis, relations of Type R (or for that matter Type A) might diverge is because of differences in the mean transitory components of income or consumption. Such differences would tend to alter the heights of such relations while leaving the slopes unaffected. Since these effects are so straightforward, we shall confine the detailed discussion that follows to other effects. For simplicity, therefore, we shall assume in the next two sections that the mean transitory components of income and consumption are zero for any group considered, so that the mean measured income and measured consumption for the group are equal to the corresponding mean permanent components.

1. *Relative Income Status Measured by Ratio of Measured Income to Average Income*

Under these conditions, from (3.10) and (3.11), the regression of consumption on measured income is given by

(6.1) $$c = k(1 - P_y)\bar{y} + kP_y \cdot y.$$

Dividing both sides by y, we have

(6.2) $$\frac{c}{y} = kP_y + k(1 - P_y)\frac{\bar{y}}{y}.$$

This is a linear relation between the consumption ratio and the reciprocal of the ratio of measured income to mean income. However, for a narrow enough interval, it can be approximated by a linear relation in terms of relative income itself.[1] More important for our purpose, equation (6.2) implies that relations of Type R will be the same for different groups, on our hypothesis, if, and only if, k and P_y are separately the same for those groups.[2] For any groups for which this is so, this variant of the relative income hypothesis gives the same results as our hypothesis, though our hypothesis is more fruitful in that it says something about the form of the function and about the determinants of its parameters.

If, in addition to k and P_y, $\bar{y}$ is also the same for different groups, then relations of Type A, namely (6.1), will also be the same for different groups, so all three hypotheses—the permanent income, relative income, and absolute income hypotheses—will give the same results. However, at least for the linear terms of the relations, this

[1] It should be noted that our hypothesis does not predict that a linear regression will fit the observed means for successive income classes. The equation (6.1) is derived by asking what the parameters of a linear regression would be if they were computed for a set of data described by our hypothesis. The observed means will in fact fall on a straight line under our hypothesis if transitory factors are equally important at all levels of permanent income, not otherwise. This is one reason why we have carried along in our theoretical discussion, and mostly used in the empirical work, the logarithmic variant of our hypothesis. Empirically, the condition of equal effect of transitory factors seems better satisfied for the logarithms than for the original data.

Similarly, our hypothesis implies that the regression of the consumption ratio on the reciprocal of relative income will be linear only under the same conditions. Again, therefore, one would expect the logarithmic variant to approximate linearity more closely than the arithmetic variant.

[2] On the logarithmic alternative

(6.1)′ $$C = K + \bar{Y}(1 - P_y) + P_y \cdot Y.$$

Subtracting Y from both sides, we have

(6.2)′ $$C - Y = K + (1 - P_y)(\bar{Y} - Y).$$

As for the arithmetic relations, logarithmic relations of Type R will be the same for different groups, on our hypothesis, if and only if K and P_y are separately the same for those groups.

160

requirement is more stringent than is necessary. In order for relations of Type A to be the same to linear terms, kP_y and $k(1 - P_y)\bar{y}$ must be the same; and any triplet of values of k, P_y, and $\bar{y}$ that makes these combinations of them the same will yield the same relations of Type A; a higher mean income for one group than for another might be offset, for example, by an appropriately higher P_y and lower k.

This is in part an obvious result: since relative income in this variant is defined as the ratio of absolute income to mean income, it must be capable of accounting for at least some differences in consumption-income regressions that reflect differences in mean incomes; and, on the other hand, it cannot account for differences between groups that have the same mean income. What are perhaps less obvious are the implications of our hypothesis about the circumstances, other than differences in mean income, under which the other two hypotheses will both fail.

Suppose we have two groups for which the regression of consumption on income is given by (6.1), i.e. for which the arithmetic variant of our hypothesis holds and for which it is appropriate to regard $\bar{c}_t = \bar{y}_t = 0$, but for which either P_y or k or both differ. How will the two relations of Type R compare? From (6.2), the consumption ratio increases as $\bar{y}/y$ increases, since $k(1 - P_y)$ is necessarily positive. But $y/\bar{y}$, or relative income, decreases as $\bar{y}/y$ increases, so the relations of Type R have a negative slope. Suppose k is the same but P_y differs. The larger P_y, the smaller the positive slope of (6.2), which means the smaller the absolute value of the negative slope of the relation of Type R, or the flatter this relation is with respect to the axis of relative income.[3] The two relations intersect at the mean income or relative income of unity, where the consumption ratio equals k. For given P_y, the larger k, the higher the consumption ratio, and so the relation of Type R; and it is higher in the same ratio for all values of relative income. For given P_y, the larger k, the greater the slope in absolute value or the steeper the relation of Type R.

These algebraic results admit of a simple interpretation on our hypothesis. Consider, for example, consumer units with measured incomes twice the average incomes of the groups to which they belong. The permanent income of these consumer units will, on the average, be somewhere between the average income of the groups to which

[3] More formally, differentiate the right hand side of (6.2) with respect to $y/\bar{y}$. The result is

$$d\left(\frac{c}{y}\right)\bigg/d\left(\frac{y}{\bar{y}}\right) = -k(1 - P_y)\left(\frac{\bar{y}}{y}\right)^2,$$

so the slope is smaller in absolute value the larger is P_y (and also the smaller is k). The derivative with respect to the savings ratio clearly has the same numerical value but the opposite sign.

they belong and their measured income. Consumption being adjusted to this permanent income, it will be less than twice the average consumption of the groups to which the consumer units belong. In consequence, the consumption ratio will be less than the ratio of average consumption for the group to average income. This is the explanation for the negative slope of relations of Type R.

Suppose, now, that some of these consumer units are from a group for which P_y is low, that is, for which transitory factors play a sizable role in producing differences in measured income, and the rest are from a group for which P_y is high. Consumption will be adjusted to a lower permanent income for the first set of consumer units than for the second set, since transitory factors will account for a larger part of the deviation of their incomes from the average. In consequence, the consumption ratio will be lower for them than for the second set even though the ratio of average consumption to average income is the same for the groups to which the two sets belong. This is the explanation for the steeper relation of Type R for a low P_y than a high P_y.

To put even more succinctly the conditions under which the relations of Type R can be expected to differ for different groups: measured relative income means the same thing for different groups only if relative income status is equally stable for the different groups. And P_y is a measure of the stability of relative income status.

One of the charts in the paper by Brady and Friedman exemplifies these effects. They plot the ratio of savings to income against both absolute and relative income for urban families for four budget studies: the 1901, 1917–19, 1935–36, and 1941 studies listed in my Table 1.[4] The use of relative income produces a striking reduction in the dispersion of the four regressions, but still leaves some important differences. The major difference in the slopes is that the regression is more steeply sloped for 1901 than for the later years; the regressions for 1917–19 and 1935–36 have roughly the same slope, and the regression for 1941, a mildly flatter slope.[5] We have seen that k does not differ systematically for these different studies. Consequently, on our hypothesis these differences imply a lower value of P_y in 1901 than in the later years and moderately lower values in 1917–19 and 1935–36 than in 1941. Our estimates of P_y from the consumption-income regressions, recorded in the final column of Table 1, are .75 for 1901, .86 and .82 for 1917–19 and 1935–36 respectively, and .87

[4] Brady and Friedman, "Savings and the Income Distribution," p. 261.

[5] Brady and Friedman plot the savings ratio against the logarithm of the income ratio rather than the income ratio itself. However, if at any value of the income ratio, the slope with respect to the logarithm is steeper for one curve than for another, so is the slope with respect to the arithmetic value.

for 1941. It should be emphasized that this is largely an illustration of the effects of differences in the value of P_y on the slopes of relations of Type R, rather than self-contained independent evidence relevant to discriminating between the two hypotheses. The reason is, of course, that the relation between the slopes of the two types of regressions is purely arithmetic and we have derived these estimates of P_y from the slopes of regressions of Type A. To discriminate between the two hypotheses would require independent evidence on the value of P_y for the four studies.

Some independent evidence is obtained by adding to the chart just considered a corresponding regression for farm families in 1935–36. Such a regression is decidedly steeper than the regressions for urban families both for the same year and for the other years.[6] On our hypothesis, this implies a lower value of P_y for farm families. And there is surely ample independent evidence, both qualitative and quantitative,[7] that P_y is lower for farm than for urban families.

2. Relative Income Status Measured by Percentile Position in the Income Distribution

In order to relate percentile position in any simple fashion to the variables that our hypothesis suggests are crucial, it is necessary to specify something about the form of the income distribution. Let us suppose that all income distributions are normal distributions, so that each is completely described by its mean and standard deviation.[8] Any measured income can be written as

$$(6.3) \qquad\qquad y = \bar{y} + g\sigma_y,$$

where $\bar{y}$, as before, designates the mean income of the group, σ_y is the standard deviation of income, and g is the deviation of income from the mean income in standard deviation units. For a normal distribution, the value of g uniquely determines the percentile position and conversely, so we can replace percentile position by g. Substituting (6.3) in (6.2), we have

$$(6.4) \qquad \frac{c}{y} = kP_y + k(1 - P_y) \cdot \frac{\bar{y}}{\bar{y} + g\sigma_y} = kP_y + k(1 - P_y)\frac{1}{1 + vg},$$

where v is the coefficient of variation of measured income, or $\sigma_y/\bar{y}$.

[6] Brady and Friedman do not plot this regression because they use the percentile measure of relative income status in comparing farm and nonfarm families. The above statement is based on a rough calculation from their Table 1, *ibid.*, p. 253.

[7] See below, Chap. VII, sec. 2 and 3.

[8] It is closer to the empirical evidence on the shape of income distributions to suppose that the logarithm of income rather than income itself is normally distributed. However, the major result is the same whichever assumption is made, so there is no loss in generality and some gain in ease of exposition in assuming absolute incomes normally distributed.

There are now three parameters that must be the same for different groups in order to render the relations of Type R the same, namely, k, P_y, and v.

In this variant, it is no longer true that the relative income hypothesis gives the same result as the absolute income hypothesis for groups with the same mean income. If the relations of Type A were the same for a set of such groups, relations of Type R, as defined by (6.4), would not be, unless the standard deviation of income were also the same for the different groups. The relation between the absolute and relative income hypotheses is therefore more complicated for this variant. If we consider only the linear part of the relations of Type R, or—what comes to the same thing—only the height and slope at the mean income, only two parameters are involved as can be seen by replacing $1/(1 + vg)$ in (6.4) by the first two terms of its Taylor's expansion around $g = 0$. This gives

$$(6.5) \qquad \frac{c}{y} = kP_y + k(1 - P_y)(1 - vg) = k - k(1 - P_y)vg \ .$$

Relations like (6.5) will be identical for different groups provided that k and $(1 - P_y)v$ are identical; so any combinations of P_y and v that keep $(1 - P_y)v$ the same will do.[9] I have been able to construct no simple interpretation of this particular combination of P_y and v,[10] so perhaps the best procedure is to consider the effects of changes in P_y and v separately, while recognizing that these can offset one another. Changes in k and P_y have the same effect on relations of Type R as for the first variant of relative income. The higher k, the higher the relation at all values of g; since it is higher by a constant percentage rather than absolute amount, the absolute value of the slope is also higher by the same percentage, so the relation is steeper (relative to the axis of g or of percentile position[11]). The higher P_y, the smaller the

[9] On the logarithmic alternative, we have

$$(6.3)' \qquad\qquad Y = \bar{Y} + G\sigma_Y \ .$$

Substituting in (6.2)',

$$(6.4)' \qquad\qquad C - Y = K - (1 - P_y)\sigma_Y G \ .$$

The logarithmic standard deviation, σ_Y, is an estimate of the coefficient of variation for arithmetic data and, like the latter, is a pure number unaffected, for example, by doubling every income. Consequently, (6.4)' yields more directly and elegantly the same result as (6.5).

[10] It can be expressed in various ways in terms of the standard deviations of the permanent and transitory components, but no one seems particularly illuminating. Thus:

$$(1 - P_y)v = \left(1 - \frac{\sigma_p^2}{\sigma_y^2}\right)\frac{\sigma_y}{\bar{y}} = \frac{\sigma_t^2}{\sigma_y^2}\cdot\frac{\sigma_y}{\bar{y}} = \left(\frac{\sigma_t}{\sigma_y}\right)\left(\frac{\sigma_t}{\bar{y}}\right) \ .$$

[11] Note that, for a given g, a change in k, v, or P_y affects the slope with respect to the percentile or the logarithm of the percentile in the same direction as the slope with respect to g.

absolute value of the slope, and hence the flatter the relation at any given value of g, and conversely. Like changes in P_y, changes in v affect only the slope, not the height at the mean income ($g = 0$). The higher v, the larger in absolute value is the slope at the mean income, and so the steeper the relation.[12]

The interpretation of these results in terms of our hypothesis is essentially the same as for the first variant. The difference is that a given value of g corresponds to the same relative income for different groups only if v is the same, which is the reason why v enters into the picture. If v is greater for one group than for another, the same value of g means a higher ratio of measured income to average income for the one group than for the other, which in turn would, of itself, imply a lower consumption ratio. In order to offset this effect, given the same ratio of average consumption to average income for the two groups, a larger part of the deviation of measured income from the mean must be accounted for by the permanent component; i.e., P_y must be higher. So the effect of a higher v can be offset by a higher P_y.

Once again, some of the material presented by Brady and Friedman serves to illustrate these effects. They found, for example, that the savings ratio rose more rapidly with percentile position for farmers than for nonfarmers, and that it was generally higher except for low incomes.[13] The difference in height presumably reflects mostly the difference in k. The difference in k also affects the slope but by itself would produce a difference in slope the reverse of that observed, so it must be more than counterbalanced by differences in $v(1 - P_y)$. According to the estimates in Table 4 of Chapter IV, there is little difference in v between farm and nonfarm groups. Consequently, the

---

[12] It should be noted that the statements about the effects of changes in k and P_y apply both to the linear approximation described by (6.5) and to the original version, (6.4), while the statement about v applies only to the former, which is why "at the mean income" is included in the above sentence.

To demonstrate these statements, differentiate (6.4) with respect to g. This gives

$$\frac{d(c/y)}{dg} = -k(1 - P_y)\frac{v}{(1 + gv)^2}.$$

For given g and v, the absolute value of the righthand side clearly increases as P_y decreases and as k increases. To determine its behavior with respect to v, differentiate the final ratio (call it z) with respect to v. This gives

$$\frac{dz}{dv} = \frac{1 - gv}{(1 + gv)^3}.$$

For g zero or negative, $dz/dv > 0$, so long as $1 + gv > 0$, as, by the definition of g, it will be for positive incomes. For g positive, $dz/dv > 0$ for $v < 1/g$, equal to zero when $v = 1/g$, and less than zero for $v > 1/g$. Thus, at or below the mean income, the relation at each value of g becomes steeper, the larger is v. Above the mean income, the relation at each value of g at first becomes steeper as v increases, then flatter, and the value of v at which it starts to become flatter is smaller, the larger is g.

[13] Brady and Friedman, op. cit., pp. 253 and 262.

substantial difference between them in P_y is again presumably the explanation. The lower value of P_y for farmers than for nonfarmers produces a steeper relation of Type R for them. Again, this is partly only an illustration of the algebraic connection among the relations of various types; it is partly, also, however, evidence in favor of our hypothesis, insofar as there is independent evidence on the relative values of P_y for farm and nonfarm families.

Another example from Brady and Friedman is a chart plotting the savings ratio against percentile position for all nonfarm white families and for Negro families in New York, Columbus, Atlanta, middle-size cities in the South, small cities in the South, and villages in the South, all based on the 1935–36 study.[14] According to their chart, the savings ratio for white families is generally above that for Negro families, at least for percentile positions above 50, and rises more rapidly with income for percentile positions in the immediate neighborhood above 50, and less clearly for higher percentile positions. Unfortunately, the chart contains only one point for a percentile below 50 for each group, so there is little evidence for this region. The relations for the different Negro groups are extremely erratic, giving evidence of considerable variation as a result of sampling fluctuations, so that fine comparisons are impossible. About the only generalization that seems justified is that the relations for the villages and small cities are flatter than the others.

From Tables 4 and 7 of Chapter IV, it will be seen that v is higher for all nonfarm families (white plus Negro) than for Negro families in four of the six communities. P_y as estimated by the elasticity of consumption with respect to measured income, is lower also for four of the six communities though the four communities involved are not the same for both v and P_y. These differences would account for the steeper slope of the Type R relation for white families. As Table 7 shows, v is decidedly lower for Negro families in the small cities and villages of the South than in the other communities, and P_y decidedly higher; both would contribute to the observed flatter relations for these groups.[15]

Duesenberry plots a more detailed chart for New York Negro and white families and for Columbus Negro and white families. Any differences between the relations for Negro and white families in each city separately is too small to be detected in view of rather substantial erratic movements. The difference between the two cities is rather

[14] *Ibid.*, p. 264.
[15] The value of $v(1 - P_y)$ is .140 for all nonfarm families; .056, .122, .166, .101, .031, and .035 for Negro families in New York, Columbus, Atlanta, middle-size cities in the South, small cities in the South, and villages in the South, respectively.

clearer: the savings ratio is generally higher for Columbus than for New York and changes more with percentile position. The higher savings ratio for Columbus presumably reflects a lower value of k; the steeper relation for Columbus, a substantially lower value of P_y without much difference in v (see Table 7).[16]

3. *The Basis for the Relative Income Hypothesis*

We have been interpreting the relative income hypothesis in terms of our own hypothesis and thus have been emphasizing relative measured income as an index of relative permanent income. But it should be noted that considerations of a very different sort recommended the relative income hypothesis to its originators. They were led to emphasize relative income on emulative and imitative grounds. Consumer units, they argued, derived their standards of consumption partly from their neighbors; a unit at any given absolute income level will spend more on consumption in a community in which this income is a relatively low income than in a community in which it is a relatively high income, partly because it must spend more to keep up with the Joneses, partly because it will have more opportunity to observe superior goods and so will be tempted by what Duesenberry calls the "demonstration" effect.[17]

This argument in effect regards measured income as permanent income; it reconciles the observed stability of the average propensity to consume over time with the tendency for the propensity to decline with income at any one time by allowing for the effect of a rise in average income on the relative income that corresponds to any given absolute income. It rationalizes the cross-section decline in the propensity with income on the usual grounds; to quote Duesenberry, "At (relatively) low incomes the desires for present consumption outweigh considerations of the future to such an extent that little or no saving occurs. At higher levels the pressure for increased current consumption is sufficiently reduced to permit some attention to the future."[18] As is shown in Chapter II, this analysis is, to say the least, most unsatisfactory on a purely theoretical level.

These very different theoretical bases for attaching significance to the relative income hypothesis lead to quite different predictions, and it is by the conformity of these predictions to experience that we can choose between them. If relative income is important because of

---

[16] The value $v(1 - P_y)$ is .086 and .056 for New York whites and Negroes, respectively; .131 and .122 for Columbus whites and Negroes.

[17] Duesenberry gives the most explicit and extensive rationalization of the relative income hypothesis along these lines. See Duesenberry, *Income, Saving, and the Theory of Consumer Behavior*, particularly Chap. III.

[18] *Ibid.*, pp. 37–38.

emulation, there is no reason why it should not have the same effect among farm families as among nonfarm families; or, in any event, something additional would have to be introduced into the hypothesis, and the hypothesis in this way made more complex, to explain why it should have a different effect. If relative income is important because of the demonstration effect, again there is no reason why its effect should differ for farm and nonfarm families. True, the demonstration might be less ubiquitous and urgent, and this might account for higher savings on the farm, but this difference would presumably be the same at all relative income levels so there is no reason why it should affect the slope of a relation of Type R. On the other hand, if relative measured income is important as an index of the ratio of permanent income to average income, there is every reason why it should have a different effect for farm and nonfarm families. Since relative measured income status is more unstable on farms than in the city, a given difference in relative measured income corresponds on the average to a smaller difference in relative permanent income status. The fact that the observed relations of Type R differ for farm and nonfarm families and differ in the direction implied by the permanent income hypothesis is therefore evidence for it and against the emulative or demonstrative interpretation of the significance of relative income.

Similarly, emulative and imitative grounds give no reason to expect systematic differences between relations of Type R for different years, for cities of different size, or for consumer units of different race. On our hypothesis, such differences are to be expected whenever these groups differ in respect of specified characteristics of the income distribution. We have seen above that the observed differences in the relations of Type R among such groups seem to conform with the implications of our hypothesis. However, this evidence is incomplete and indirect. One relevant characteristic of the income distribution, namely, P_y, has not been observed directly but inferred from consumption behavior, and this inference is justified only if our hypothesis is accepted, so to some extent we have begged the crucial question. To complete this evidence we must demonstrate independently, as we shall in the next chapter, that P_y as inferred from consumption behavior is an estimate of P_y computed from income data. This done, the comparisons in question do become relevant evidence in favor of our hypothesis and against the emulative or demonstrative interpretation of the significance of relative income.

The permanent income hypothesis seems to me superior to the relative income hypothesis on three grounds: first, it has a simpler and more attractive theoretical basis in that it uses the same constructs to account for cross-section and temporal results, whereas the relative income hypothesis introduces very different considerations to account for the declining ratio of consumption to measured income in budget study regressions of consumption on income and for the constant ratio of aggregate consumption to aggregate income over long spans of time; second, it is more fruitful, in that it predicts a wider range of characteristics of observed consumption behavior; and finally, the evidence that we have cited seems to fit it somewhat better. In respect of the third point, however, this evidence is by no means sufficient to justify a firm rejection of the relative income hypothesis. It is much to be desired that a fuller test be made of the two hypotheses.

As with change in income, it should be emphasized here too that acceptance of the permanent income hypothesis does not imply rejection of relative income as a meaningful and relevant variable. The permanent income hypothesis explains why relative income is meaningful and relevant, and under what circumstances conversion of relations of Type A into relations of Type R can be expected to replace heterogeneity with homogeneity and under what circumstances it cannot be expected to do so.

4. *The Relative versus the Absolute Income Hypotheses*

The writers who have suggested the relative income hypothesis have offered empirical evidence—much of which we have referred to in the preceding sections of this chapter and in earlier chapters—in support of their contention that the relative income hypothesis interprets existing data better than the absolute income hypothesis. This evidence, while by no means conclusive, is certainly persuasive. In light of it, I am inclined to interpret the deficiencies of the relative income hypothesis recorded in the preceding sections as meaning only that the permanent income hypothesis is superior to the relative income hypothesis and as in no way contradicting the view that the relative income hypothesis is superior to the absolute income hypothesis. However, as noted in Chapter I, James Tobin has examined the compatibility of the absolute and relative income hypothesis with a number of pieces of empirical evidence and has reached a different conclusion. Although he regards the import of the evidence he examines as mixed, he concludes that on the whole it supports a somewhat modified absolute income hypothesis rather better than it does the relative income hypothesis. His analysis deserves examination in some detail both because of its intrinsic interest, and in order to see whether the discrepancies he finds between the evidence and the relative income hypothesis constitute evidence against the permanent income hypothesis as well, or can be explained by it.

169

Tobin examines four pieces of evidence bearing on the relative acceptability of the two hypotheses: budget data (1) for two samples of families over a period of three consecutive years, (2) on the savings patterns of Negroes and whites, and (3) on consumption-income relations in different cities, and (4) time series data on the ratio of aggregate savings to aggregate income. He concludes that items (1) and (3) favor the absolute income hypothesis, items (2) and (4) the relative income hypothesis. To resolve the conflict, Tobin suggests modifying the absolute income hypothesis by introducing the amount of financial resources other than income as an additional variable affecting consumption. He presents some indirect evidence to show that this modified hypothesis fits item (2) at least as well as the relative income hypothesis, and may also fit item (4). Tobin's modified hypothesis is in the spirit of our hypothesis, though not identical with it.

We have already examined items (2) and (4) in considerable detail.[19] Both for this reason and because Tobin's case for the absolute income hypothesis, even in its modified form, rests primarily on items (1) and (3), we need consider further only these two items.

a. CONTINUOUS BUDGET DATA

These data are for two samples of farm families in Illinois, Iowa, and Minnesota for which budget records are available for the three years 1940–1942.[20] One set of budgets was collected by the Farm Security Administration from families who had incurred loans from the FSA to purchase farms—these are the data we used in Chapter IV in our analysis of the effect of change in income; the other, by agricultural experiment stations, or extension services. Tobin presents a detailed analysis of the first sample and states that the second yields similar results.

The average income of the FSA sample rose sharply from 1940 to 1942—by nearly 75 per cent in money terms, and by 37 per cent in real terms; yet this rise was only half as large as the contemporaneous rise in real per capita farm income for the United States as a whole. Average consumption expenditures of the group rose also, but by less than 15 per cent in real terms so that the ratio of consumption to income fell rather sharply. This result is clearly consistent with the absolute income hypothesis, in the sense that budget studies show consumption to be a lower percentage of income, the higher the income. It is inconsistent with the relative income hypothesis. If the relevant income distribution is regarded as that of the sample itself,

---

[19] See above, pp. 79–85, 116–124.
[20] Willard W. Cochrane and Mary D. Grigg, *op. cit.*

the relative position of the group as a whole obviously remained unchanged, so that the ratio of consumption to income should have been unchanged also. If the relevant income distribution is for farmers as a whole, this group fell in relative position, which should imply a rise, not a fall, in the ratio of consumption to income.

Tobin plots the ratio of consumption to income for different income classes and different years against the corresponding (a) absolute real income and (b) ratio of income to the mean income of the group as a whole. Plotted against (a), the consumption ratios for the three years fall on a single well-defined curve, with little scatter about it. Plotted against (b), the consumption ratios define three curves, one for each year; the consumption ratio is lower for a given relative income, the later the year.

Two considerations are important in judging the weight to be attached to this evidence. In the first place, the sample analyzed is highly special, as is to be expected from its method of selection. Average consumption is only 53 per cent of average income in 1940, 48 per cent in 1941, and 43 per cent in 1942. These ratios of consumption are drastically lower than the ratios generally observed for farm families, or than the corresponding estimates for farmers as a whole in the corresponding years, yet the average income of the sample is not greatly different from the average income of all farm families in the corresponding states.[21] In view of the difficulties in measuring both income and consumption expenditures for farmers, these abnormal ratios raise doubts about the accuracy of the data.

In the second place, the two respects in which the FSA sample appears to contradict the relative income hypothesis—the behavior of the consumption-income ratio for the sample as a whole, and the behavior of this ratio for different income classes—are really only one: the second is the first in disguise. The correlation between measured consumption and measured income is very low so that the regression of consumption on income is very flat—on our hypothesis, P_y is rather small, in the neighborhood of .3 to .5.[22] The negative relation for any one year between the ratio of consumption to income and absolute real income that shows up on Tobin's Figure 1 is mainly the result of dividing almost constant consumption expenditures by successively higher incomes; it is only slightly flatter than the rectangular hyperbola that would be produced by strictly constant expenditures. Average real consumption rises only mildly—by 12 per cent—over the three year period. The corresponding rectangular

[21] See Reid, "Effect of Income Concept upon Expenditure Curves of Farm Families," p. 154.

[22] *Ibid.*, pp. 154, 165–166. See also Chap. VII below for direct evidence on P_y.

hyperbolae for the three years would differ only by the same amount, and three slightly flatter curves intersecting these hyperbolae successively farther to the right (because of the rise in average real income) would differ even less. Their essential coincidence in Tobin's figure therefore reflects primarily the small change in average consumption plus the low correlation between consumption and income. When the consumption ratios are plotted against relative incomes, curves only slightly flatter than rectangular hyperbolae are again produced, but this time the difference in the level of the rectangular hyperbolae is given by the difference in the ratio of average consumption to average income, which is about 20 per cent, and there is no offset, since the conversion to relative incomes places the mean of all three samples at the same point on the horizontal axis (namely 100), so the flatter curves intersect the hyperbolae one above the other.

While these qualifications lessen the weight that can be assigned to the evidence of the FSA sample, they by no means justify disregarding that evidence. As far as it goes, it speaks for the absolute income hypothesis and against the relative income hypothesis, at least in the variant in which income position is measured by the ratio of the income of the unit to the mean income of the group to which it belongs. We saw in section 1 above that this hypothesis gives the same results as the permanent income hypothesis if (1) k and P_y are the same for the different groups compared, and (2) the mean transitory components of income and consumption are zero for each group considered. There seems no reason to suppose that (1) is not reasonably well satisfied for the three years: on our hypothesis, differences in (1) would produce differences in the slope of the regression of consumption or the consumption ratio on income or relative income, yet the regressions for the three years show no sizable differences in slope. There is, on the other hand, good reason to suppose that point (2) is seriously in error: the mean transitory component of income was almost certainly positive in 1941 and 1942, and of consumption, almost certainly negative in 1942. Both 1941 and 1942 were years of abnormal prosperity, and by 1942 wartime shortages of goods were making themselves felt.

These effects are in the right direction to explain the differences in consumption ratios. Are they of the right magnitude? A rough test can be made with the help of Figure 13. Let us assume that this Figure is correctly described by the permanent income hypothesis so that the points on it can be regarded as generated from the central heavy line by the addition of transitory components of income and consumption. In order to estimate the mean transitory component of income in 1940, 1941, and 1942, let us further set the mean transitory component of consumption in these three years equal to zero. This is clearly implausible, particularly for 1942, but makes little difference to the final result since the effect of setting this component equal to zero when it might more plausibly be regarded as negative is to make the resulting estimate of the mean transitory component of income too large. But these errors are offsetting, since a negative mean transitory component of consumption has roughly the same effect as a positive mean transitory component of income. On these assumptions, we can estimate from Figure 13 the ratio of measured income to permanent income, the estimates being 1.00, 1.04, and 1.25 for 1940, 1941, and 1942, respectively.[23] These estimates are for the nation as a whole. Let us suppose them to hold also for the FSA sample. If we multiply them by the observed ratios of consumption to measured income, which, we may recall, were .53, .48, and .43 for the three years, the resulting figures are estimates of the ratio of permanent consumption to permanent income, and it is these ratios that should remain the same on our hypothesis. The numerical estimates obtained in this way are .53, .50, and .54 for 1940, 1941, and 1942, respectively. These are certainly enough alike to justify regarding the evidence for the FSA families as consistent with our hypothesis, albeit in a somewhat more sophisticated version than that in which it yields the same results as the relative income hypothesis.

b. GEOGRAPHICAL BUDGET COMPARISONS

For each of six communities,[24] Tobin compares two regressions: the regression of the ratio of consumption to income on percentile position in the income distribution computed by Duesenberry from Consumer Purchases Study data for 1935–36 for native-white non-relief families;[25] and the regression of the ratio of consumption to income on absolute income computed by Mendershausen from the same data,[26] corrected for estimated intercity differences in cost of living. He selects four values of the percentile position (1.0, 3.4, 30.2,

[23] From (5.2),

$$\frac{c_p^*}{y^*} = k^* \frac{y_p^*}{y}.$$

Replace c_p^* by c^* and write r for the observed ratio of consumption to income. It then follows from (5.2) that

$$\frac{y^*}{y_p^*} = \frac{k^*}{r}.$$

In Figure 13, we set $k^* = .8875$. r is equal to .886 in 1940, to .853 in 1941, and to .712 in 1942.

[24] Columbus, Providence, Denver, Chicago, Omaha, and the merged cities, Butte and Pueblo.

[25] *Op. cit.*, p. 54.

[26] Horst Mendershausen, "Differences in Family Saving," pp. 122–137.

and 90.2). For each value he determines the consumption ratio for Denver from the percentile regression, and the value of real income for which the absolute income regression for Denver gives the same consumption ratio (the matching real incomes are $9,800, $5,000, $2,380, and $1,470). For each value of the percentile position he computes the consumption ratios for each of the six cities from the percentile regressions, and the coefficient of variation of these six values. Similarly, for each real income value, he computes the consumption ratio for each of the six cities from the absolute income regressions, and the coefficient of variation of these six values. For each of the four points, the coefficient of variation of the percentile estimates exceeds substantially the coefficient of variation of the absolute income estimates. Tobin concludes that the consumption ratio is more homogeneous among cities for a given absolute income than for a given percentile position, and hence that this evidence favors the absolute income hypothesis.

This evidence does not, however, justify this conclusion, both because the evidence is poorly suited to provide a test of the two hypotheses and because the statistical analysis is inadequate. An alternative analysis of these and similar data leads to results that are much less clear cut.

As was noted in section 2 above, the absolute and relative income hypotheses yield divergent results for different groups of families only if the groups differ in the distribution of income, so that the same percentile point corresponds to different values of real income. It so happens that the six groups of consumer units Tobin compares differ little in average real income; the largest average real income is only 20 per cent above the smallest, the next to the largest only 10 per cent above the next to the smallest.[27] While the groups differ in the dispersion of the distributions about the mean, inspection of the data suggests that these differences, too, are moderate. All in all, therefore this set of communities is a most unsatisfactory set on the basis of which to test the two hypotheses. The difference in results that could be expected from the two hypotheses for communities so homogeneous as these is small enough to be easily swamped by extraneous factors affecting the comparison.

Such extraneous factors are clearly present, thanks not only to chance variation and observational error, but also to differences in

[27] These statements are based on mean incomes for native-white nonrelief families taken from U.S. Bureau of Labor Statistics, Bulletins 642, 644, 645, 646, deflated by cost of living in different cities as given by Mendershausen (*ibid.*). Duesenberry excluded some of the lower income classes (those for which an average of less than forty-eight full weeks of employment was reported) in computing his regressions, so these statements may not apply in detail to his figures. But the error can hardly be large.

the statistical procedures used by Duesenberry and Mendershausen. In consequence, the computed coefficients of variation reflect both whatever "real" differences there may be among the regressions for the different cities, and what may be regarded as sampling errors in the estimates of the parameters of the computed regressions. Tobin does not attempt to separate out these two sources of variation, or to test whether the coefficients of variation are larger than could readily be accounted for by sampling error alone. Supplementary calculations for the percentile regressions indicate that the coefficients of variation for them are roughly twice the value that could be expected on the average from chance alone, a difference somewhat greater than can readily be attributed to chance.[28]

There are at least three reasons why the sampling error of the percentile regressions might be expected to exceed the sampling error

[28] Duesenberry gives the standard deviations of his parameters. From these and other data that he gives it is possible to compute for each city for each percentile point the variance of the ordinate of the regression. The square root of the mean of these variances for the six cities is an estimate of the standard deviations to be expected by chance alone. The standard deviations computed in this way compare with the observed standard deviations as follows:

Percentile Point	Estimated Theoretical Standard Deviation	Observed Standard Deviation
1.0	2.3	4.6
3.4	1.4	3.3
30.2	1.4	2.7
90.2	2.2	3.5

The observed standard deviations given in this table are larger than those used by Tobin, because they were computed by dividing the sum of squares by 5, the number of degrees of freedom, whereas Tobin divided the sum of squares by 6, the number of observations.

If the estimated theoretical standard deviation is accepted as strictly correct, the significance of the difference between the observed and theoretical standard deviations can be readily tested, since the ratio of 5 times the observed variance to the theoretical variance is then distributed as χ^2 with 5 degrees of freedom. By this test, the observed variances are significantly larger than the theoretical variances, the probabilities that the observed χ^2 would be exceeded by chance varying from slightly less than .05 to less than .001. Of course, not all four comparisons are independent. The regressions being compared have two parameters, so only two independent comparisons are possible. A direct test of the differences among the parameters would be both more straightforward and statistically more efficient.

It should be noted that the procedure used for deriving the theoretical standard deviations is an approximation on a number of scores. It is noteworthy that the observed standard deviations, though higher, follow the pattern of the theoretical standard deviations.

Similar calculations were not made for Mendershausen's regressions because they would have required extensive recomputations from the original data.

of the absolute income regressions: first, the percentile regressions contain only two parameters, the absolute income regressions, three; second, the estimated percentile position is subject to a source of sampling error that does not affect the estimated real income since it depends on the frequency distribution of the sample incomes, which is only an estimate of the distribution in the community as a whole; third, Duesenberry excluded some of the lower income classes (those for which an average of less than forty-eight full weeks of employment was reported), whereas Mendershausen computed his regressions from all the data.[29]

This expectation is confirmed by the results. The correlation coefficients reported by Duesenberry for his regressions for the six communities tend to be lower than those reported by Mendershausen. The mean variance (square of the standard deviation) of the observations about the regressions computed from these correlation coefficients is roughly 2.6 times as large for the percentile as for the absolute income regressions.[30] The mean variance among communities computed from Tobin's four sets of figures is 2.3 times as large for the percentile as for the absolute income regressions.[31] It looks very much as if the whole of the difference between the coefficients of variation for the two hypotheses simply reflects Duesenberry's lower correlation coefficients. These lower correlation coefficients might themselves be interpreted as evidence that the percentile hypothesis fits the data less well than the real income hypothesis. But this evidence is for each

[29] It should be noted that Duesenberry's exclusion of these classes, while perhaps called for by the rationalization he presents for the relative income hypothesis, is not justified by the permanent income hypothesis.

[30] The square of the coefficient of correlation (r^2) is the fraction of the total variance accounted for by the regression; unity minus r^2 is the fraction not accounted for. The average value of $1 - r^2$ is .103 for Duesenberry's regressions; .040 for Mendershausen's. Note that this method of averaging implicitly weights the variances about the regressions by the reciprocal of the total variance.

One ambiguity of this comparison is that Duesenberry does not state explicitly whether he computed his correlation coefficients from the mean values for income classes or from the original observations. The former tends to yield a higher coefficient than the latter. I have assumed, on the basis of internal evidence, that he did the former, as Mendershausen explicitly states he did.

[31] The variances were computed for each level of income or percentile point; the four resulting percentile variances averaged and divided by the average of the four resulting real income variances. These averages are an unweighted average of the variances, not a weighted average, as for the ratio of 2.6 just cited. The average ratio of the percentile variance to the real income variance is 3.0. This ratio is not strictly comparable with the ratio of the variances of observations about the regressions. For any given regression, the variance of the ordinate of the regression for a given value of the abscissa is proportional to the variance about the regression. The proportionality factor, however, will in general vary from one type of regression to another, as well as from one value of the abscissa to another on the same regression. For Mendershausen's regressions, I cannot compute these proportionality factors on the basis of his published figures. I see no reason to expect that adjustment for this defect would substantially alter the results.

community separately; it does not reflect differences among communities. More important, the different statistical procedures used in calculating the percentile and absolute income regressions render highly dubious any such interpretation of the lower correlation coefficients.

Tobin's analysis of these data is not only incomplete but also statistically inefficient. Tobin gives ordinates of the regressions for four selected points; he could equally well have done so for forty; but such a multiplication of points would add no new information. Knowledge of the ordinates of a percentile regression for any two points, and of an absolute income regression for any three, permits the calculation of the ordinates for all other points, since the percentile regressions have two parameters, and absolute income regressions, three. At most, therefore, three independent comparisons among the regressions are possible.

Much of the difficulty of interpreting Tobin's results arises, as noted above, from differences between Duesenberry's and Mendershausen's computations other than the difference between the absolute income and the relative income hypothesis: their use of different forms of regression equations, different kinds of independent variables, and slightly different bodies of data to estimate the regressions. These can all be eliminated by using Mendershausen's regressions alone to test whether the absolute or relative income hypothesis gives estimates that vary less from city to city. By a simple transformation, Mendershausen's regressions can be written so that they express the ratio of consumption to income as a function of either (a) absolute real income or (b) the ratio of the income of a consumer unit to the average income of the community.[32] The latter is a variant of the relative income hypothesis, though not the percentile variant used by Duesenberry. It can be seen whether the parameters differ more when the regressions are written in form (a) or in form (b). There are three parameters in the regression used by Mendershausen. However, one is the same for both forms of the regression, so differences can appear in only two.

---

[32] Mendershausen fits regressions of the form $s' = a + by + c(1/y)$, where s' is the ratio of saving to measured income, y is total family income, and a, b, and c, statistically estimated parameters. Following Tobin, let k be the ratio of the cost of living in Columbus to the cost of living in the city in question. The parameters of the absolute real income regression are then a, b/k, and kc, obtained by making the transformation $y' = ky$, where y' is "real" income as defined by Tobin. A regression in terms of relative income is obtained by making the transformation $y'' = y/\bar{y}$ where y'' is relative income and $\bar{y}$, average total family income in the city in question. The parameters of the relative income regression are then a, $b\bar{y}$, $c/\bar{y}$. The ratio of consumption to income is unity minus s', so the parameters of the relation described at the head of Table 16 are related to a, b, and c by $\alpha = 1 - a$, $\beta = -b$, $\gamma = -c$.

Table 16 summarizes the results of comparisons along these lines for the six communities compared by Tobin, ten communities including these six for which estimates of intercity differences in cost of living are available, 20 communities including these 10 for which Mendershausen reports regressions for white families,[33] four communities for which he reports regressions for Negro families, and

TABLE 16

Comparison of Relative and Absolute Income Hypotheses
for Different Groups of Communities, 1935–1936

Comparison based on parameters of regression:

$$c' = \alpha + \beta y + \gamma \frac{1}{y},$$

where

c' = ratio of measured consumption to measured income,

y = alternatively, absolute nominal income (measured income in nominal units), absolute real income (measured income deflated for cost of living differences), relative income (ratio of measured income to mean income of group), and

Coefficient of variation = standard deviation divided by mean.

	Coefficient of Variation of Estimates of:						
	β			γ			Coefficient of Variation of Mean Income
	Absolute Income		Relative Income	Absolute Income		Relative Income	
Groups Compared	Nominal	Real		Nominal	Real		
White families in:							
6 communities	.33	.32	.32	.20	.18	.23	.04
10 communities	.53	.51	.54	.33	.30	.35	.11
20 communities	.71		.71	.38		.40	.13
Negro families in 4 communities	.23		.34	.79		.72	.35
White families in 20 communities and Negro families in 4 communities	.74		.64	.53		.49	.24

Source:

All estimates are based on parameters reported by Horst Mendershausen, "Differences in Family Saving between Cities of Different Size and Location, Whites and Negroes," *Review of Economic Statistics*, XXII (August, 1940), pp. 122–37. Cost of living also taken from Mendershausen. Mean incomes are from Department of Labor, B.L.S. Bulletins Nos. 642–647 and Department of Agriculture, B.H.E., Miscellaneous Publications 339, 345.

[33] This count refers to the individual communities. Mendershausen also reports regressions for combinations of these communities. I have made no use of these.

finally, all 24 groups for which he reports regressions. Except for the six and ten communities, the comparison must be made for an inferior variant of the absolute income hypothesis, namely, one in which no allowance is made for price differences. The comparisons in the first two lines of the table show that correction for price differences systematically reduces the divergence among the parameters. However, the effect is moderate and we can allow for it qualitatively in making the remaining comparisons; as a result, the gain from broadening the scope of comparison seems clearly greater than the loss from being unable to make direct corrections for prices.

For each of the three sets of white families, the absolute real income hypothesis seems either equal or superior to the relative income hypothesis for both of the parameters, if for the third set we may judge from the nominal income results. The differences are small and may well be within the range of sampling errors, and the comparisons are not independent since the several sets have communities in common; yet the results are consistent and agree with Tobin's original finding. For the Negro families, the parameters give conflicting results; for one parameter, the absolute income hypothesis is superior; for the other, inferior. Finally, for all groups, the relative income hypothesis gives better results for both parameters; conceivably, these would be reversed if cost of living corrections could be made, but it seems hardly likely.

The reason for the much better showing of the relative income hypothesis in the last two comparisons is suggested by the final column of the Table, which gives measures of the dispersion of mean incomes in the different communities. This dispersion is markedly wider in the last two comparisons than in the first three; in these, there is considerably more of a difference in mean incomes to produce differences among absolute income regressions of the kind predicted by the relative income hypothesis. In the first three comparisons, as already noted, there is so little difference in mean incomes that there is hardly anything for the relative income hypothesis to do. The fact that the performance of the relative income hypothesis improves relative to that of the absolute income hypothesis as the dispersion of mean incomes increases must be regarded as evidence in favor of the relative income hypothesis.

The comparisons that are summarized in Table 16 are not themselves fully satisfactory because they deal with each parameter separately; they do not allow for the possibility that the differences in the parameters may either offset or reinforce one another.[34] In work done

[34] I am indebted to James Tobin for calling my attention to this deficiency of these tests arising from their neglect of the interaction between the parameters.

since the publication of the article under discussion, Tobin has made some comparisons that allow for this possibility. However, these are only for the six and the ten communities, which is why I have included the less satisfactory comparisons in Table 16. Tobin subjected the data to an analysis of variance by computing the sum of squared deviations about a regression of Mendershausen's form fitted to the data for each city separately—the corresponding mean square, entered in column (2) of Table 17, is the same for the two hypotheses since, as

TABLE 17

Comparison of Relative and Absolute Income Hypotheses Based on
Analysis of Variance for Two Groups of Communities, 1935–1936

| Groups Compared (1) | Variance Estimated from Deviations | | | Ratio of Variance between Cities to Variance from Regressions | |
| | From Separate Regressions (2) | Between Cities on | | | |
		Absolute Hypothesis (3)	Relative Hypothesis (4)	Absolute (5)	Relative (6)
White families in					
6 cities	.046	.213	.478	4.7	10.5
10 cities	.067	.498	.555	7.4	8.2

Source: Unpublished computations by James Tobin kindly made available to me.

noted earlier, for any one community a relation of Type R is simply a transformation of a relation of Type A and yields the same predictions of the consumption ratio. He then fitted regressions of the same form to the data for all the cities combined, using absolute real income in one case and relative income in the other as his independent variable. The sum of squared deviations about this regression reflects the effect of differences both within and between cities; the excess of this sum over the sum of squares about the separate regressions is attributable to differences between cities. The corresponding mean squares are entered in columns (3) and (4). These are markedly larger than the variance within cities as is shown by the ratios in the final two columns, all of which are much larger than the ratio that could plausibly be expected to arise from chance.[35] On this evidence, neither the absolute nor the relative income hypothesis can be regarded as accounting satisfactorily for the differences between cities; factors accounted for by neither must be at work to produce differences of this size between cities.

[35] The .01 value of F for the number of degrees of freedom involved is approximately 2.4 for the six communities and 1.9 for the ten communities.

The mean square between cities is more than twice as large for the relative as the absolute income hypothesis for the six communities; about 10 per cent larger, for the ten communities. Unfortunately, there seems no simple way to determine the probability that such a difference would arise by chance; I conjecture that the difference for the six communities is larger than can readily be attributed to chance, and for the ten communities almost certainly small enough to be readily accounted for in this way.[36] This difference in results for the two sets of communities can again be explained by the difference in dispersion of mean incomes. According to Table 16, the dispersion, though small for both sets of communities, is nearly three times as large for the ten communities as for the six. Again, therefore, the relative income hypothesis shows up better when there is more scope for it to operate. It seems not unlikely that if this comparison could be extended to a more heterogeneous set of communities, the result would be, as in Table 16, to reverse the relative size of the mean squares between cities.

It may be that the significant differences between cities left unaccounted for by either the absolute or relative income hypothesis can be accounted for, at least in part, by our hypothesis, that is, by differences in P_y or in the numerical value of k which reflect differences in its determinants. However, I have been unable to uncover any independent evidence on these magnitudes that would enable us to determine whether this is so.

C. SUMMARY EVALUATION OF EVIDENCE

Our re-examination of Tobin's evidence suggests that it is much less favorable to the absolute income hypothesis and more favorable to the relative income hypothesis than he regarded it. Of the four pieces of evidence Tobin examines in some detail, two are admittedly more favorable to the simple relative income hypothesis than to the simple absolute income hypothesis. The remaining two, on which Tobin rests his case, can be regarded as speaking with a rather weak voice for the absolute income hypothesis. But for one, the FSA sample, the reason seems to be that transitory components of income and expenditure were introduced by World War II. For the other, the comparison among communities, the reason seems to be that the two

[36] If the mean squares between cities for the relative and absolute income hypotheses were statistically independent estimates, their ratio would have the F distribution, and the probability of exceeding the observed ratio by chance would be a trifle over 5 per cent for the six communities, well over 20 per cent for the ten communities. However, the two estimates are not statistically independent, since they are computed from the same degrees of freedom. I conjecture that their interdependence is such as to make large F's less likely to arise from chance, but I cannot demonstrate that this is so.

hypotheses are compared under conditions that give little scope to the forces emphasized by the relative income hypothesis. As these conditions are expanded to cover a wider range of variation in average income, the performance of the relative income hypothesis improves relative to that of the absolute income hypothesis, so that this piece of evidence can equally be regarded as favoring the relative income hypothesis. All in all, therefore, I see little justification for rejecting, on the basis of this evidence, the prior conclusion that the relative income hypothesis is superior to the absolute income hypothesis.

One of the apparent failures of the relative income hypothesis is, as already implied, readily accounted for on the permanent income hypothesis and therefore is another piece of evidence for the latter as compared with either of the other hypotheses. With respect to differences among communities, we have no evidence whether they can or cannot be accounted for by the permanent income hypothesis.

CHAPTER VII

Evidence from Income Data on the Relative Importance of Permanent and Transitory Components of Income

THE distinguishing feature of the permanent income hypothesis is the central role it assigns to certain characteristics of the income distribution in explaining empirical evidence on consumption behavior. In examining the consistency of our hypothesis with available evidence, we have so far restricted ourselves to inferring these characteristics from paired data on consumption and income; from data for either a number of consumer units in the same year, or a number of years for a group of consumer units. As has been noted several times, however, these characteristics can be determined from income data alone. An estimate of P_y, the fraction of the variance of incomes contributed by the permanent component, can be constructed from data on the incomes of identical consumer units in different years.[1] This possibility provides an independent means of testing our hypothesis; in addition, it enhances its potential usefulness by broadening the range of data that it can be used to interpret.

Consider a group of consumer units whose measured incomes we know for two successive years. Suppose that the differences among the incomes of the members of the group in each year are entirely attributable to differences in permanent components of income, and that we can neglect "aging" from one year to the next (alternatively, assume that all members of the group are affected alike by aging). The relative measured income position of the members of the group would then, in some sense yet to be defined precisely, be the same in the two years; there would be perfect correlation, also in a sense yet to be defined precisely, between their incomes in the two years. At the other extreme, suppose all differences in income among members of the group in at least one of the years are attributable to transitory

---

[1] Similarly, estimates of P_c, the fraction of the total variance of consumption expenditures contributed by the permanent component of consumption, can be constructed from data on the consumption expenditures of identical consumer units in different years. The discussion that follows about P_y applies with suitable changes equally to P_c.

factors that exhaust their effect in that year. Incomes in the second year would then tend to be uncorrelated with those in the first year. The size of the correlation between incomes in two successive years therefore provides some evidence on the importance of the permanent component in producing differences in measured income.

1. *A Method of Estimating* P_y

Let $\bar{y}_i$ stand for the mean measured income and s_i, for the standard deviation of measured income in year i; r_{ij}, for the product moment correlation coefficient between measured incomes in years i and j; b_{ji}, for the slope of the computed regression of year j's measured income on year i's; b_{ij} for the slope of the regression of year i's measured income on year j's; and P_i for the fraction of the total variance of measured income contributed by the permanent component in year i. I have elsewhere suggested two alternative statistical estimates of P_i, differing in the precise meaning attached to constancy of the permanent component.[2] One is derived for what I have called the *mean assumption*, which is that permanent components maintain the same ratio to the mean of the group in different years, so that the relative variability of the permanent component is unchanged. Under this assumption,[3]

(7.1)
$$\begin{cases} P_i = b_{ji}\dfrac{\bar{x}_i}{\bar{x}_j} = r_{ij}\dfrac{s_j\bar{x}_i}{s_i\bar{x}_j}, \\[2ex] P_j = b_{ij}\dfrac{\bar{x}_j}{\bar{x}_i} = r_{ij}\dfrac{s_i\bar{x}_j}{s_j\bar{x}_i}. \end{cases}$$

The other measure is derived for what I have called the *variability assumption*, which is that the fraction of the total variability contributed by the permanent components is the same in successive years, i.e. that P_y is the same in years i and j. Let P' designate the common

[2] What follows is essentially a restatement and summary of Friedman and Kuznets, *Income from Independent Professional Practice*, pp. 325–338, 352–364, which contains full proofs of the formulas that follow.

[3] Under the logarithmic variant, the mean assumption can be broadened without affecting the results. If the absolute values of the permanent components are in a common ratio, whether the ratio of the arithmetic means or any other common ratio, estimates of P_Y are given by

(7.1′)
$$\begin{cases} P_{Yi} = B_{ji}, \\ P_{Yj} = B_{ij}, \end{cases}$$

where B_{ji} is the regression coefficient of the regression of the logarithm of income in year j on the logarithm of income in year i, and B_{ij} the same with i and j interchanged.

value of P_y. Then, under this assumption,[4]

(7.2) $$P' = \sqrt{P_i P_j} = r_{ij} .$$

It is obvious from the formula that the contribution of the permanent component as estimated under the variability assumption is a geometric average of the contributions in the two years as estimated under the mean assumption. Although the variability assumption leads to mathematically simpler results, it is less attractive theoretically than the mean assumption. Further, some statistical tests made by Margaret Reid suggest that the mean assumption yields the better results in interpreting consumption data.[5] These formulas are for incomes in absolute units; however, very similar formulas apply when the data are expressed in logarithms, and the logarithmic variant in general seems to fit the empirical evidence rather better.

Consider three successive years, say years 1, 2, and 3. Suppose that two estimates of P_3 are computed by (7.1): first, from data for years 2 and 3 (call this $P_{3.2}$); second, from data for years 1 and 3 (call this $P_{3.1}$). Clearly, the two results need not be identical. In general $P_{3.2}$ can be expected to be larger than $P_{3.1}$ since the correlation between incomes in two consecutive years can be expected to be higher than in two nonconsecutive years with one year intervening. This difference in numerical results reflects an implicit difference in the definition of the permanent component—a point that we have mentioned at several points but have not hitherto had occasion to state precisely. In taking $P_{3.2}$ as an estimate of the fraction of variance contributed by the permanent component in year 3, we implicitly define the permanent component as the component that is attributable to factors affecting income alike in two or more successive years, and the corresponding transitory component, as the component that is attributable to factors affecting income in one and only one year. In taking $P_{3.1}$ as an estimate of P_3, we implicitly define the permanent component as the component that is attributable to factors affecting income alike in three or more successive years, and the corresponding transitory component, as the component that is attributable to factors affecting income in one or two but not three successive years.

[4] Under the logarithmic variant, the formula is essentially the same if the variability assumption is interpreted as meaning that the same fraction of the logarithmic variance is contributed by the permanent component in successive years, namely,

(7.2') $$P'_r = \sqrt{P_{r_i} P_{r_j}} = r_{r_i r_j}$$

[5] The results are contained in an unpublished paper by Margaret Reid, entitled "The Relation of the Within-Group Transitory Component of Incomes to the Income Elasticity of Family Expenditures."

More generally, we can conceive of income as the sum of a continuum of components, classified by the length of the period for which the corresponding factors affect income and the time unit in which they make their first appearance. For simplicity, we can represent this continuum by a trichotomy of permanent, quasi-permanent, and transitory components, where the "truly" permanent component is attributed to factors affecting income over the longest period considered; the "truly" transitory component, to factors affecting income in only a single time unit; the quasi-permanent component, to other factors affecting income in more than one, but not all, time units. Given data on incomes in a series of years, statistical estimates can be constructed of the fraction of the total variance of income contributed by each component.[6]

As the permanent income hypothesis is used to interpret empirical data, it may be necessary to elaborate it by allowing for the separate influence of quasi-permanent components, or even additional sub-components.[7] For the present, however, it seems better to stick to the simpler formulation in terms of permanent and transitory components alone; this still leaves considerable leeway in the precise definition of the permanent component, which, as noted earlier, should be determined empirically, not imposed a priori.[8]

The approach to the analysis of income data just described can be used to estimate not only the contribution of the various components to the variance of income for the group as a whole but also their contribution to the deviation of the average income of a particular income class from the average income of the group as a whole. If the fraction of this deviation contributed by the permanent component (when we classify all components of income into the dichotomy of permanent and transitory components) is the same for all income classes in year i, then the regression of year j income on year i income will be linear, and conversely. These are also the conditions, therefore, under which, on our hypothesis, the regression of consumption on income will be linear for year i.

It should be noted that this analysis applies only to differences in income; it does not, for any one group, give evidence on the mean transitory component of income. Some such evidence can be obtained, however, by applying the same analysis to data on the mean incomes of a number of groups, say to the mean incomes in two successive years of a set of communities.

[6] See Friedman and Kuznets, *op. cit.*, pp. 352–64.

[7] This is equivalent to allowing for different "short-run" and "long-run" marginal propensities to consume.

[8] See above, pp. 23–25, 92–93, 142, 150–151.

TABLE 18

Correlation Coefficients between Incomes of Identical Units
in Different Years

Group	Income Definition	Years Correlated	Number of Years Intervening between Years Correlated	Correlation Coefficient
1. Physicians	Earnings from independent practice	[a]	0	.93
		[b]	1	.91
		1929 & 1932	2	.88
2. Dentists	Earnings from independent practice	[a]	0	.92
		[b]	1	.88
		1929 & 1932	2	.76
3. Lawyers	Earnings from independent practice	[c]	0	.84
		1932 & 1934	1	.80
4. Certified public accountants	Earnings from independent practice	[d]	0	.88
		[e]	1	.78
		1929 & 1932	2	.82
5. Consulting engineers	Earnings from independent practice	1929 & 1930	0	.67
		1929 & 1931	1	.63
		1929 & 1932	2	.52
6. Families in 33 cities	Total family income	1929 & 1933	3	.74[t] (.63 to .86)
7. Wisconsin taxpayers grouped in family unit	"Economic income" of family unit	[g]	0	.84
		[h]	1	.78
		[i]	2	.76
		[j]	3	.71
		[k]	4	.70
		1929 & 1935	5	.69
8. Urban spending units	Total income	1947 & 1948	0	.83
9. Farm families reporting to agricultural experiment station	Logarithm of family net cash income	[l]	0	.41
		1940 & 1942	1	.33[m]
10. FHA families	Logarithm of family net cash income	[l]	0	.48
		1940 & 1942	1	.46[m]
11. Groups 9 and 10	Logarithm of family net cash income	[l]	0	.52
		1940 & 1942	1	.47[m]

(cont. on next page)

187

TABLE 18 (cont.)

[a] Average of coefficients for 1929 and 1930, 1932 and 1933, 1933 and 1934.
[b] Average of coefficients for 1929 and 1931, 1932 and 1934, 1934 and 1936.
[c] Average of coefficients for 1932 and 1933, 1933 and 1934.
[d] Average of coefficients for 1929 and 1930, 1932 and 1933, 1933 and 1934, 1934 and 1935, 1935 and 1936.
[e] Average of coefficients for 1929 and 1931, 1932 and 1934, 1934 and 1936.
[f] Average of coefficients for 33 different cities. The individual coefficients vary from .63 to .86, with 5 less than .7, 12 from .7 to .75, 12 from .75 to .8, and 4 from .8 to .86.
[g] Average of six coefficients for all consecutive pairs of years from 1929 to 1935.
[h] Average of coefficients for 1929 and 1931, 1933 and 1935.
[i] Average of coefficients for 1929 and 1932, 1932 and 1935.
[j] Average of coefficients for 1929 and 1933, 1931 and 1935.
[k] Average of coefficients for 1929 and 1934, 1930 and 1935.
[l] Average of six coefficients: for 1940 and 1941, 1941 and 1942 for three separate state groups: Illinois, Iowa, and Minnesota.
[m] Average of three coefficients for separate state groups in Illinois, Iowa, and Minnesota.

Source:
Items 1 to 5
Milton Friedman and Simon Kuznets, *Income from Independent Professional Practice*, National Bureau of Economic Research, 1945, Table 56, p. 305.
Item 6
Horst Mendershausen, *Changes in Income Distribution during the Great Depression*, Studies in Income and Wealth, VII, National Bureau of Economic Research, 1946, Table 30, p. 90.
Item 7
Frank A. Hanna, Joseph A. Pechman, Sidney M. Lerner, *Analysis of Wisconsin Income*, Studies in Income and Wealth, IX, National Bureau of Economic Research, 1948, Part III, by Frank A. Hanna, "The Accounting Period and the Distribution of Income," Table 15, p. 232.
Item 8
Based on data from Survey of Consumer Finances reinterview sample collected by Michigan Survey Research Center for Federal Reserve Board. Coefficient taken from Margaret Reid, "The Relation of the Within-Group Transitory Component of Incomes to the Income Elasticity of Family Expenditures," unpublished paper.
Items 9 to 11
Ibid.

2. *Empirical Evidence on* P_y

A collection of computed correlation coefficients between incomes in different years is given in Table 18.[9] These can be taken as estimates of the contribution of the permanent component in the corresponding years, under the variability assumption, or of the average contribution in the corresponding years, under the mean assumption. As expected, the coefficients decline with an increase in the number of years intervening between the years correlated. The decline is, however, on the whole moderate; the results are therefore not likely

[9] The correlations summarized in Table 18 are all that, to the best of my knowledge, are available for the data in question. Omissions from the list—e.g. the absence of a correlation for physicians for 1930 and 1931—correspond with omissions in the original source.

188

to be greatly affected by the precise definition of the permanent component that is adopted.

The most striking feature of the table is the consistency among the correlation coefficients for such different groups and time periods, with the exception of farm families. The summary in Table 19 of the

TABLE 19

Summary of Correlation Coefficients in Table 18
for Three Principal Bodies of Nonfarm Data

Number of Years Intervening between Years Correlated	Average Coefficient of Correlation for		
	Professions	Wisconsin Taxpayers	Urban Families
0	.85	.83	.83
1	.80	.78	
2	.74	.76	
3		.71	.74
4		.70	
5		.69	

correlation coefficients for the three principal bodies of nonfarm data emphasizes this consistency.

The differences among the various groups are clearly small enough to be attributed to sampling variation. According to these data, for nonfarm families, the contribution of the permanent component to the variance of income cannot be set higher than about .85, on the broadest definition of the permanent component, nor lower than about .70 on a rather narrow definition. For a three year permanent component span—that is, for one year intervening between the years correlated—the relevant value of P_y is about .80. The correlation coefficients for farm families are distinctly smaller than for urban families, as general knowledge would lead one to expect. For the small and unrepresentative samples covered in Table 18—unfortunately the only ones for which we have data—the coefficient is between .4 and .5 for consecutive years and between .3 and .5 for nonconsecutive years with one year intervening.

Part of this difference between the coefficients for farm and nonfarm families may reflect the use of logarithms in computing the farm correlations and of absolute incomes in computing the others. Some bits of evidence suggest that for data like these, the computed correlation coefficient between the logarithms is generally lower than between the absolute values. But this can at most account for a small part of the difference.[10]

[10] Margaret Reid has computed logarithmic correlations matching 14 of Mendershausen's 1929–33 correlations. The logarithmic correlation was lower in every case and the average correlation coefficient was .64 for the logarithms and .74 for the original values.

3. *Comparison of Estimates of P_y with Estimated Income Elasticity of Consumption*

On our hypothesis, the elasticity of consumption with respect to measured income computed from budget data is also equal to P_y, so the correlation coefficients in Tables 18 and 19 can be regarded as estimates of corresponding income elasticities.[11] The numerical values in these tables are clearly of the right order of magnitude to be estimates of the income elasticity of consumption. According to Table 1, the elasticity computed directly from the consumption-income data varies from .70 to .87 for various groups of nonfarm consumer units in the United States, with something like .83 as a reasonably typical value, and is .65 and .69 for two samples of farm units. For the nonfarm groups, these values are as good a summary of the correlations in Tables 18 and 19 as of the elasticities in Table 1. For the farm families, the correlations in Table 18 are lower than the elasticities in Table 3, but, as we shall see, so are elasticities computed for the particular farm groups covered by Table 18, so again the agreement is excellent.

The agreement between the values of P_y estimated from income data alone and from the regression of consumption expenditures on measured income must be regarded as strong evidence in favor of our hypothesis. Two considerations make this agreement particularly striking: first, most of the data underlying Table 18 are entirely independent of the data underlying the elasticities in Table 1; second, we were led to compare these two kinds of data as we have just done solely by our hypothesis and not by any previously noted similarity between the two magnitudes. To the best of my knowledge, no one has hitherto made a comparison of this kind, or indeed, of any kind, between these two kinds of data. It should perhaps be noted explicitly that there is nothing in the arithmetic of the computations to produce the observed measure of agreement. The correlation coefficients are constrained within the range -1 to $+1$; the elasticities can have any value from $-\infty$ to $+\infty$, though we know that empirically they are uniformly less than $+1$.

Our comparison has so far been without regard to the length of the horizon that defines the permanent component. We have been able to neglect this feature because, as noted, the effect of the length of the horizon on P_y is moderate, causing it to vary—for nonfarm groups—only from about .70 to about .85, so that leaving it undefined still gives a narrow enough range of values to provide an impressive

---

[11] This statement is exact for arithmetic linear regressions only at the mean point and for zero mean transitory components; for logarithmic linear regressions, it is exact more generally.

check on the coincidence predicted by our theory between the two sets of estimates of P_y. Given this general coincidence, we can use these data to estimate the appropriate length of horizon. For nonfarm groups the correlation coefficients for consecutive years, which corresponds with a two-year horizon, are in general somewhat higher than the income elasticities computed from the budget data: one correlation coefficient is .67, the other six vary from .83 to .93 and the seven average .84. The elasticities for nonfarm groups vary from .70 to .87, the .70 being for 1944. The four others for the period after World War I are between .80 and .87. All eight average .80, the five for the period after World War I, .81. The correlation coefficients for nonconsecutive years with one year intervening, which corresponds with a three-year horizon, match the elasticities somewhat better: one is .63, the other five vary from .78 to .91, and the six average .80. On this evidence, a three-year horizon gives the definition of the permanent component that fits these data the best.[12]

Margaret Reid has made a more precise and detailed test of the relation between estimates of P_y computed from income data alone (strictly speaking, P_Y, since she used logarithms throughout) and elasticities computed from consumption-income regressions.[13] For a number of different groups of families for which income data were available for a number of consecutive years and expenditure data for one or more of these years, she has compared income elasticities computed from the budget data with estimates of P_Y computed from incomes in different years. Construction of both estimates for the same families eliminates one source of noncomparability that affected the preceding comparison between the elasticities in Table 1 and the correlation coefficients in Table 18. In addition, she has been able to estimate P_Y from the income data on the mean assumption and so get estimates for each year separately.

Much of Reid's data are for the farm families analyzed also by Tobin (see Chapter VI, section 4 above) and used in Chapter IV in considering the effect of change of income. As noted earlier, there is considerable doubt about the representativeness and accuracy of these data. Although these defects should affect the direct estimate of P_Y and the income elasticities in much the same way, and so do not

---

[12] One qualification that is required in connection with this comparison is that the elasticities were estimated from logarithmic regressions by graphic methods, the correlations computed from arithmetic data. It is not clear what the net effect of these differences is: the use of logarithms would probably reduce the correlations (see footnote 10); on the other hand, computation of the elasticities from all the data rather than graphic estimation would probably reduce the estimated elasticities (see Chapter IV, footnote 11). So these two differences probably offset one another, at least in part.

[13] Described in Reid, "The Relation of the Within-Group Transitory Component of Income to the Income Elasticity of Family Expenditures."

destroy the value of the data for the present purpose, they probably introduce a good deal of variability into the results.

Figure 15, taken from Miss Reid's unpublished paper, summarizes the results. Both the income elasticities and the estimates of P_Y from income data were computed from the logarithms of the original observations. For such data, our hypothesis implies that the observed income elasticity of consumption should be equal to P_Y, provided, of course, that the "permanent component" is appropriately defined. If the data conformed precisely to this expectation, the observations would all fall on the diagonal lines in the panels.

In Panel 1, P_Y is estimated from data on income in two consecutive years, which implies the broadest definition of permanent component. The resulting values might be expected to be upper estimates of the appropriate P_Y or of the income elasticities. The results conform to this expectation. The cluster of points follows the pattern of the diagonal line, but tends to be to the right of it, an effect which overestimates of P_Y would produce. In judging this figure, it should be noted that (1) all but one of the points are for farm families, and the one exception is the point corresponding to the highest recorded value of P_Y, which is for the urban sample collected by the Michigan Survey Research Center; (2) the points are for years varying from 1937 to 1948; (3) the points for farm families are all computed from relatively small samples, varying from 60 to 229 families; (4) as just noted, at least some and perhaps many of the farm samples may be highly unrepresentative.

For some of the samples, data were available for three consecutive years. For these, Reid estimated P_Y from data for the first and third years, which implies a more restrictive definition of the permanent component. The results are plotted in Panel 2. As was to be expected, the substitution of a three-year for a two-year permanent component shifts the cluster of points to the left; one-third of the points are above the diagonal, whereas in Panel 1 only one-seventh are. The points in Panel 2 appear to follow the pattern of the straight line less well than in Panel 1; and taken at their face value, a flatter line than the diagonal seems called for. However, this difference should be given little weight. The appearance of flatness is produced entirely by points for the more dubious set of farm samples; the points for this set of samples alone show the same tendency in Panel 1, but it is there concealed by the larger number of other points in the chart.[14]

Panel 2 suggests that the appropriate definition of permanent component is for a period of three years or slightly longer. This is the

[14] The points in question are all for the Farm Security Administration samples analyzed explicitly by Tobin and discussed above.

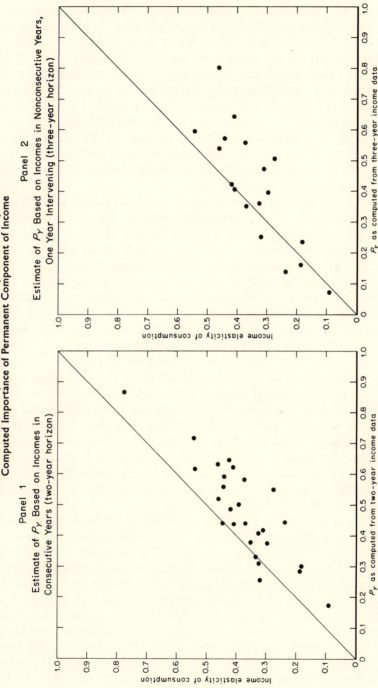

FIGURE 15

Relation between Computed Income Elasticity of Consumption and
Computed Importance of Permanent Component of Income

Panel 1

Estimate of P_Y Based on Incomes in
Consecutive Years (two-year horizon)

Panel 2

Estimate of P_Y Based on Incomes in Nonconsecutive Years,
One Year Intervening (three-year horizon)

Source: Margaret Reid, "The Relation of the Within-Group Transitory Component
of Incomes to the Income Elasticity of Family Expenditures," unpublished paper.

same as the conclusion reached earlier from data, primarily for urban families, none of which is used in Panel 2. This common result is also consistent with the evidence from time series data. The expected-income regression computed in Chapter V between real per capita consumption and a weighted average of current and past incomes gave an estimate of 2.5 years for the average time lag or of 5 years for the effective horizon. This is longer than the horizon implied by the cross-section data. And it is plausible that it should be. Vagaries that reduce the effective horizon for individuals tend to cancel out in average data. It is encouraging to find such close agreement in the precise definition of permanent components suggested by three independent bodies of data.

After the preceding part of this section was written and circulated in mimeographed form, some additional data were transmitted to me by John Frechtling of the Federal Reserve Board on the relation between P_y as estimated from income data alone and the income elasticity of consumption as estimated from data on income and consumption (Table 20). These additional data are from a reinterview sample taken in connection with the 1953 Survey of Consumer Finances and cover the incomes and some wealth items of a limited number of spending units for 1951, 1952, and early 1953. Perhaps their most serious limitations for our purposes are: (1) Income is before rather than after taxes. (2) Data on all forms of savings are not available, so savings were approximated by the change in liquid assets plus the change in short-term debt. The major items omitted are savings in the form of real estate and other contractual items. (3) As is also the case with most of the other data used, no part of expenditures on durable consumer goods is treated as savings. What I have designated "consumption" in Table 20 is income less the indicated approximation to savings, which means that it includes personal taxes, some items of positive or negative savings, and expenditures on durable consumer goods.

The deficiencies in the definition of saving presumably explain why the average propensity in line 2 for independent business units is so much higher than in other data; the average propensities for the other two groups are not out of line. The income elasticities in line 4 seem somewhat higher than for most of the other studies we have examined, especially for the two nonfarm groups; this may well reflect not only the truncated saving definition but also the implicit inclusion of personal taxes as consumption. The alternative direct estimates of P_y in the last three lines of the table are strikingly similar to the income elasticities. The agreement is particularly close for the correlation coefficients in line 5, which are estimates of P_y under the variability assumption. It is decidedly less close for the estimates of P_y under the mean assumption, particularly for 1952 in line 7, and at least as much weight should be given to this comparison, since some very limited evidence has led me to prefer slightly the mean assumption to the variability assumption.

While this piece of evidence agrees with the other evidence presented above in showing a close relation between the income elasticity as

TABLE 20

Alternative Estimates of P_y and Other Data from Survey of Consumer Finances, 1953 Reinterview Sample, for Three Occupational Groups

	Independent Nonfarm Business	Farm Operators	Clerical and Sales
1. Number of cases	83[a]	99	132
Measures based on income and consumption data for 1952:			
2. Average propensity to consume	.99	.89	.95
3. Marginal propensity to consume[b]	.83	.62	.85
4. Income elasticity of consumption[c]	.83	.69	.90
Measures based on income data for 1951 and 1952:			
5. Correlation coefficient (estimate of P')	.83	.68	.88
6. Estimate[d] of P_{1951}	.85	.52	.94
7. Estimate[d] of P_{1952}	.81	.91	.83

[a] Omits one case with exceptionally high income in 1951 and 1952.
[b] Slope of computed arithmetic linear regression of consumption on income.
[c] Marginal propensity divided by average propensity, i.e. elasticity at mean income.
[d] Computed from formulas (7.1) in text.
Source:
Based on sums of observations, squares, and cross-products kindly made available to me by John Frechtling when he was with the Board of Governors of the Federal Reserve System. All computations are unweighted, which means that upper income groups are overrepresented.

computed from consumption-income data and estimates of P_y computed directly from data on income in two years, it differs in one important respect. The elasticities here are about the same as or larger than the correlation coefficients for successive years, whereas in the other comparisons they have been smaller. I am inclined to attribute this divergence to an overestimate of the elasticities as a result of both the truncated savings definition and the inclusion of personal taxes in consumption, but I have no independent evidence to test this conjecture.

4. *Correlation of the Ratio of Savings to Income in Consecutive Years*

In a discussion of the variability of consumer behavior based largely on the Survey of Consumer Finances reinterview sample for 1947 and 1948 (the source of the correlation coefficient in line 8 of Table 18), Katona gives a correlation table showing the relation between savings as a percentage of income in 1947 and in 1948 for 655 urban units.[15] This table serves as an additional piece of evidence on the permanent income hypothesis, and, even more directly, on the appropriate length of horizon.

Let us treat these data as if they were for a group of consumer units that all had the same numerical value of k. Suppose transitory components of both consumption and income were zero for every consumer unit. The ratio of consumption to income (so of saving to income) would then, on our hypothesis, also be the same for all, namely k (or $1 - k$ for saving to income). For a given k, differences among consumer units in this ratio therefore reflect the effect of transitory components of income and consumption alone. If the relevant horizon were two years, factors would be regarded as transitory only if they affected income and consumption in just one year, so transitory components in successive years would be uncorrelated. It follows (as is demonstrated in the Appendix to this Chapter) that the ratio of consumption to income in the two years would also be uncorrelated.[16] Suppose the horizon were three years. Some factors would then be regarded as transitory even though they affected income in two years, so transitory components in successive years would be correlated, though in years separated by a year they would be uncorrelated. The result would be to introduce correlation between the ratios of consumption to income in successive years, while leaving the ratios in two years separated by a year uncorrelated. In general, the longer the horizon, the higher tends to be the correlation between the ratios of consumption to income in consecutive years, and the longer the span of years for which a correlation exists.

It is clear, I trust, even from this brief sketch that, according to the permanent income hypothesis, the extent of correlation between incomes in pairs of years, both consecutive and nonconsecutive, and the length of the horizon are critical factors determining the extent of correlation between the ratios of consumption to income in two

[15] George Katona, "Variability of Consumer Behavior and the Survey Method," Chapter II in Katona, Klein, Lansing, Morgan, *Contributions of Survey Methods to Economics*, p. 71.

[16] Note that the correlation between the ratios of consumption to income in two years is numerically identical with the correlation between the corresponding ratios of saving to income.

consecutive years. It is perhaps less clear that such information alone is enough, on rather general assumptions, to determine the numerical value of the correlation coefficient. Yet the Appendix to this Chapter demonstrates that this is so. The correlation for Katona's table for a horizon of three years is there estimated in this way to be .25; the computed correlation is .26.[17] We may perhaps regard this as a fourth piece of evidence for a three-year horizon.

Katona analyzes his table to determine whether particular patterns of savings ratios are systematically related to other characteristics of consumer units, whether and how the patterns carry over to particular forms of saving, and the like. Needless to say, his results are almost wholly negative, except where they are of the nature of arithmetical necessities.[18] If our interpretation of his table is correct, his procedure is comparable with tossing a thousand fair coins twice, classifying the coins according as they come up heads both times, heads once and tails once, or tails both times; and then examining the resultant groups of coins to see why they behaved differently. The only respect in which this analogy is inexact is that there may be some systematic differences in k among the consumer units covered by the table. However, on the basis of our earlier quantitative results, such differences might be expected to be much smaller than the differences introduced by transitory components. It is as if the thousand coins, instead of all being perfectly fair, varied slightly in the probability of a head, or were mostly fair but included a few that were biased. It would take a good many more than two tosses apiece to classify the coins confidently by the probability of a head, or to isolate with confidence the few slightly biased coins.

Appendix:

Correlation between Savings Ratios in Two Consecutive Years

We shall deal throughout with the ratios of consumption to income rather than of savings to income. However, this amounts

---

[17] Such close agreement is to be regarded as an accident. It does not, however, in any way reflect a choice of the assumptions of the calculations in the Appendix to fit the observed value; I estimated the correlation as .25 before I computed the actual correlation.

[18] For example, he regards the table as revealing "one further significant fact. Repetitiousness, which is more frequent in positive than in negative saving, appears to be concentrated among people who save a small percentage of their income" (*ibid.*, p. 70). The greater frequency of repetitiousness in positive than in negative saving simply reflects the fact that in each year separately there are more positive than negative savers. Given that about two-thirds are positive savers and one-third zero or negative savers in each year, four-ninths would be positive savers in both years in the absence of any correlation, only one-ninth zero or negative savers in both. The explanation of the concentration of repetitiousness among small savers is the same: small savers are much the most numerous in both years; it would be phenomenal if they were not the most numerous among repeaters as well.

only to a change of coordinates and so does not affect the correlation.

Let us use the logarithmic variant of our hypothesis, and write out the equations in full, so that

$$(7.3) \qquad\qquad \log c = \log c_p + \log c_t ,$$

$$(7.4) \qquad\qquad \log y = \log y_p + \log y_t .$$

Subtract (7.4) from (7.3) and express in arithmetic terms:

$$(7.5) \qquad\qquad \frac{c}{y} = \frac{c_p}{y_p} \frac{c_t}{y_t} = k \frac{c_t}{y_t} .$$

Suppose k is the same for all consumer units in question. The correlation between c/y in the two years and between c_t/y_t is then identical, since the only difference is in the unit of measure. So our problem reduces to the correlation between c_{t1}/y_{t1} and c_{t2}/y_{t2}, where the years are indicated in the subscripts. Expressed in logarithmic terms, our problem is to determine the correlation between $\log c_{t1} - \log y_{t1}$ and $\log c_{t2} - \log y_{t2}$, or between $C_{t1} - Y_{t1}$ and $C_{t2} - Y_{t2}$. For simplicity, assume the transitory components of both consumption and income to average zero in each year. Then

$$(7.6) \qquad r_{(C_{t1}-Y_{t1})(C_{t2}-Y_{t2})} = \frac{E(C_{t1} - Y_{t1})(C_{t2} - Y_{t2})}{[E(C_{t1} - Y_{t1})^2 E(C_{t2} - Y_{t2})^2]^{\frac{1}{2}}} .$$

On our hypothesis,

$$(7.7) \qquad r_{C_{t1}Y_{t1}} = r_{C_{t2}Y_{t2}} = r_{C_{t1}Y_{t2}} = r_{C_{t2}Y_{t1}} = 0.$$

For simplicity, assume further that

$$(7.8) \qquad \begin{cases} \sigma^2_{C_{t1}} = \sigma^2_{C_{t2}} = \sigma^2_{C_t} , \\ \sigma^2_{Y_{t1}} = \sigma^2_{Y_{t2}} = \sigma^2_{Y_t} . \end{cases}$$

Expanding (7.6) and using (7.7) and (7.8), we get

$$(7.9) \qquad r_{(C_{t1}-Y_{t1})(C_{t2}-Y_{t2})} = \frac{r_{C_{t1}C_{t2}}\sigma^2_{C_t} + r_{Y_{t1}Y_{t2}}\sigma^2_{Y_t}}{\sigma^2_{C_t} + \sigma^2_{Y_t}} .$$

Assume that

$$(7.10) \qquad r_{C_{t1}C_{t2}} = r_{Y_{t1}Y_{t2}}$$

so that

$$(7.11) \qquad r_{(C_{t1}-Y_{t1})(C_{t2}-Y_{t2})} = r_{Y_{t1}Y_{t2}} .$$

If the horizon were two years, transitory components of both consumption and income would be uncorrelated: indeed, this may be regarded as a definition of a two year horizon. In this case, (7.9) as well as the special case (7.11) would be zero.

The analysis in section 2 of the Appendix to Chapter 7 of *Income from Independent Professional Practice* can be used to give an estimate of $r_{Y_{t1}Y_{t2}}$. The term "transitory" was used there to designate a component affecting income in one year only, and "quasi-permanent", to designate components affecting income in more than one year. In the notation used there for a three-year horizon, our $Y_{t1} = t'_1 + q'_{11} + q'_{12}$, our $Y_{t2} = t'_2 + q'_{22} + q'_{23}$, where t'_1 and t'_2 are the components affecting year 1 and year 2 alone, q'_{11} and q'_{12} are two-year components affecting year 1 income and ending their effect in years 1 and 2 respectively, and q'_{22} and q'_{23} are two-year components affecting year 2 income and ending their effect in years 2 and 3 respectively (see *ibid.*, p. 353). If we extend (7.8) to apply to each component of Y_{t1} and Y_{t2} separately, we can make a transformation which will make $q'_{12} = q'_{22}$, since these are the quasi-permanent components produced by a factor common to both years; the other components are all uncorrelated between the two years. In consequence, the correlation between Y_{t1} and Y_{t2} is the variance of the common item over the common total variance, or

$$(7.12) \qquad r_{Y_{t1}Y_{t2}} = \frac{\sigma^2_{q'_{22}}}{\sigma^2_{t'_2} + \sigma^2_{q'_{22}} + \sigma^2_{q'_{12}}} .$$

If we divide numerator and denominator by σ^2_Y, and recall that our assumptions imply the variability assumption, this reduces to

$$(7.13) \qquad r_{Y_{t1}Y_{t2}} = \frac{Q^*_{22}}{1 - P^*} = \frac{r_{12} - r_{13}}{1 - r_{13}} ,$$

where Q^*_{22} is the proportionate contribution of q_{22}, and P^* of the components lasting more than two years, estimated under the variability assumption; r_{12} is the correlation between incomes in years 1 and 2, that is, in two consecutive years; and r_{13} is the correlation between incomes in years 1 and 3, that is, in two nonconsecutive years, with one year intervening. From Tables 18 and 19, for urban units (Katona's table is for urban units), r_{12} appears to be approximately .85; r_{13}, approximately .80. Inserting in (7.13) we have

$$(7.14) \qquad r_{Y_{t1}Y_{t2}} = \frac{.85 - .80}{1 - .80} = \frac{.5}{.20} = .25 .$$

By (7.11), this is also an estimate of the correlation between ratios of savings in the two years.

This is a very rough approximation, not only because of the approximation involved in going from (7.9) to (7.11), but also because I have used correlations between arithmetic values to estimate logarithmic correlations.

199

CHAPTER VIII

A Miscellany

THIS chapter comments on a few items that do not fit into the organization of the preceding chapters, yet seem to deserve some mention. The common feature of the sections that follow is that all are primarily tentative speculations about possible further work rather than records of completed work; this is the reason why they have not been covered by the preceding chapters and yet why they seem to me to deserve inclusion. The items considered are: (1) the regression of income on consumption; (2) the extension of the permanent income hypothesis to expenditures on particular categories of consumer goods; (3) the relevance of the hypothesis to analyses of the distribution of income; (4) the connection of the hypothesis with the observed distribution of wealth; and (5) additional tests of the hypothesis.

1. *Regression of Income on Consumption*

In the preceding chapters, we have dealt almost exclusively with the regression of measured consumption on measured income, and have paid little attention to the regression of measured income on measured consumption. Yet as noted at various points in the theoretical discussion, these two regressions are symmetric; for every statement about the one, there exists a dual for the other. The reason we have concentrated on the consumption-income regression is that this regression is the one mainly considered in consumption research and the only regression that can be computed from most published budget study data; the published tables almost always classify consumer units by measured income classes and give average values of income, total consumption expenditures, and other magnitudes for such classes; they seldom give comparable data for measured consumption classes.

The absence of such data is much to be regretted; they would add to our substantive knowledge of consumption behavior and provide additional evidence on the acceptability of the permanent income hypothesis. Just as, on our hypothesis, the elasticity of consumption with respect to measured income can be viewed as a measure of P_y, the fraction of the variance of income contributed by the permanent component of income, so the elasticity of income with respect to measured consumption can be viewed as a measure of P_c, the fraction of the variance of consumption contributed by the permanent component of consumption.[1] Just as this interpretation requires that the measured income elasticity of consumption be less than unity and would be contradicted by observed elasticities greater than unity, so it requires that the measured consumption elasticity of income be less than unity and would be contradicted by observed elasticities greater than unity.[2] To put it in terms that may be clearer, this interpretation requires that the elasticity of consumption with respect to income be less than unity when it is computed from the regression of consumption on income and greater than unity when it is computed from the regression of income on consumption.[3] Just as the value of P_y estimated from the regression of consumption on income can be combined with the observed variation in income to give estimates of the dispersion of the permanent and transitory components of income so the value of P_c estimated from the regression of income on consumption can be combined with the observed variation in consumption to give estimates of the dispersion of permanent and transitory components of consumption. And just as correlations between incomes of the same consumer units in different years can be used to construct independent estimates of P_y, so correlations between consumption of the same consumer units in different years can be used to construct independent estimates of P_c.

Among the various bodies of data examined in preceding chapters, I have been able to estimate readily the regression of income on measured consumption for only one, the Survey of Consumer Finances data for 1947–48 analyzed by Morgan and used in Chapter IV, section 4, as evidence on the effect of change in income. Some comparisons for income and consumption from these data are summarized in Table 21. These comparisons are extremely suggestive. According to line 1, P_c, as estimated from the regression of income

[1] In both cases, the same conditions must be satisfied for these statements to hold true: for arithmetically linear regressions, the elasticities must be computed at the mean and transitory components average out to zero; for logarithmically linear regressions, the equality holds more generally.

[2] For arithmetically linear regressions, this implication of our hypothesis is that the intercepts of both regressions be positive.

[3] Though we have ample direct evidence that the first condition is satisfied almost uniformly, we have too few estimated regressions of income on consumption to be able to assert with anything like the same confidence on the basis of direct evidence that the second condition is. A few pieces of direct evidence are cited later in this section, in the text and in footnotes.

TABLE 21

Relative Dispersion of Measured Income and Measured Consumption and
Their Permanent and Transitory Components, Based on Survey of
Consumer Finances Data, 1947 and 1948

	Income	Consumption
1. Fraction of variance attributable to permanent components	.82	.98
Relative dispersion of:		
2. Permanent components	.68	
3. Transitory components	.32	.09
4. Total	.75	.69

Source:
Computed from sums of observations on income and savings, squares of observations, and cross-products kindly made available to me by James Morgan of the Michigan Survey Research Center.
Derivation:
Line 1
Income = elasticity of consumption with respect to income computed from least-squares arithmetic linear regression of measured consumption on measured income at mean income. Consumption = elasticity of income with respect to consumption computed from least-squares arithmetic linear regression of measured income on measured consumption at mean consumption.
Line 2
Ratio of square root of product of line 1 and corresponding variance of original observations to corresponding mean. See footnote 5 of text for proof that result is the same for income and consumption.
Line 3
Ratio of square root of product of complement of line 1 and corresponding variance of original observations to corresponding mean.
Line 4
Ratio of standard deviation of original observations to mean.

on consumption,[4] while less than unity as the hypothesis predicts, is decidedly larger than P_y, as estimated from the regression of consumption on income. Transitory factors apparently account for only some 2 per cent of the variance of measured consumption compared with some 18 per cent of the variance of measured income. Expressed as a ratio to the mean, the estimated standard deviation of the transitory component is only 9 per cent for consumption, over 30 per cent for income; the ratio for income is very nearly the same as the corresponding ratio estimated for all urban or nonfarm

[4] Elasticities of income with respect to consumption can be computed for the separate change of income classes in the same way as the elasticity entered in Table 21. However, these cannot be interpreted as estimates of P_c because the condition that the mean transitory components be zero cannot be regarded as holding for them. In computing the income elasticities in Table 11, we avoided this problem by determining graphically the slope of log-log regression lines of consumption on income. I do not have the data for the corresponding regression lines of income on consumption. The computed elasticities of income with respect to consumption are .849, .961, .998, .952, .995 for the

families in 1935–36 and 1941 (see Table 4). Only one number is recorded in the table for consumption and income for the estimated relative dispersion of the permanent component. The reason is that a common relative dispersion is implied by the permanent income hypothesis; it asserts that permanent consumption is simply a common multiple (k) of permanent income, which means that the two must have the same relative dispersion; and this requirement is embodied in the computational procedures for deriving the estimates in Table 21.[5]

It certainly seems plausible that transitory factors should affect total consumption expenditures to a much smaller extent than they affect income. Total measured consumption is the sum of expenditures on a large number of separate consumption items. Some transitory factors doubtless affect all or many of these items alike, for example, a decision to spend a year abroad; others affect different items in opposite directions, for example, an illness that raises medical expenses and lowers clothing or recreational expenses; still others, and perhaps the most important, affect separate items more or less independently, for example, the accidental state of inventories of various consumer goods, variations in weather, fluctuations in relative prices. The third class of transitory factors tends to average out; the variance of their sum is the sum of their variances and so the relative dispersion of their sum is less than the (weighted) average of their relative dispersions—this is the so-called "law of averages" or "law

down more than 25 per cent, down 5 to 25 per cent, down 5 per cent to up 5 per cent, up 5 to 25 per cent, and up more than 25 per cent classes, respectively; all are less than unity; however, it is possible that correction for the non-zero mean transitory components would push one or more over unity. A corresponding elasticity can also be computed for the 123 spending units for which the change in income was not known; the computed value is 1.152; this contradiction to the hypothesis cannot be given much weight, both because of the small number of cases and because the nonavailability of income-change data may well mean abnormality in other respects as well.

See also footnote 6 below.

[5] The estimates of P_y and P_c in Table 21 are given by

$$P_y = r_{cy} \cdot \frac{\sigma_c}{\sigma_y} \cdot \frac{\bar{y}}{\bar{c}},$$

$$P_c = r_{cy} \frac{\sigma_y}{\sigma_c} \cdot \frac{\bar{c}}{\bar{y}},$$

where r_{cy} is the correlation coefficient between income and consumption, and σ_y, σ_c are the standard deviations, and $\bar{y}$ and $\bar{c}$, the arithmetic means of income and consumption, respectively. The estimated relative dispersion of the permanent components of income and consumption are:

$$\frac{\sigma_{y_p}}{\bar{y}} = \frac{1}{\bar{y}} \sqrt{P_y \cdot \sigma_y^2} = \sqrt{r_{cy} \cdot \frac{\sigma_c \cdot \sigma_y}{\bar{c} \cdot \bar{y}}} \; ,$$

$$\frac{\sigma_{c_p}}{\bar{c}} = \frac{1}{\bar{c}} \sqrt{P_c \cdot \sigma_c^2} = \sqrt{r_{cy} \cdot \frac{\sigma_c \cdot \sigma_y}{\bar{c} \cdot \bar{y}}} \; .$$

of large numbers." The second class makes for an even larger reduction in the relative dispersion: these factors tend systematically to offset one another, and so the variance of their sum is less than the sum of their variances. Only the first class transmits its impact in full to total consumption. Measured income, too, is the sum of a number of items; but the number of sources of income that can be regarded as independently or offsettingly affected by transitory factors is much smaller than the corresponding number of consumption categories, and generally one source, the earnings of the principal earner, is the major source of measured income and cannot itself be broken into many constituents that can be regarded as independently affected by transitory factors. In short, there is much less opportunity for or likelihood of the averaging out of the effect of the accidental forces impinging on measured income than of those impinging on measured consumption.[6]

[6] Some evidence on the regression of income on consumption is also available for two other studies: the 1934–36 Bureau of Labor Statistics wage-earner study, and the 1941 study. I have relegated this evidence to a footnote because for both studies the effect of classifying by consumption is confounded with the effect of adjusting for size of family; the tabulations by consumption classes are for consumer units classified by consumption per equivalent adult. There might be much merit for our purposes in segregating families of different size; I am inclined to believe that it lessens the value of the data to express them per equivalent unit. The scales generally used for this purpose have the effect of putting large families in the lower income and expenditure classes and small families in the higher classes; and they do this to a much greater extent than the tendency for income to rise with size of family produces the opposite result for unadjusted data. Insofar as large families have a higher k than small families, the result is to introduce a systematic difference in k along the income or consumption scale.

For the 1934–36 data, the elasticity of consumption with respect to income, graphically estimated from data unadjusted for family size, is .89; the relative dispersion of measured income, .34; of the permanent component of income, .32; of the transitory component of income, .11. The elasticity of income with respect to consumption, graphically estimated from average family income and expenditure for classes determined by "unit expenditures," the term used for expenditures per equivalent adult, is .94. If we assume that the same elasticity would be obtained for classes determined by family expenditure, this would imply a relative dispersion of the transitory component of consumption of about .08. Presumably, however, the systematic differences in k mentioned in the preceding paragraph mean that the elasticity for classes determined by family expenditure would be lower than for classes determined by expenditure per equivalent adult, so .08 must be regarded as an underestimate. Without this adjustment, it is close to the .09 entered in Table 21. The relative dispersion of total family expenditures, computed from the averages for classes determined by "unit expenditures," is .20, which would imply a relative dispersion of the permanent component of consumption of .20 and of the transitory component, of .05. As might be expected, these are decidedly lower than those implied by the other classification, for the variance computed from average consumption for classes formed by a variable other than consumption itself is necessarily smaller than for classes formed by consumption. These results on the whole clearly conform well to our hypothesis and give numerical results similar to those recorded in Table 21 for the 1947–48 data. For the data used in the above calculations, see Williams and Hanson, *Money Disbursements of Wage Earners and Clerical Workers*, pp. 12, 22, 52, 56.

The evidence for the 1941 study comes from special tabulations that were obtained

The small dispersion of the transitory component of consumption, if it should be confirmed by other evidence, gives empirical justification to a proposal by William Vickrey that measured consumption replace measured income as the primary basis for classifying families in tabulating data from family budget studies.[7] On our hypothesis, this method raises the same problem in principle as classification by measured income; the disturbing effects of transitory components of consumption are simply substituted for the disturbing effects of transitory components of income; and just as comparisons of consumption-income regressions reflect not only differences in consumption behavior but also differences in the strength of transitory forces impinging on the income distribution, so comparisons of income-consumption regressions reflect not only differences in consumption behavior but also differences in the strength of transitory forces impinging on the distribution of consumption. But these effects are all matters of degree, and if transitory components of consumption were sufficiently small, their disturbing effects might not be serious, in which case, measured consumption, adjusted so far as possible to an accrual basis, could be used as a reasonably good approximation to permanent consumption.

Of course, it is better to eliminate or adjust for the disturbing

---

by William Vickrey. These combine Bureau of Labor Statistics data for urban communities and Bureau of Home Economics data for rural nonfarm communities, with weights of 2 and 1. The data are given in the form of a cross-tabulation, the variables of classification being income per equivalent adult and expenditures per equivalent adult. The graphically estimated elasticity of consumption per equivalent adult with respect to income per equivalent adult is .87; of income per equivalent adult with respect to expenditure per equivalent adult, 1.00; the relative dispersion of income per equivalent adult is .93, of the corresponding permanent component, .87, of the corresponding transitory component, .33. The coefficient of variation of expenditures per equivalent adult is .78. It is clear that these data do not conform well either to our hypothesis or to the results in Table 21. On our hypothesis, the elasticity of income with respect to consumption should be less than unity, and the relative dispersion of permanent components should be the same for consumption and income. Put differently, these numbers imply a zero or negative relative dispersion for the transitory component of consumption, which is impossible. I do not know whether these results deserve to be regarded as a significant contradiction of the hypothesis or simply as a reflection of the deficiencies of the variables used to classify the consumer units. As noted above, we might expect an elasticity of income with respect to consumption computed from data unadjusted for family size to be less than one computed from per equivalent adult data, and this difference is in the right direction to account for the divergence of the above results from expectation. Unfortunately, however, I have no evidence on the likely magnitude of this effect. For the data underlying the above calculations, see William Vickrey, "Resource Distribution Patterns and the Classification of Families," *Studies in Income and Wealth*, X (New York: National Bureau of Economic Research, 1947), pp. 276–277.

[7] *Ibid.*, pp. 266–297; see also the comments by Alice C. Hanson, Margaret G. Reid, Dorothy S. Brady, and Jerome Cornfield, *ibid.*, pp. 305–324, and Vickrey's reply, *ibid.* pp. 324–329.

effects of both transitory components when this can be done readily and at little additional cost. But it may sometimes be difficult, unduly costly, or impossible to do so. And when this is the case, comparisons among regressions of income on consumption may come closer to being dominated by differences in consumption behavior proper than comparisons among regressions of consumption on income.

2. Application of Permanent Income Hypothesis to Individual Categories of Consumption

The permanent income hypothesis, which we have applied only to total consumption expenditures, clearly has implications also for individual categories of consumption. The planned expenditures of a consumer unit on, say, food, may be expected to be related, via the consumer unit's tastes and preferences, to the prices that it expects to have to pay for food and other items, and to the income that it expects to receive, or the permanent component of income. Its measured expenditures on food differ from its planned expenditures because of a transitory component of food expenditures, and its measured income differs from its permanent income because of a transitory component of income. When the regression of measured expenditures on measured income is computed from budget data for a group of families—the regression that has come to be called an "Engel curve"—the transitory component of food expenditures tends to average out, but the transitory component of income does not, for reasons that have been emphasized repeatedly above. In consequence, the elasticity of measured expenditures with respect to measured income reflects not only the consumer unit's tastes and preferences but also the importance of transitory components of income.

Let c_f stand for the mean observed consumption on food of families with a given measured income, and assume that the transitory component of food expenditures is uncorrelated with the permanent or transitory component of income and averages zero for the group as a whole, so that c_f can be regarded as the mean permanent component of food expenditures. The elasticity of c_f with respect to measured income then is

$$\eta_{c_f y} = \frac{dc_f}{dy} \cdot \frac{y}{c_f} = \frac{dc_f}{dy_p} \frac{dy_p}{dy} \cdot \frac{y}{y_p} \cdot \frac{y_p}{c_f}$$

(8.1)

$$= \frac{dc_f}{dy_p} \cdot \frac{y_p}{c_f} \cdot \frac{dy_p}{dy} \cdot \frac{y}{y_p} = \eta_{c_f y_p} \eta_{y_p y}.$$

206

But, on our hypothesis, $y_p = c_p/k$, which means that

$$(8.2) \qquad \eta_{y_p y} = \frac{dy_p}{dy} \cdot \frac{y}{y_p} = \frac{1}{k} \frac{dc_p}{dy} \cdot \frac{ky}{c_p} = \frac{dc_p}{dy} \cdot \frac{y}{c_p} = \eta_{c_p y},$$

so that

$$(8.3) \qquad \eta_{c_f y} = \eta_{c_f y_p} \cdot \eta_{c_p y}.$$

The first elasticity on the righthand side, between permanent food expenditures and permanent income, reflects the influence of tastes and preferences proper; the second, the influence of transitory factors affecting income.

It follows that differences among groups of families in the observed income elasticity of particular categories of consumption cannot be interpreted as reflecting solely the influence of differences in tastes or of differences in prices or similar factors affecting opportunities; they may reflect a third set of forces, namely, differences in a particular characteristic of the income distribution, the importance of transitory components of income.

If the permanent income hypothesis is accepted, and if, further, permanent income is taken to mean the same thing for the different categories of consumption as for total consumption, the effect of this third set of forces can be readily eliminated. From equation (8.3), the ratio of the observed measured income elasticity of expenditures on the particular category to the corresponding elasticity of total consumption is an estimate of the elasticity of expenditures on that category with respect to permanent income. An alternative is to classify the families by measured income, to compute mean expenditures on an individual category of consumption and on all categories combined for each such class. Under the relevant assumptions about correlations and mean transitory components of consumption, these means are estimates of the mean permanent components of the individual category and of total consumption. The relation between them is then an estimated relation between permanent components.[8]

One possible source of difficulty with this approach is the necessity of taking permanent income to mean the same thing for the different categories of consumption. We have interpreted the exact meaning of permanent income in terms of the horizon of the consumer unit. Now there seems to be no reason why the horizon should be the same for all individual categories of consumption and some reasons why it should differ systematically. For example, it seems highly

---

[8] Note that this is *not* the same as the procedure suggested by Vickrey and discussed in the preceding section of classifying families by total consumption expenditures and then relating expenditures on individual categories to total expenditures. See Reid, "Effect of Income Concept upon Expenditure Curves of Farm Families," pp. 170–174.

plausible that housing expenditures are planned in terms of a longer horizon, and so a different concept of permanent income, than expenditures on, say, food.[9] If this turns out to be a meaningful way of looking at the problem, the concept of permanent income applicable to total consumption will have to be regarded as an average of the concepts applicable to each category and our roughly estimated horizon of three years, as an average of shorter and longer horizons.

I have not myself done any work with the individual categories of consumption, so I have no basis for judging whether this difficulty will in practice turn out to be serious or whether, on the contrary, the use of the same concept of permanent income for all categories will yield acceptable results.

Though these comments are phrased in terms of budget data, they clearly apply equally to time series data and to the numerous attempts to estimate demand functions, or price and income elasticities, from such data.[10] The elasticities that are generally computed are elasticities with respect to measured magnitudes; yet they are interpreted as if they were elasticities with respect to permanent components; and the result is systematically to bias the estimates and the conclusions.

We have already commented on another feature of current practice in such demand studies that the permanent income hypothesis brings into question, namely, the combination of budget and time series data by using elasticities computed from budget data as equally valid for time series data (see Chapter V, section 2c above). The preceding comments suggest one way in which the two kinds of data might validly be combined: compute from budget data the elasticity with respect to the permanent component, say by using equation (8.3); estimate from time series data the relative importance of transitory components, say by computing the fraction of the variance of the observations accounted for by deviations from a three or four year moving average of the original observations; use this to convert the budget data elasticity to a time series elasticity. Though this procedure seems free from bias, it probably would be preferable to go still farther and to restate the demand function to be computed in terms of permanent and transitory components. Besides permitting

[9] This range of considerations was impressed on me primarily as a result of conversations with Margaret Reid about a study she is making of the determinants of housing expenditures.

[10] Guy H. Orcutt, "Measurement of Price Elasticities in International Trade," *The Review of Economics and Statistics*, XXXII (May, 1950), pp. 117–132, and Arnold C. Harberger, "A Structural Approach to the Problem of Import Demand," *American Economic Review*, XLIII (May, 1953), pp. 148–159, discuss biases in such estimates that, while not described by them in these terms, can be regarded as reflecting the effects of transitory components and the use of measured price or measured income as a direct estimate of "permanent price" or "permanent income."

the direct use of information from budget data, this has the great advantage that the results are not wedded to the length of the particular time series from which they have been computed, but, sampling fluctuations aside, are invariant with respect to the length of the series.

3. *Relevance to the Analysis of the Distribution of Income*

The permanent income hypothesis makes information from studies of the distribution of income relevant to the analysis of consumption behavior. Clearly, the relation is reciprocal. If accepted, the hypothesis makes information from studies of consumption behavior relevant to the analysis of the distribution of income.

One example may suggest the rich possibilities opened up in this way by the coordination of two previously distinct problems and bodies of data. Distributions of income by size are generally based on the measured income of individual income units for a single time period, typically a year. These distributions reflect the influence of differences among individual units both in what we have called the permanent component of income and in what we have called the transitory component. Yet these two types of differences do not have the same significance; the one is an indication of deep-seated long-run inequality, the other, of dynamic variation and mobility. In consequence, comparison of such distributions of income for different countries or periods may be extremely misleading if the relative importance of permanent and transitory differences is not the same in the different countries or periods compared. This problem has been one motivation for the studies of the incomes of identical units in different time periods that we used in Chapter VII.

On our hypothesis, the income elasticity of consumption expenditures is a measure of the fraction of the total variance of income attributable to the permanent component. The host of budget studies for different countries over a wide period of time are thereby made available to supplement and extend the data on the incomes of identical units in different years—a body of data that is much more limited in scope than the rich store of family budget data.

An obvious example is the comparative degree of inequality of income in Britain and the United States. Casual observation suggests that relative income status is decidedly less variable—the transitory component of income less important—in Britain than in the United States, so that distributions of annual income are a misleading basis for judging the degree of underlying inequality. But how much of a correction is needed on this account? On our hypothesis, the comparison made in Chapter IV, section 2b, between the income elasticity of consumption in the two countries gives a measure: according to this comparison, something like 13 per cent of the variance is accounted for by transitory components in Britain, something like 18 per cent in the United States. This comparison was for a single pair of studies and so the resulting estimates must be regarded as rather crude even though the studies are an exceptionally favorable pair for comparative purposes. However, much additional data could almost surely be brought to bear to improve these estimates.

4. Connection between the Permanent Income Hypothesis and the Distribution of Wealth

The distribution of wealth—by which is meant here only nonhuman wealth—is typically very much more widely dispersed than the distribution of measured income. At first sight, this difference seems inconsistent with the permanent income hypothesis.[11] If planned savings—by which we mean again only savings embodied in non-human wealth—are the same fraction of permanent income at all levels of permanent income, does this not imply a tendency for the distribution of wealth to become similar to the distribution of income? True, at some initial point there might be a discrepancy, but would not the tendency for savings to accumulate at a constant percentage of permanent income tend to eliminate the discrepancy? Would not income from property tend to become the same fraction of income at all income levels?

A minor reason why there is, or at any rate need be, no inconsistency between the hypothesis and the stated facts is that the numerical value of k differs among groups; these differences may not be produced by differences in permanent income, yet they may be associated with them. For example, nonfarm entrepreneurs have higher average income than nonfarm nonentrepreneurs and also a lower k. Such differences in k are cumulative in their effect.

The major reason why there need be no inconsistency is precisely the very difference between measured income and permanent income that is the heart of the hypothesis. The hypothesis asserts that planned savings are the same fraction of permanent income at all income levels and have the same relative dispersion as permanent income. But equally, it asserts that the actual savings of any unit equal its planned savings plus the transitory component of income, positive or negative, minus the transitory component of consumption, positive or negative. The result is that the absolute dispersion of measured savings is necessarily higher than that of planned savings; insofar as the transitory components of income average out, average

[11] I am indebted to Simon Kuznets for calling this to my attention.

savings are unaffected, so the relative dispersion of measured savings is also higher. A few figures will illustrate the magnitudes involved. Let us take the value of k to be .9 for each of a group of consumer units for whom the dispersion of the various components of income and consumption is of the magnitude specified in Table 21, and suppose that transitory components average out for the group as a whole. We can then summarize the elements determining the relative dispersion of measured savings as follows:

Relative dispersion of permanent component of savings (equals relative dispersion of permanent component of income or consumption)	.68
Dispersion of transitory component of income as a ratio to average savings (10 times relative dispersion of transitory component of income, since savings average one-tenth of income)	3.20
Dispersion of transitory component of consumption as ratio to average savings (9 times relative dispersion of transitory component of consumption, since savings average one-ninth of consumption)	.81
Estimated relative dispersion of measured savings (square root of sum of squares of above three figures, since the several components are assumed uncorrelated)	3.37
To be compared with estimated relative dispersion of measured income from Table 21	.75

Given these estimates, therefore, our hypothesis implies that the relative dispersion of measured savings is some $4\frac{1}{2}$ times that of measured income, 337 per cent instead of 75 per cent.[12]

Wealth is the accumulation of savings. The process of accumulation brings into play the law of averages and so, on this account, tends to reduce the relative dispersion of wealth below that of savings. The size of the effect depends critically on the correlation of transitory components in successive years: clearly if a large positive transitory component in one year tends systematically to be associated with a large positive transitory component in the next, there will be much less averaging out than if successive years are uncorrelated. Now as we saw earlier (Chapter VII, section 4), the assumed zero correlation

[12] To avoid confusion, it may be worth pointing out explicitly how the dispersion for total savings can be larger than the figure recorded for each of the components, a result that seems at first sight to run counter to the "law of averages." The reason is that the *average* of each of the two transitory components separately is zero, so that adding these components adds nothing to the denominator of the relative dispersion, while it increases the standard deviation in the numerator. The figures recorded for the transitory components are not their own coefficients of variation—these are infinite under the assumed conditions—but the ratio of their standard deviations to the mean of the first item, the permanent component. This is the difference between this and the case that follows. Accumulating savings in different years add to the denominator as well as the numerator of the ratio defining the coefficient of variation.

between transitory and permanent components of income or consumption in any one year does not imply zero correlation of transitory components in successive years; the size of the correlation between years depends on the horizon of the consumer unit, and is larger, the longer the horizon.

But the process of accumulation also has another effect that works in the direction of increasing the variance of wealth for any population as a whole, namely, it introduces differences in the number of years of accumulation and so introduces divergences between consumer units of different ages that are not present in the distribution of the savings of a single year. Differences in age are a source of dispersion in permanent income and of correlation between transitory components; but they are an even more potent source of differences in nonhuman wealth: the process of using up a particular piece of human capital, if I may speak so cold-bloodedly, consists very largely of replacing it by nonhuman capital.

To illustrate these effects, consider a simple hypothetical case. Suppose the only source of transitory components of income is the age cycle in earnings, that transitory components of consumption are zero and that we take the individual as our elementary consumer unit. To avoid negative wealth, suppose that each individual separately comes into our purview only at age 20, when he begins to receive, say, $4,500 per year as earnings, that he receives identically the same earnings in each of 40 years to age 60, when he goes into partial retirement, receiving $2,000 a year earnings and using up his accumulated savings until he dies at age 70, that all individuals follow identically the same course, and that the population as a whole consists of an equal number of individuals of each age. To avoid the necessity for tedious computation, assume that the interest rate is zero. Suppose, as seems reasonable under the bizarre circumstances assumed, that the individual's horizon is his lifetime. His permanent income in each year is then $4,000; he saves $500 per year for each of the 40 years of earnings and accumulates thereby $20,000 to provide a supplement to earnings of $2,000 a year to support consumption of $4,000 a year for 10 years of semiretirement. What are the associated distributions and dispersion of permanent income, measured income, and wealth? For permanent income, dispersion is zero; everyone has a permanent income of $4,000. For measured income the distribution is:

> 80 per cent of the population receive $4,500
> 20 per cent of the population receive   2,000

or a mean measured income of $4,000, a standard deviation of $1,000, and a coefficient of variation of .25. For wealth, as of the end of the accounting year, including those who die then but not including the new entrants, the distribution of wealth is:

For the 80 per cent of the population who saved during the year:

2 per cent have	$500
2 per cent have	1,000
....	
2 per cent have	20,000

For the 20 per cent of the population who dissaved during the year:

2 per cent have	18,000
2 per cent have	16,000
....	
2 per cent have	0

The mean wealth is $10,000; the standard deviation of wealth is $5,788; the coefficient of variation, .579; or over twice that for income. I hasten to add that this result depends on the particular numbers assumed; it is possible to choose numbers that yield a dispersion of income greater than the dispersion of wealth.[13] But the example does show some of the complications involved in connecting the distribution of measured income with the distribution of wealth under our hypothesis.

One complication which this example does not exemplify and may rather conceal is worth noting explicitly, though it is implicit in the general statement that preceded the example. The example is one in which transitory components average out to zero for each individual separately during his lifetime. This is so only because the age-earnings cycle is the only source of transitory components considered. More generally, transitory components need not and will not tend to average out to zero for each individual during his lifetime. This point is important, because it is easy to confuse our hypothesis with the very different one that the appropriate time unit for studying consumption behavior is the individual's horizon, whether it be his lifetime or a shorter period, and that the individual is to be regarded as making and, more important, carrying out successfully, plans for that period—what might be called a "planning period" hypothesis. Our hypothesis is quite different: the horizon determines only what factors he regards as transitory; his estimate of permanent income is not for a defined period but an estimate of a rate at a moment of time that is revised over time and may never conform to experience.

[13] For this kind of an example, let p be the fraction of years at the higher income, q at the lower, and r, the ratio of the lower income to the higher, and suppose people to be distributed continuously by age. Then, under the special assumptions of this hypothetical case, the coefficient of variation of wealth is always .578, of measured income, it is $(1 - r)\sqrt{pq}/(p + qr)$, which can vary from 0 to ∞ for r between 0 and 1.

The analogy is an estimate that a particular coin is fair. I may use this estimate to judge the outcome of, let us say, 100 tosses. This does not, however, mean that I expect the number of heads to equal precisely the number of tails over the particular 100 tosses; if 52 heads come up, 50 is the permanent component and 2 is the transitory component for the 100 tosses. The permanent component in our hypothesis is the same kind of concept. Transitory components need not average out for each individual or for each group; their failure to do so is a source of variation in wealth holdings that is not taken into account in the preceding simple example.

5. *Additional Tests of the Permanent Income Hypothesis*

The various tests of the permanent income hypothesis made in earlier chapters can obviously be extended to a wider range of data and can be improved in detail and precision in many respects. The two kinds of tests that it would probably be most interesting to extend in this way are those involving the effect of change in income (Chapter IV, section 4) and those using data on incomes in different years (Chapter VII), both because these tests are in some ways the most searching and precise, and because the data we have been able to use in making these tests are so incomplete.

In respect of these tests, and of others that we have made, there are three improvements that are sufficiently important and sufficiently general to justify mention. Perhaps the most important would be to take explicit account of the effect of the life cycle of income and consumption. Again and again, we have implicitly or explicitly supposed that changes in permanent income or relative income status from one year to the next could be neglected. This seems a reasonably good approximation, to judge from our results; yet it certainly would be a much better approximation, and one that could be relied on over longer spans of time, if it were made for groups of consumer units at the same stage in the life cycle, so that the effects of "aging," instead of simply being neglected, could be allowed for explicitly. Another improvement of the same kind would be a more satisfactory treatment of durable consumer goods. Though our theoretical analysis calls for treating the purchase of such goods as a capital transaction and including in consumption only their use value, we have in the main, particularly for budget data, been forced to use a concept of consumption that includes as current consumption expenditures on durable goods other than housing. The third improvement would be a more satisfactory treatment of sampling error. I have resorted again and again to intuitive judgments about the likelihood that a particular difference could or could not be regarded as attributable to sampling fluctuation. It would be highly desirable to have such judgements supplemented by formal tests of statistical significance wherever possible.

In addition to tests of this kind, which follow so directly from our earlier discussion that they need little explicit consideration, there are others that justify somewhat more extended consideration.

A crucial element in our hypothesis is the asserted lack of correlation between transitory components of income and consumption. The first two tests listed below seem likely to be especially sensitive to a failure of this element of our hypothesis. The other tests are less specific.

a. In 1950, a special life insurance payment was made by the government to veterans.[14] This payment seems to have been largely unexpected and so to qualify as a "windfall" or clearly transitory element. It was made only to some veterans and there seems no reason to expect that the veterans who received the payment differ systematically from those who did not. The Bureau of Labor Statistics made an extensive budget study for 1950 covering a large number of consumer units. If it is possible to distinguish veterans from others, and to subclassify the veterans into those who did and those who did not receive the special insurance payment, a comparison of their consumption-income behavior would provide almost a controlled experiment. On our hypothesis, the windfall should affect consumption only insofar as it raises permanent income; for the rest it should be treated as a transitory component. If consumption can be defined to exclude major consumer durables, the hypothesis predicts that the elasticity of consumption with respect to income excluding the special payment will turn out to be the same for veterans who did and those who did not receive the payment; and that the regression for the former will be higher than for the latter by an amount that is a small fraction of the average insurance payment—on the basis of our estimate that the horizon is about 3 years, say under one-third. If the insurance payment were the same for different veterans, this would be the whole of the story. Insofar as it differs fairly widely, additional tests are possible. Deviations from the regressions described above can be correlated with the size of the payment; the correlation should be low and the regression coefficient small, about .3 or so.

b. We have so far simply taken the permanent component of income for granted and have not inquired into the factors responsible for its size. It is clear, however, that the permanent component of income is itself a resultant of a host of factors many of which are

---

[14] I owe the suggested test that follows to Irwin Friend.

specifiable and observable, such as location, age, occupation, education, and the like.[15]

Suppose a regression were computed for a broad group of consumer units, say a sample of all units in the United States, and the corresponding elasticity estimated. Suppose this broad group were broken down into subgroups, say by the communities in which they reside, and separate regressions computed for each community. An appropriately weighted average of the corresponding elasticities should then be smaller than the elasticity for the group as a whole, and smaller by an amount calculable from the income data for the separate communities. The classification by communities eliminates one source of variability in permanent components, and so should reduce the variance of permanent components and hence the elasticity.

This process can be continued. For each community, the groups can be classified by occupation; within occupation by education; within education by age and family size, and so on. At each stage in the hierarchy the average of the elasticities of the different groups should be lower than the elasticity for the broader group of which they are part. As the groups are more and more rigorously defined, the elasticity should approach zero.

c. The time unit used in the material cited in preceding chapters is a year. Suppose data were available for a shorter time unit, say a quarter. The effect would be to increase the variance of the transitory component without affecting the variance of the permanent component and so, on our hypothesis, to reduce the measured income elasticity of consumption. Conversely, the use of a longer time unit, say a biennium, would have the opposite effect. These results could be expected for either family budget data or time series data.

One test piece of evidence along these lines has already been cited: that from Klein's analysis of some Consumer Finances data (see Chapter IV, section 2f). Another is available from a comparison made by Reid.[16] The 1941 budget study cited in preceding chapters covered both 1941 and the first quarter of 1942. Reid computed elasticities for the year 1941 and for the first quarter of 1942 for urban, rural nonfarm, and farm families. In each case, the elasticity was noticeably higher for the annual data. Both these pieces of evidence are from budget data. It would be desirable to have similar evidence from time series data.

d. Section 2 above suggests a test using data on expenditures for

[15] See Friedman and Kuznets, *Income from Independent Professional Practice*, pp. 361–362, for an attempt to estimate the quantitative influence of some of these factors.

[16] Contained in an unpublished paper by Margaret Reid, "The Relation of the Within-Group Transitory Component of Incomes to the Income Elasticity of Family Expenditures."

particular categories of consumption. Classify the consumer units covered by a family budget study into a number of groups that can be expected to have much the same tastes and preferences and to be faced with the same prices but to differ in the relative importance of transitory components of income—for example, different occupational groups in the same community, especially salaried versus independent groups; or even better, farm and nonfarm groups. Compute the elasticity of various categories of consumption with respect to measured income for each group. Divide each of these by the corresponding measured income elasticity of total consumption expenditures; according to (8.3), the result is an estimate of the elasticity of expenditures on the particular category with respect to permanent income. Our hypothesis would lead us to expect such elasticities to differ less from group to group than the elasticities with respect to measured income.

It may be, as suggested in section 2, that different concepts of "permanent" are required for the several categories. In that case, the ratio of the measured income elasticity for one category to that for total consumption is not a satisfactory estimate of the relation between permanent components. Nonetheless, it is plausible that the procedure described in the preceding paragraph would yield values differing less from group to group than the measured income elasticities. The reason is that one might expect that, while a change in the definition of the permanent component would change the fraction of the variance attributable to it, differences among these fractions from group to group would be highly correlated for different definitions. For example, if a smaller fraction of the variance is accounted for by permanent components for entrepreneurial groups than for others when "permanent" refers to a horizon of three years, then it seems plausible that the same result will hold when "permanent" refers to a horizon of ten years. Of course, even if true, this does not guarantee that the adjusted elasticities will be more homogeneous than the original; "over-correction" will occur and may be sufficient to spread them more widely.

e. Data for groups of consumer units like those described in the preceding test could also be used in another way. Choose groups for which there is reason to expect the relative importance of transitory components of income to differ but of consumption to be roughly the same. From regressions of consumption on income, estimate P_y; from regressions of income on consumption, P_c. Our hypothesis would lead us to expect the estimates of P_c to be more alike for the different groups than the estimates of P_y.

f. Another way to estimate P_c is from data on consumption of identical units in different years. If such data were available, as well as income for the same units in at least one year, they would of course, permit a comparison of alternative estimates of P_c like the comparison of alternative estimates of P_y in Chapter VII. In addition, however, if the data included incomes in both years, estimates of P_y and P_c for the same group would be available, both based on the interyear correlation data. The implied ratio of transitory components $(1 - P_c)\sigma_c^2 / (1 - P_y)\sigma_y^2$ is then the information needed to compute for each year the so-called "mutual regression," which in the present context is the relation between the permanent components. Compute those regressions, including a constant term if the data are used in arithmetic form; and not restricting the regression coefficient to unity, if the data are used in logarithmic form. On our hypothesis, the constant term of the arithmetic relation should not differ significantly from zero if the transitory components of income and consumption can be regarded as averaging out to zero, and the slope of the logarithmic relation should not differ significantly from unity. Further, the computed variances of "error terms" yield independent estimates of P_y and P_c.

g. By the method in item f, estimates of k can be computed for some groups of families. For other groups for which the mean transitory components of expenditure and income can be taken to be zero, k can be computed from the ratio of mean income to mean expenditures. On our hypothesis, the k's so computed are related to variables such as the rate of interest, the ratio of wealth to income, and the importance of the transitory component of income. The latter two variables might be expected to differ most among groups and therefore to be the most promising variables to investigate.

h. A test that is a special case of the one just mentioned is to estimate the variance of the transitory component of income for any group of families by multiplying the observed variance of income by the complement of the measured income elasticity of consumption. The larger the corresponding measure of relative dispersion of transitory components, the greater the need for a reserve against emergencies and the lower, therefore, should be k. If mean transitory components of income and consumption are zero, k is given by the ratio of mean consumption to mean income for the group of families considered. Accordingly, our hypothesis leads us to expect a negative correlation between the relative dispersion of transitory components, computed as described, and the average propensity to consume or the ratio of consumption to income at the mean of the group.

If these parameters were available for a large number of groups of families, this correlation should, on our hypothesis, emerge despite the fact that mean transitory components of income and expenditures may not be zero and despite other differences among groups that may affect k. For there seems no reason why these features of the groups considered should themselves be correlated with the size of the transitory component, hence no reason why they should do more than reduce the closeness of correlation.

This is doubtless only a partial list of the kinds of confrontation of the hypothesis with empirical evidence that will be suggested in the course of using the hypothesis. They are listed here and described as "tests" primarily to give a taste of the breadth of evidence relevant to the hypothesis, rather than because I believe their completion to be a prerequisite for the use of the hypothesis in substantive empirical research. On the contrary, the hypothesis has, in my view, been tested searchingly enough on a sufficiently broad range of data, and has yielded sufficiently good results, to justify its acceptance as a working hypothesis. Further evidence on it will develop, and improvements in it be suggested, in the course of using it, and it is as by-products of this kind that the tests listed above should probably be made.

From this point of view, the analyses of data listed above as "tests" could equally be termed ways of using the hypothesis to discover empirical regularities, describe basic characteristics of consumption behavior, and summarize efficiently masses of detailed evidence. This is particularly so for items b, d, and g; it applies in some measure to every item in the list.

CHAPTER IX

Summary and Conclusion

THE central theme of this monograph can be illustrated by a simple hypothetical example. Consider a large number of men all earning $100 a week and spending $100 a week on current consumption. Let them receive their pay once a week, the pay days being staggered, so that one-seventh are paid on Sunday, one-seventh on Monday, and so on. Suppose we collected budget data for a sample of these men for one day chosen at random, defined income as cash receipts on that day, and defined consumption as cash expenditures. One-seventh of the men would be recorded as having an income of $100, six-sevenths as having an income of zero. It may well be that the men would spend more on pay day than on other days but they would also make expenditures on other days, so we would record the one-seventh with an income of $100 as having positive savings, the other six-sevenths as having negative savings. Consumption might appear to rise with income, but, if so, not as much as income, so that the fraction of income saved would rise with income. These results tell us nothing meaningful about consumption behavior; they simply reflect the use of inappropriate concepts of income and consumption. Men do not adapt their cash expenditures on consumption to their cash receipts, and their cash expenditures on consumption may not be a good index of the value of services consumed—in our simple example, consumption expenditures might well be zero on Sunday.

Lengthening the period of observation from a day to a week would eliminate entirely the error introduced into our simple example by the use of inappropriate concepts of income and consumption. It is the central theme of this monograph that the use of a period as long as a year does not render the error in actual data negligible, let alone eliminate it entirely. The results obtained from such annual data conform in broad outline to those of our simple example: recorded consumption is on the average positive when recorded income is zero, and the fraction of income saved rises with income. If the thesis of this monograph is correct, these results are to be explained in the same way. They too reflect the use of inappropriate concepts of income and consumption.

Our analysis accordingly distinguishes sharply between income as recorded—which we term measured income—and the income to which consumers adapt their behavior—which we term permanent income—and, similarly, between measured consumption and permanent consumption. The concept of permanent income is easy to state in these general terms, hard to define precisely. Permanent income cannot be observed directly, it must be inferred from the behavior of consumer units. And this is equally true of permanent consumption and its relation to permanent income.

The wide range of empirical material examined in this monograph turns out to be consistent with a rather simple relation between permanent consumption and permanent income suggested by purely theoretical considerations, namely, a ratio between permanent consumption and permanent income that is the same for all levels of permanent income but depends on other variables, such as the interest rate, the ratio of wealth to income, and so on. The widespread belief that the ratio of consumption to income declines as income rises can be explained entirely by the considerations stressed in our example.

Our conclusion about the meaning of permanent income cannot be stated so simply. We can think of the factors affecting the consumer's receipts as having a range of time dimensions: some factors affect his receipts only for a day, others for a week, a year, two years, and so on. We have approximated this continuum by a dichotomy. Effects lasting less than a certain time period are considered transitory, those lasting for a longer time, permanent. The length of this time period we call the consumer unit's horizon. A number of different pieces of evidence support the highly tentative conclusion that the horizon so defined is about three years.

On our interpretation of the evidence, the transitory components of a consumer unit's income have no effect on his consumption except as they are translated into effects lasting beyond his horizon. His consumption is determined by longer-range income considerations plus transitory factors affecting consumption directly. The transitory components of income show up primarily in changes in the consumer units' assets and liabilities, that is, in his measured savings.

This approach to the interpretation of consumption data and the particular hypothesis to which it has led have far-reaching implications. The rest of this chapter states the hypothesis more formally, summarizes the evidence adduced in support of it, lists generalizations about consumer behavior derived from it, and outlines some of its implications for research, economic understanding, and economic policy.

1. *Summary Statement of Hypothesis*

The permanent income hypothesis can be summarized in a system of three simple equations for the individual consumer unit:

(α) $$c_p = k(i, w, u)y_p \,,$$

(β) $$y = y_p + y_t \,,$$

(γ) $$c = c_p + c_t \,.$$

Equation (α) asserts that planned or permanent consumption (c_p) is a fraction (k) of planned or permanent income (y_p) that does not depend on the size of permanent income but does depend on other variables, in particular, the interest rate (i), the ratio of nonhuman wealth to income (w), and other factors affecting the consumer unit's tastes for current consumption versus accumulation of assets (u), such as the degree of uncertainty attached to the receipt of income, the consumer unit's age and its composition, and objective indexes of cultural factors like race or national origin. This is the simplest equation that seems consistent with the pure theory of consumer behavior as presented in Chapter II.

Equations (β) and (γ) assert that measured income (y) and measured consumption (c) can each be regarded as the sum of two components: (1) the permanent component that enters into (α), and (2) a transitory component reflecting the influence of factors regarded as chance or random by the consumer unit, as well as errors of measurement. As they stand, these equations have no substantive content; they are purely definitional.

The permanent components of income and consumption can never be observed directly for an individual consumer unit; we can only observe *ex post* what it spends and what it receives. We can, however, make inferences about the permanent components for groups of families from observed data if we accept certain assumptions about the relation between permanent and transitory components. The particular assumptions I have made are that the transitory components of consumption and income can be taken to be uncorrelated with the corresponding permanent components and with each other; these are an essential part of the hypothesis presented in this monograph. In addition, I have on occasion assumed the mean transitory components of consumption and income to be zero. This is not essential to the hypothesis and has been done only for the convenience or simplicity of the particular application.

These assumptions breathe substantive content into equations (β) and (γ). Equations (α), (β), and (γ) then imply an observed regression of measured consumption on measured income for which the ratio of consumption to income declines as measured income increases—as in our simple introductory example and for the same reasons. They imply also a computed elasticity of measured consumption with respect to measured income that is proportional to the fraction of the total variance of income for the group concerned that is contributed by the permanent component (P_y), and a height of the regression that depends on the mean level of the permanent and transitory components of income and consumption and on the variables affecting k. The regression is shifted upward by a rise in mean permanent income and by an increase in k. Thus changes in neither the elasticity nor the height of the observed regressions need imply any changes in consumer tastes and preferences for current consumption versus accumulation of wealth, or in opportunities for exchanging the one for the other. They may instead reflect simply changes in certain characteristics of the income distribution. The appearance of changing consumer behavior may simply be a disguised reflection of the fact of changing income structure.

For simplicity of exposition, the hypothesis has been described in its arithmetic form. A variant is to retain (α) but to replace (β) and (γ) by similar expressions in the logarithms of the various terms, and to assume zero correlation between the logarithmic transitory components of income and consumption and each of these and the corresponding logarithmic permanent component. This logarithmic variant seems to fit the empirical evidence better than the arithmetic variant and is the one that has been used in most of the empirical work of the preceding chapters. Its implications are essentially the same as those of the arithmetic variant, since the one can be regarded as a first order approximation to the other, and most verbal statements of the implications apply equally to both; its advantage is that the implications hold over a wider range.

The relation between aggregate consumption and aggregate income depends not only on the consumption function for individual consumer units but also on the distribution of consumer units by the variables affecting their behavior. Under simplifying assumptions, however, the aggregate function has the same form as the individual function and can likewise be described by (α), (β), and (γ), with the exception that the variables determining the ratio of permanent consumption to permanent income (designated k^* for aggregate data) are different. They are now the distribution of consumer units by i, w, and u, or such summary measures of these distributions as their means and variances. Given the same assumptions of zero correlation between transitory and permanent components and between transitory components of consumption and income, the hypothesis then has the same implications for the regression of consumption on income computed from aggregate data as for the regression computed from data for individual consumer units. In neither case is stability of the observed regression a necessary consequence of stability in consumer behavior with respect to current consumption and current saving.

The hypothesis has many empirical implications in addition to those already stated about the regression of measured consumption on measured income. For example, it can be used to decompose the dispersion of measured income, and also of measured consumption, into the parts attributable to transitory and permanent components. It implies that if consumer units are classified by the change in income from one year to another, the regressions of consumption on income for such groups will, under plausible conditions, be parallel and differ in height by amounts that can be specified in advance; and that the common slope will be steeper than the slope of the regression for all units combined by an amount that can be calculated from a characteristic of the income distribution for the group as a whole. It can be used to predict the correlation between the ratio of measured saving to measured income of the same units in different years. For aggregate data for a country like the United States that has been experiencing secular growth, it implies that the elasticity of consumption with respect to measured income computed from time series will be higher, the longer the period spanned by the data, and the longer the elementary time unit of observation; that it will also be higher when computed from data on aggregate consumption and income than from per capita data and when computed from data in current prices than from data in constant prices.

2. *Evidence on the Acceptability of the Permanent Income Hypothesis*

The implications of the permanent income hypothesis explain the major apparent anomalies that arise if the observed regression between measured consumption and measured income is interpreted, as it generally has been, as a stable relation between permanent components—though, of course, this is not the name that has been attached to the measured magnitudes. On such an interpretation the observed regression of consumption on income for a single group of consumer units implies (a) that inequality of income will increase over time—since consumption exceeds income for low income units and is less than income for high income units so apparently the poor are getting poorer and the rich richer; (b) that savings must have become an increasing fraction of income over time in the United

States and similar countries—since real income has been increasing more or less steadily; and (c) that regressions computed from budget studies made at widely spaced dates will not differ systematically. Yet there is ample evidence that (a) inequality of income has, if anything, decreased over time in the United States, (b) savings have been a roughly constant fraction of income over time in the United States, (c) computed regressions have steadily been higher, the later the date of the budget study. All three observations are entirely consistent with the permanent income hypothesis presented in this monograph.

The consistency of the hypothesis with these broad facts is only a small part of the evidence in its favor. In addition, the hypothesis is consistent with numerous detailed findings about consumption behavior that have accumulated from analyses of both budget data for individual consumer units and time series data on aggregate consumption and income; in particular, each of the implications listed in the preceding section has been compared with observation and no serious discrepancy has been found in either qualitative or quantitative elements of the implications. Perhaps the two most striking pieces of evidence for the hypothesis are, first, its success in predicting in quantitative detail the effect of classifying consumer units by the change in their measured income from one year to another; and, second, its consistency with a body of data that have not heretofore been used in analyzing consumption behavior or, indeed, even regarded as relevant to consumption behavior, namely, data on the measured income of individual consumer units in successive years. An estimate of the fraction of the variance of measured income contributed by permanent components (i.e. of P_y) can be made from such data by techniques that I developed much earlier for another purpose, namely, the analysis of the stability of relative income status. On the permanent income hypothesis the measured income elasticity of consumption is also an estimate of this same fraction.[1] These two estimates are derived from two largely independent bodies of data. Comparison of them for a variety of groups of consumer units show that they are highly correlated and approximately of the same order of magnitude.

There is some leeway in the hypothesis in the precise meaning to be assigned to the permanent component of income. The broadest definition would regard this component as attributable to any factors whose influence extends over more than one elementary time unit (a year, in most studies). Successively narrower definitions would include

[1] If computed from an arithmetically linear regression, at the mean income and for zero mean transitory components of income and consumption.

225

only factors affecting income in three or more years, four or more years, and so on until the narrowest definition would identify the permanent component with expected lifetime income. The comparisons mentioned in the preceding paragraph as well as a number of other pieces of evidence suggest that the empirically appropriate definition is to regard the permanent component as reflecting the influence of factors affecting income for a period of three or more years. But this must still be regarded as a highly tentative conclusion.

A number of hypotheses have been suggested in recent years to explain the contradictions mentioned above between the available evidence and the hypothesis that consumption expenditures are a stable function of absolute income. The chief such hypotheses can be regarded as special cases of the permanent income hypothesis under special conditions. This is true of the hypothesis that the ratio of consumption to income for a consumer unit depends on the relative income position of the consumer unit as measured by either the ratio of its income to the mean income of the group of which it is regarded as a member or its percentile position in the income distribution. It is equally true of the hypothesis that aggregate consumption depends not only on current aggregate income but also on the highest previous income, which has been considered a special case of the relative income hypothesis. Regarded as an alternative theory, the relative income hypothesis has fewer empirical implications than the permanent income hypothesis, so is less fruitful; in addition, such empirical evidence as I have examined, for circumstances when the implications of the two hypotheses differ, favors the permanent income hypothesis rather than the relative income hypothesis.

3. *Generalizations about Consumer Behavior Based on the Hypothesis*

Empirical evidence has been considered in this study primarily from the standpoint of its consistency with the permanent income hypothesis rather than of its contribution to the understanding of consumer behavior. In the process of using the evidence to test the hypothesis, however, we have necessarily been led to use the hypothesis to extract generalizations from the evidence; these are two sides of the same coin. It may illuminate these tests and this evidence if we summarize here this by-product, taking for granted that the agreement of the hypothesis with the available evidence is sufficient to justify its tentative acceptance. It should be emphasized that the generalizations that follow are all for personal consumption and personal savings; they do not cover corporate savings or governmental savings.

226

a. We have found no evidence of any structural change in the behavior of consumer units in the United States with respect to spending and saving over at least the past sixty years. The data for this period all conform to the pattern defined by our hypothesis, including not only the general equations (α), (β), and (γ) but also the more specific assumptions about the lack of correlation between the transitory components of income and of consumption and between each of these and the corresponding permanent component. And they conform to this pattern in the sense not only that the general functional relations apply but also that the parameters of the relations seem to have been unchanged over the period in question. A horizon of about three years seems to have characterized the outlook of consumer units, though it should be noted that the results are not very sensitive to the length of the horizon.

b. Over this period, k, the ratio of permanent consumption to permanent income has been decidedly higher for wage earners than for entrepreneurial groups; from .90 to .95 for wage earners, from .80 to .90 for entrepreneurs, probably close to the lower end of this range for nonfarm entrepreneurs and to the middle or upper end for farmers.

The difference between entrepreneurial and nonentrepreneurial groups in the size of k seems larger and better established than any other we have examined. The value of k is perhaps a trifle higher for Negroes than for whites; this difference, which is small and not well established, is opposite in direction from that which has been inferred from conventional analysis of the data. The value of k is probably higher for large than for small families, but again this cannot be regarded as well established.

c. At least part of the reason why k is lower for entrepreneurial than for nonentrepreneurial groups is the greater uncertainty of income prospects for the former, which makes the need for a reserve against emergencies greater.

For nonentrepreneurial consumer units living in urban communities of at least moderate size, the dispersion of transitory components of income is about 20 to 25 per cent of their average income; that is, about two out of three will in any year be within plus or minus 20 or 25 per cent of what they regard as their permanent position.

For nonentrepreneurial groups in small cities and villages, it seems likely that the transitory component is even less widely dispersed, though the evidence for this statement is very limited.

For entrepreneurial consumer units, whether farm or nonfarm, the relative dispersion of transitory components of income seems to be upwards of 40 per cent, perhaps as high as 50 per cent, of average income, or something like twice as great as for nonentrepreneurial groups.

For the various nonfarm groups combined, including entrepreneurs and others, the average relative dispersion of transitory components is about 30 per cent.

d. Part of the reason why k is lower for entrepreneurial than for nonentrepreneurial groups may be the ability of the entrepreneurial group to earn a higher rate of return on accumulated capital; a similar difference between nonfarm and farm entrepreneurs may also explain why k is lower for the nonfarm entrepreneurs. However, this conclusion is highly conjectural and cannot be regarded as well established.

e. In terms of permanent income status, farmers are less dispersed than nonfarm groups as a whole, though perhaps about as dispersed as nonfarm wage and clerical workers. Nonfarm entrepreneurial groups are more widely dispersed than either farmers or other nonfarm groups. Our estimates of the size of the dispersion vary from about 60 to 70 per cent for farmers to 80 to 90 per cent for nonfarm entrepreneurial groups.

f. The variability in permanent income status has accounted for something like 80 to 85 per cent of the variability of measured annual income for broad nonfarm groups in the United States; for a much smaller fraction, for farm groups. It has apparently accounted for a larger fraction in Great Britain and Sweden than in the United States. This means that the distribution of annual income exaggerates the inequality of long-run income status by more for farmers than for nonfarmers, and by more for the United States than for Great Britain or Sweden.

g. There is limited evidence that transitory components are much less important for consumption than for income, having a relative dispersion of the order of perhaps 10 per cent instead of the 30 per cent recorded for income.

h. There is no evidence of a lag in the adjustment of consumer expenditures to changes in circumstances beyond that which is implicit in the idea that consumers adapt their expenditures to longer-run income status as measured by permanent income rather than to their momentary receipts. The effects of changes in measured income on consumer expenditures can all be accounted for in this way.

i. The ratio of aggregate consumption to aggregate income for the United States (k^*) has remained roughly constant for more than half a century at about .88 for a definition of consumption that excludes expenditures on major consumer durable goods and includes their estimated use value. Accumulation of durables has accounted for an increasing fraction of savings, so the ratio of consumption to income would be slightly higher and would show a moderately rising secular trend for measures of consumption that treated expenditures on durables as consumption. These conclusions are supported by both budget data and time series data.

j. The constancy of the numerical value of k^*, though consistent with the permanent income hypothesis, is not required by it, even in the absence of structural change and even when the conditions are satisfied for the aggregate function to be described by equations like (α), (β), and (γ). The constancy of k^* means that the variables determining k and the distribution of consumer units by these variables have been either constant or offsetting in their effects. Probably the two major offsetting forces have been (1) the declining relative importance of farming, which would tend to raise k^*, and (2) the declining size of family, which would tend to lower k^*. A third major factor, the changing role of the state in the provision of security, has itself had offsetting effects on k^* as it is measured from the available statistics.

k. Permanent income for the community as a whole can be regarded as a weighted average of current and past measured incomes, adjusted upwards by a steady secular trend and with weights declining as one goes farther back in time. The average time span between the measured incomes averaged and current permanent income is about $2^{1}/_{2}$ years.

The corresponding aggregate consumption function is

$$c^*(T) = k^*\beta \int_{-\infty}^{T} e^{(\beta-\alpha)(t-T)} y^*(t)\, dt$$

where c^* is aggregate or per capita consumption and y^* aggregate or per capita income, T designates the time unit in question, t designates time in general and is simply a variable of integration that does not appear in the final function, and k^*, α, and β are the parameters of the function. k^* is to be interpreted as the ratio of permanent consumption to permanent income, α as the secular rate of growth of income, and β as the damping coefficient which describes the process of forming estimates of expected or permanent income from current and past measured income; the higher β, the more rapidly the weights decline as one goes back in time, and the shorter the average lag between permanent income and the incomes averaged. For the period 1905 to 1951, and Raymond Goldsmith's data on deflated per capita savings and deflated per capita personal income,

229

the estimated values of the parameters are

$$k^* = .88$$
$$\alpha = .02$$
$$\beta = .40 \ .$$

The values of α and β should be fairly insensitive to the precise data used, whereas k^* will be quite sensitive. The value cited is for a concept of consumption that includes only the use value of major consumer durable goods, treating accumulation in the stock of consumer durables as savings, and that includes additions to social security reserves as personal savings and income.

4. *Implications of the Hypothesis for Research*

The broader implications of acceptance of the permanent income hypothesis affect two very different areas of human effort: (1) research into consumption behavior and income structure and (2) economic understanding and policy.

A major part of the effort in consumption research, both with respect to total consumption and consumption expenditures on particular categories, has been directed toward determining the regression of consumption on income. This emphasis reflects the belief that current income is the major determinant of current consumption expenditures and that comparison of regressions is a way of eliminating the influence of income and so isolating the effects of other factors affecting consumer behavior. This partial correlation approach underlies most of the data collection and presentation; it explains alike why the Study of Consumer Purchases, perhaps the largest and most carefully planned budget study ever undertaken, collected expenditure data from a controlled rather than representative sample; and why measured income is the major, and often the only, variable used to classify consumer units in tabulations of budget data. This partial correlation approach characterizes also the bulk of the analytical research into consumer behavior, from Engel's original enunciation of his famous laws which led to his name being attached to regressions of consumption on income, to current self-consciously complex econometric research; from the examination of data for a small group of consumer units, to the calculation of demand functions from a combination of time series and budget data for a nation as a whole and for many separate commodities. Sophistication has taken the form of adding more and more variables, and of using more refined statistical techniques to estimate their effects and to allow for sampling and measurement errors; it has not changed the basic orientation or direction of the research.

Acceptance of the permanent income hypothesis implies that much or most of this research has been misdirected. What has been held constant is not income in the sense that is relevant to consumption behavior but a more or less arbitrary mixture of income in this sense and accidental elements. Statistical measures that have been taken to reflect the influence of differences in consumer behavior in fact reflect features of the income distribution. In consequence, the discovery of regularities in consumer behavior has been bedeviled by the confounding of such behavior with unrelated though not irrelevant features of the distribution of income. The result has been the introduction of increasing complexity into the analysis in an effort to rationalize the data within the same general framework.

This complexity is frequently pointed to with pride by workers in the field as evidence of the subtlety of their analysis. It is tempting to make a virtue of necessity by asserting that the consumer *is* a complex creature who is influenced by everything under the sun and hence that only an analysis in terms of a large number of variables can hope to extract a consistent pattern from his behavior. In fact, the necessity of introducing many variables is a sign of defeat and not of success; it means that the analyst has not found a truly fruitful way of interpreting or understanding his subject matter; for the essence of such a fruitful theory is that it is simple. The consumption analyst, as it were, has been priding himself on his success in adding yet more epicycles. The possibility of dispensing with these does not, of course, mean that his empirical findings are in error, that the variables he finds related to consumer behavior are not related to it, any more than acceptance of the Copernican view rendered non-existent the astronomical movements that it was necessary to introduce additional epicycles to explain. What it does mean is that these empirical relations can all be inferred from a much simpler structure, that they can all be regarded as manifestations in different guise of a single and simpler set of forces rather than as the result of largely irreducible ultimate variables.

Acceptance of the permanent income hypothesis means that much less emphasis should be attached to the regressions of consumption on income, especially in the analysis of total consumption and savings. The principal task in this area at the present stage of knowledge is to find the major determinants of k and to measure their influence. The data needed for this purpose, at least for the first attack on the problem, are average consumption and average income for groups of consumer units for which transitory components can largely be expected to average out; for example, communities, or moderately homogeneous occupational groups within cities. I know, myself, of

231

only one study, by Dorothy Brady, which has used the community as the unit of observation and has dealt with relations among averages.[2] We need to determine whether and how the ratio of such averages, which we have been calling the average propensity to consume, is connected with the variables our hypothesis leads us to put into the forefront: the rate of interest, the relative dispersion of transitory components of income and of consumption, the ratio of wealth to income, the age and composition of consumer units. Much can be done along these lines with existing data, though thanks to their different orientation, community averages are either not available for many such data or can be computed only with difficulty. With respect to future collection of data, acceptance of this approach in many ways simplifies the problem, by enabling emphasis to be put almost entirely on samples giving good estimates of means. This can be done with a smaller sample and perhaps a simpler sampling design than is required to get good estimates of multivariate relations including current income of the consumer unit as a major variable.

From the point of view of the permanent income hypothesis, the regression of consumption on income not only should receive much less exclusive emphasis in consumption research than it has heretofore, it also serves a different function and use. Its function is primarily to provide a means to decompose the total variation in income into the parts contributed by permanent and transitory components. The result is useful for consumption research in providing an estimate of one variable that may be expected to influence k, namely, the relative dispersion of transitory components. Its main use, however, is not in consumption research at all but in analyzing the distribution of income. It enables the mass of consumer budget data to be used to interpret data on the distribution of income and to convert them into estimates of the distribution of permanent income status.

Curiously enough, while the hypothesis converts the regression of consumption on income into a tool for analyzing income distribution, it gives the regression of income on consumption, which has heretofore been almost entirely neglected, significance for consumption research. For this regression enables us to decompose the total variation in consumption into the parts contributed by permanent and transitory components and so to estimate the relative dispersion of transitory components of consumption. The regression of income on consumption needs to be computed from any existing data for which it is possible to do so, and in future studies, the two regressions should be treated symmetrically.

A final implication of the hypothesis for research that deserves

[2] "Family Savings in Relation to Changes in the Level and Distribution of Income."

mention is the importance it confers on data on the consumption or income of the same consumer units in different years, especially on such data giving both the consumption and income of the same units. It is likely that data of this kind now exist which have not been exploited, and these are one of the kinds of consumption data that should receive highest priority in future collection of data.

5. Substantive Implications of the Hypothesis

Acceptance of the permanent income hypothesis necessarily has implications for any problem of economic understanding or policy in which the determinants of savings play a significant role. At least in recent years, there have been two main classes or problems of this kind: those connected with the process of economic development, particularly of so-called underdeveloped economies, and those connected with economic fluctuations.

a. ECONOMIC DEVELOPMENT

Students of economic development tend to give a major role to the availability of resources for capital formation. One source is, of course, domestic savings. Their availability has, in turn, been taken to depend largely on the level of real income, on the one hand, and the inequality of income on the other.

The level of real income has been regarded as playing a dual role. First, the level of income defines the total amount available for consumption and savings; if, by some criterion, the total is low, so is the potential amount available for either purpose. This is, of course, a purely arithmetical truism and is unaffected by the hypothesis accepted about the factors determining the division of the total between consumption and savings. Second, acceptance of the absolute income hypothesis led to the belief that a low real income was unfavorable to savings in the further sense that it made for a relatively low ratio of savings to income.

The relative income hypothesis, which has received increasing acceptance in recent years, removed the direct connection between low real income and a low savings ratio but substituted an indirect connection. True, it argued, in an isolated community, the level of real income would have no effect on the savings ratio. But in a community connected with the rest of the world it would. According to the most widely accepted theoretical justification for the relative income hypothesis, that of Duesenberry, relative income is important within a community because of emulation and the demonstration of the availability and usefulness of superior goods. But these same effects work as well between communities. The "demonstration

233

effect" of the level of consumption in high income countries, or of citizens of high income countries resident in underdeveloped countries, tends, it has been argued, to lead the citizens of the underdeveloped countries to devote an unduly high percentage of their low level of income to current consumption and, especially, to use in that way any increases in income.

Acceptance of the permanent income hypothesis removes both the direct and this particular indirect connection between low real income and a low savings ratio. According to it, the savings ratio is independent of the level of income. Relative income, as measured, is empirically related to the savings ratio within a country not because of emulation or the demonstration effect but because relative measured income is a biased index of relative permanent income status. If the emulation and demonstration effects are not present within a community, there is no reason to expect them to operate between communities. It may be that a country or group with a relatively low real income will also have a low aggregate ratio of savings to income; but it may also have a high ratio, and in either case the explanation is to be sought not in the level of income but in other factors.

Although, on the permanent income hypothesis, a low level of real income does not make for a low savings ratio, a rapid rate of rise in income, whatever the level, may do so. The reason is that a rise expected to continue tends to raise permanent income relative to measured income and so to raise consumption relative to measured income. I conjecture that whether this effect shows itself is likely to depend critically on the source of the rise in real income. If it reflects development financed at least in part from domestic capital in an environment which makes for a high rate of return on domestic capital, the high rate of return to savings is an offset to the high ratio of permanent to current income and may well be more important. On the other hand, if the rise in income reflects primarily an external stimulus that gives little or no role to domestic capital, there may be no offset and one might expect the savings ratio to fall. An example of this second possibility might be the rising income among Okinawan natives as a result of its development as a United States military base, though I know too little about the details to be confident that it is. At any rate, if some examples of the two kinds of developments could be found, they might offer a rather nice test of the present analysis and of the applicability of the permanent income hypothesis across countries.

Thanks to the widespread acceptance not only of the absolute income hypothesis but of a very special form of it, the inequality of the distribution of income has been regarded as a major factor explaining the aggregate savings ratio.[3] Wide inequality of income is thought to tend toward a high savings ratio, and an approach toward equality, toward a low savings ratio. This consideration has frequently been a major argument offered in defense of inequality by people who are in other respects egalitarians: inequality in an underdeveloped country, they say, is a necessary evil since there is no other way to generate the savings needed for economic development.

According to the permanent income hypothesis, the effect of inequality depends critically on the source of the inequality. Insofar as the inequality is attributable to differences in permanent income status, it has no effect on the savings ratio. Insofar as it is attributable to differences in transitory components, it does, because inequality then means uncertainty about income prospects and hence increases the need for a reserve against emergencies. What is favorable to a high savings ratio is not inequality per se but uncertainty, provided, of course, it is uncertainty of a kind that does not reduce the average rate of return on capital—a qualification that is entered to allow for the clearly unfavorable effect on savings of increased uncertainty about the security of property such as might arise from fears of confiscation or close regulation by government.

This distinction between the sources of inequality seems to me of great importance. If I may speculate on the basis of utterly inadequate knowledge in the hope of provoking further study by better qualified students, it seems to me that the kind of inequality characteristic of many so-called underdeveloped countries is precisely the kind that is irrelevant to the savings ratio. Such countries frequently have rigid social systems, sharp separations between classes, great stability in the membership of classes within generations and from generation to generation; in short, wide inequality in permanent income status. The process of development, of industrialization, breaks down these rigid class distinctions; historically, it tends not only to produce a smaller degree of inequality in measured income but, what is more important for our purposes, also to substitute inequality arising from transitory factors for inequalities of permanent income status. The reduction of the inequality of permanent income status, whatever its importance in other connections, is neutral with respect to the savings ratio. This kind of inequality, which interestingly is generally the kind that is most distasteful to egalitarians, cannot be defended

[3] If consumption is a linear function of absolute income, the aggregate savings ratio depends only on the mean income and not on its distribution, although savings are a larger fraction of income the higher the income, so long as the intercept of the consumption function is positive. For the relation described in the text to hold, the consumption function must be concave downward on the average.

as required to generate savings. On the other hand, the fluidity introduced into relative income status, the emergence of fresh possibilities of moving from one class to another, of possibilities of large gains and large losses over short periods of time—changes which the egalitarian may welcome as increasing equality of opportunity even if resulting in inequality of outcome—these changes are favorable to the savings ratio.

To continue these speculations outside my own field of competence, I wonder whether undue attention has not been given to the magnitude of the savings ratio at the expense of the form that savings take. Savings may well have been at least as large a fraction of income in the Middle Ages as in modern times; they then in considerable measure, perhaps in major part, took the form of cathedrals, which, however productive of ultimate satisfaction and of social security in more than one sense of that term, were not productive of worldly goods. I understand that budget studies for India, which at first sight seem to give very different results from corresponding studies for the United States, are found largely to duplicate the latter if the category "ornaments" is interpreted as savings or, in the jargon of budget studies, as "net changes in assets and liabilities." The East was for long regarded as a "sink" for the precious metals, surely evidence both of substantial savings and of the particular form that it took. Perhaps the crucial role that has been assigned to the savings ratio in economic development should be assigned instead to the factors determining the form in which wealth is accumulated; to the investment rather than saving process, as it were.

b. ECONOMIC FLUCTUATIONS

There has been widespread acceptance in recent years of explanations of economic fluctuations that interpret them as primarily a resultant of the interaction of unstable investment and a relatively stable relation between consumption and current income. While I do not myself accept this income-expenditure theory as a valid and tested interpretation of experience, the acceptance of the permanent income hypothesis clearly has important implications for it that are worth recording.

The combination of this interpretation with a belief in a shortage of investment opportunities and in a rising ratio of savings to income as real income rises led, particularly in the United States in the late 1930's, to a fear of "secular stagnation": "mature" economies, it was argued, tend to have limited investment opportunities and high savings ratios at full employment. Acceptance of the permanent income hypothesis removes completely one of the pillars of the "secular stagnation" thesis; there is no reason to expect the savings ratio to rise with a secular rise in real income. In addition, it destroys the case for one proposed remedy. To counter the danger of secular stagnation, it was argued, requires raising the average propensity to consume at a full employment income. Acceptance of a particular version of the absolute income hypothesis led to the belief that one way to do so was to reduce the inequality of income, so the fear of secular stagnation was used as an argument in favor of income redistributive measures. Acceptance of the permanent income hypothesis means that, whatever may be the merits or demerits of raising the consumption ratio, changes in the inequality of income, at least of permanent income, cannot be expected to have this result. Apparently the permanent income hypothesis is evenhanded—if it removes the justification for inequality as a necessary evil to produce required savings, it also removes the justification for reducing inequality as a means of reducing attempted savings.

Postwar expansion and apparently widespread investment opportunities have on occasion led some proponents of the income-expenditure theory to fear "secular exhilaration." Consistency would have required them to favor measures designed to increase inequality as a means of reducing the ratio of consumption to income at full employment and so reducing the danger of inflation. However, to the best of my knowledge, none has done so. Clearly, on the permanent income hypothesis no such conclusion would be justified.

As was noted in Chapter I, the permanent income hypothesis has relevance not only to these arguments about inequality based on particular empirical judgments, but also to the underlying Keynesian theoretical structure, in both its long-run or structural, and its short-run or cyclical, aspects.

In its long-run aspect, the central analytical proposition of the structure is the denial that the long-run equilibrium position of a free enterprise economy is necessarily at full employment; there may be, it is asserted, no monetary equilibrium at all, unless some *deus ex machina* such as rigid nominal wage rates is introduced to produce one; and the "real" equilibrium may be at a less than full employment position. Acceptance of the permanent income hypothesis in its most general form does not render these propositions invalid, for they do not depend on the proposition that savings is an increasing ratio of income as income rises and could be valid even if savings were a constant ratio. What does render these analytical propositions invalid is acceptance of the special feature of the hypothesis that w, the ratio of wealth to income, is a significant variable affecting k, the ratio of permanent consumption to permanent income, and that an increase in w tends to raise k.

In its short-run aspect, as an interpretation of cyclical fluctuations, the central role in the income-expenditure theory is played by the relation between consumption and current income. The permanent income hypothesis has, so far as I can see, no implications for the empirical validity or acceptability of this interpretation of cyclical fluctuations; that must be decided by comparing its predictions with the predictions of alternative theories. But it does have important implications for the form of the consumption function and, in consequence, for the cyclical characteristics of an economy for which the income-expenditure explanation of fluctuations holds. The permanent income hypothesis leads to an aggregate consumption function like that presented above in point k of section 3, in which current consumption is largely determined by past incomes. One need not accept this particular form; the general result follows simply from the idea that current consumption is adapted to some measure of longer-run income status rather than to current receipts. The effect is almost certain to be a much smaller estimate of the marginal propensity to consume out of current income than would be obtained from a function that makes consumption dependent on current income alone. To put it in other terms: it means that a much larger part of current consumption is interpreted as autonomous and a much smaller part as dependent on current income and hence, through the multiplier process, on investment. The result is a smaller investment multiplier, and an inherently cyclically more stable system. For the particular consumption function we have estimated from the data, the multiplier of personal disposable income with respect to autonomous expenditures is only about 1.4, and this takes no account of the stabilizing effects of the progressive personal tax structure, corporate taxation and savings, and the like.[4] To avoid misunderstanding, I hasten to repeat that these are not intended to be assertions about the actual empirical characteristics of our economy; they are conditional assertions and dependent for their validity on the prior acceptance of the income-expenditure theory as an explanation of economic fluctuations.

An enumeration of the implications of acceptance of a new hypothesis can never hope to be exhaustive. Indeed, one of the main implications is that it will stimulate people to think in new directions

[4] A more extended treatment of this point is contained in Milton Friedman and Gary Becker, "A Statistical Illusion in Judging Keynesian Models," *Journal of Political Economy*, February, 1957.

and new ways that cannot possibly be specified in advance. Even though I have ventured in this section well beyond my empirical evidence and the areas of my own competence, I have no doubt omitted more of the ultimate implications of the acceptance of the permanent income hypothesis than I have included. This is at once the appeal and the justification of what we flatter ourselves by calling "pure" research.

Index

Age, and consumption-income ratios, 90–97

Average propensity to consume (*see* Consumption-income ratios)

Becker, Gary S., 85n, 238n

Boulding, Kenneth E., 7n

Brady, Dorothy S., 4, 37, 42n, 62nn, 63n, 79n, 93f., 122, 123n, 157, 162, 163n, 165f., 205n, 232

Brumberg, Richard, 6n, 29n

Budget data on consumption-income ratios:
  and age, 90–97
  and changes in income, 100–114, 170–173
  and changes in inequality of income, 39–40, 224
  changes over time in, 40–54
  characteristics of studies, 41–43, 50–53, 55, 59–61, 73–75
  country differences in, 40–43, 54–59
  as evidence on permanent income hypothesis, 38–114
  farm and nonfarm, 59–69, 165–166
  occupational group and, 69–81, 227–228
  race differences in, 79–85, 166
  and the relative income hypothesis, 162–163, 165–167, 168, 170–182

Cagan, Philip, 143, 145, 149n, 150f.

Cochrane, Willard W., 100n, 102n, 170n

Changes in income, and consumption-income ratios, 100–114, 170–173

Consumption function (*see* Budget data on consumption-income ratios, Consumption-income ratios, Income elasticity of consumption, Marginal propensity to consume, *and* Permanent income hypothesis)

Consumption-income ratios (*see also* Budget data on ———):
  cyclical factors in, 118–119, 152
  historical stability of, 3–4, 119–124
  and interest rates, 8–14, 17, 78, 120
  related to current and past income, 4–5, 137–152
  relation between individual and aggregate, 18–19, 115

and size of family, 121–123

and social insurance and assistance, 123

theoretical analysis, 3–17

and wealth-income ratios, 5, 16–17, 28, 86–87, 120, 170, 237–238

Cornfield, Jerome, 205n

Cyclical stage and consumption-income ratios, 118–119, 152

Douglas, Paul H., 50n, 52n

Duesenberry, James S., 4, 14n, 37, 137–142 *passim*, 146ff., 157, 166f., 173–177 *passim*, 233

Durable goods purchases, treatment as capital expenditures, 20, 28, 40, 43, 116, 214, 236

Epstein, Lenore A., 79n

Ferber, Robert, 125, 126n, 132n, 134, 139–142 *passim*

Fisher, Irving, 7n

Fisher, Janet A., 90, 91n, 96n

Frechtling, John, 95n, 194f.

Friedman, Milton, 6n, 9n, 21n, 49n, 93n, 186n, 188n, 216n, 238n

Friedman, Rose D., 4, 37, 63n, 79n, 157, 162, 163n, 165f.

Friend, Irwin, 215n

Grigg, Mary D., 100n, 102n, 170n

Goldsmith, Raymond W., 40, 42n, 63n, 73n, 116, 117n, 120n, 122, 123n, 124, 125, 126n, 132n, 134, 135, 142, 145, 229

Goldsmith, Selma, 40n

Haberler, Gottfried, 5

Hamburger, William, 5

Hanna, Frank A., 49n, 188n

Hanson, Alice C., 53n, 79n, 204n, 205n

Harberger, Arnold C., 208n

Hickman, W. Braddock, 120n

Hicks, J. R., 10n

Houthakker, H. S., 42n

Income distribution and the consumption function, 17, 19, 39–40, 224, 234–236

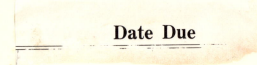